INTRODUCTION TO
COMMUNICATION

COURSE BOOK

7

SPEECH COMMUNICATION,
PUBLIC RELATIONS
AND
ADVERTISING

INTRODUCTION TO COMMUNICATION

COURSE BOOK

7

SPEECH COMMUNICATION, PUBLIC RELATIONS AND ADVERTISING

GC Angelopulo
(editor)

THE COURSE BOOK SERIES
The series is written by lecturers of
the Department of Communication,
University of South Africa.

Series Editor
Prof Trudie du Plooy

First published in 1997
Reprinted 1997

ISBN 0 7021 3801 0

© Juta & Co. Ltd.
P O Box 14373, Kenwyn 7790

Subediting: C Balchin, Cape Town
Book design and typesetting: C Bate, Cape Town
Cover design: J Wrench, Cape Town
Printed and bound by Creda Press, Eliot Ave, Eppindust II

Contents

List of Figures

List of Tables

List of Cases

Foreword

Communication exists at the core of our experience as human and social beings. Far from being an abstract, intangible phenomenon, communication is the cause and result of much of that experience. Communication makes most of our informal interaction possible, but it is also manifested in, and makes possible, the more formal activities of our lives. Three applied disciplines of communication that illustrate this very clearly are speech communication, public relations and advertising. Each describes an area of research and endeavour that, in application, has an intrinsic effect upon the success or failure of our social activities as individuals, groups and as a society.

As an **introductory course book**, this publication is aimed at introducing undergraduate students to speech communication, public relations and advertising.

The course book is written with the following general **teaching aims** in mind:

1 To explain and illustrate how the applied areas of speech communication, public relations and advertising have developed and evolved into disciplines of communication that play a central role in our society.

2 To identify the theoretical foundation of the three areas that are the focus of this book.

3 To illustrate and explain the dominant theories that exist in the study and application of advertising, public relations and speech communication.

4 To illustrate the practical application of the theories of public relations, speech communication and advertising.

An **interactive approach** is followed in this course book. We have adopted an informal writing style and have included activities throughout to encourage the active involvement of the reader. These activities challenge the reader to apply theoretical concepts, research approaches, methods and techniques in practical situations. The activities are also a form of self-evaluation. Furthermore, the four units contain a number of **learning aids**. Each unit begins with an *overview* that briefly outlines the contents of that unit, a list of the most important *key terms* relevant to the unit and a list of learning *objectives*, which students should aim to achieve. Each unit ends with a brief *summary* of the contents of that unit, as well as a list of additional sources that can be consulted as *suggested reading*.

Unit 1 is an introduction to speech communication. The unit begins with a short history of speech communication, and deals with the historical development of the study of the subject of communication. The unit proceeds with a discussion of types of speech and the prominent considerations in the preparation of a speech. Attention is also given to the delivery and evaluation of a speech. Because so much of our modern communication exists within the arena of the mass media, the unit concludes with a consideration of the application of speech communication to the mass-media interview. The unit was written by Rudolph de Jager. In addition to speech communication, his fields of specialisation include political communication and the South African mass media.

Unit 2 is an introduction to the study of public relations. It focuses upon the role of public relations in society, and the position of the discipline in the operations of the modern organisation. As this unit is introductory, some attention is given to its historical development and the position of public relations as a social science. Attention is given to a number of the most prominent theoretical approaches in public relations, and the essential role of planning in the practice of the discipline. The unit was written by Christien Bredenkamp, whose areas of interest are centred on public relations and the broader field of organisational communication.

Public relations is dealt with in more detail in Unit 3. The primary functions and effects of public relations are analysed in the context of a number of communication effects theories. The predominant techniques and processes that are used to achieve the objectives of public relations are discussed, and the confusion that sometimes arises in the distinction between these processes and public relations is addressed. A number of the issues that are considered to be critical in the development of public relations are also discussed and examined. Unit 3 was written by Berendien Lubbe, whose academic interests lie in the field of public relations and business communication.

Unit 4 is an introduction to advertising. The history of advertising is discussed with particular attention to its development in South Africa. The essential relationship between advertising and marketing is explored, and some of the more pertinent theories of advertising are noted. Particular attention is given to the Relevance Accessibility Model of advertising effectiveness, and a model for the implementation of advertising campaigns is described. The unit ends with an overview of the functions and powers that are ascribed to advertising. This unit was written by Danie du Plessis and George Angelopulo. Danie du Plessis's fields of specialisation are intercultural, development and organisational communication, and George Angelopulo's research interests lie in the communication of organisations and the mass media.

This course book is the last in a series of seven books which cover the undergraduate communication courses at the University of South Africa. The other courses on undergraduate level deal with introductions to the basics of communication; communication research; communication and the production of meaning; communication planning and management; journalism, press and radio studies; and film and television studies.

The authors wish to thank and acknowledge the following individuals and institutions:

▶ *Beeld* for the use of the photographs in Figures 1.1, 1.2, 1.3, 1.4 and 1.5.

▶ The *South African Communication Service* for the provision of the speeches in Case 1.1 and Case 1.2 of Unit 1.

▶ *Greenpeace* in London and *African Business* for permission to reproduce the photograph in Figure 3.3.

▶ *Emirates Air* for permission to reproduce the advertisement in Figure 3.4.

▶ *Air Austral* for permission to reproduce the advertisement in Figure 3.5.

▶ The *Bureau for University Teaching* at *UNISA* for the use of the logos in Figure 3.6.

▶ Mr Ruurd de Haan of *South African Airways* for providing the information and visual material in Case 3.1.

▶ Mr E K Wilshere-Preston of *Affinity Advertising & Publishing* for permission to reproduce page 97 of *Brands & branding in South Africa, volume 1*, as used in Figure 4.2.

▶ Mr Rodney Leech of *Saatchi & Saatchi Klerck & Barrett* for permission to reproduce the advertisements in Figures 4.3, 4.4, 4.5, 4.6, 4.7, 4.8, 4.9, 4.10, 4.12 and 4.13.

▶ *Hunt Lascaris TBWA* and *BMW SA* for permission to reproduce the advertisements in Figures 4.14 and 4.15.

▶ Mr G P du Plessis of *UNISA* for permission to reproduce the advertisement in Figure 4.11.

▶ Ms Thea Venter for the graphic design of Figure 4.1.

George C Angelopulo
April 1996

Introduction to Speech Communication

Rudolph de Jager

Overview

This unit begins with a short history of speech communication. Thereafter we define speech communication and discuss the different types of speech, as well as all aspects to be taken into consideration when preparing a speech. The next section focuses on the delivery of a speech. Models of speech evaluation follow, and we conclude this unit by discussing speech in mass-media interviews.

Objectives

At the end of this unit you should be able to:

1 Identify at least four historic writers on speech communication whose contributions are still valid today.

2 Define *speech communication*.

3 Name and give examples of the three main types of speech.

4 Explain the factors that should be taken into consideration when analysing an audience.

5 Describe the principles on which a speech outline is based, and formulate the outline of a speech on a topic of your choice.

6 Name the different types of speech designs and provide examples of each.

7 Explain why supporting materials/evidence are important when preparing a speech.

8 Describe two types and tests of reasoning using examples of your own.

9 Identify what is important when dealing with language and style in a speech.

10 Compare the different methods of speech delivery and explain which methods you regard as the most appropriate for particular occasions.

11 Evaluate a speech from one of the cases in this unit using the SMMA system or the dramatistic system of evaluation.

12 Explain the Toulmin model and construct an argument of your own.

13 Identify fallacies of reasoning during a debate.

14 Explain which factors you should take into consideration when speaking on radio or television.

Key terms to understand and remember

probabilities
settings
speech communication

Technically advanced communication media have become a part of every-day life in South Africa. Examples include cellular phones, satellite transmissions and the Internet which connects computer networks all over the world. Speech remains an integral part of most of these modern communication media despite the far-reaching technological advances involved. Examples of the use of speech in these media include radio and television presentations, satellite conferences, and interactive television and speech through multimedia computers.

But *speech communication* is not limited only to these media: we use speech communication in all the settings in which communication takes place (cf. Steinberg 1994). While we are speaking to an audience we may receive feedback through nonverbal communication, for example audience members may avoid eye contact, and the speaker may then decide (through **intrapersonal communication**) to speak with more enthusiasm. In **interpersonal communication** a lecturer may explain a difficult concept to a student by means of a lecture, or two people may debate a specific topic. In **small-group communication** one person may deliver a speech to introduce a group discussion. In **public speaking** the speaker delivers a speech to a large number of people in a face-to-face situation. In **mass communication**, speech communication is used in presentations, debates and interviews on radio and television.

The importance of speech communication in public relations (Units 2 and 3) and advertising (Unit 4) must be briefly considered because of its relevance to this course book as a whole. Speeches are an integral component of public relations in communicating with, for example, employees, shareholders or representatives from the mass media at a news conference (cf. Skinner & Von Essen 1991:66–72, 151–171). In advertising, a prospective advertisement (or series of advertisements) is usually presented to the client through speech communication, which may also be part of the advertisement itself (cf. Sinclair & Barenblatt 1993:196–198). Knowledge of the types and principles of speech and argumentation can therefore help us in planning and executing a public relations or advertising campaign. In other words, by integrating the content of the different units in this course book, we come to realise the applicability of speech communication in other forms of communication.

A short history of speech communication

One remarkable aspect of speech communication is its long history. The oldest essay ever discovered, addressed to Kagemni, the eldest son of the pharaoh Huni, was written about 3000 BC and consists of advice on how to speak effectively. This essay and other works of the Egyptians (for example the book *Precepts* written around 2675 BC by Ptah-Hotep) contributed little to speech theory as we know it today. But these works are significant because they show us that interest in speech is at least 5000 years old.

Another interesting aspect of speech communication is that contributions made 2500 years ago are still valid today, and form an integral part of the subject. Therefore, in the sections that follow, we distinguish between six periods in the development of speech communication (cf. McCroskey 1978:289–302); these periods are presented in chronological order. We highlight the most important contributions from writers on the subject that are still valid today and relevant to this unit.

The Greek period

During the fifth century BC at Syracuse in Sicily, Corax and his pupil Tisias formulated the first works on speech communication in Greece. Their contribution was a theory of how arguments should be developed from probabilities (which Aristotle developed more fully later on), and the organisation of a message into roughly the equivalent of an **introduction**, a **body** and a **conclusion.** Today, we still maintain that a speech should follow this structure.

Protagoras of Abdara, a sophist (i.e. a teacher who sets up a small school and charges tuition fees for tutoring) contended that each proposition (i.e. a point to be discussed or maintained) has two sides, and that speakers should be able to argue both sides. Gorgias of Leontini was one of the first writers on speech communication to emphasise the importance of **emotions** in a speech.

Isocrates was regarded as the most influential of the Greek sophists and made contributions on style and the importance of education and training in order to become an ideal orator. Plato, in his dialogue *Gorgias,* criticised the rhetoric of the day as merely a form of flattery, referring to some of the sophists' rhetoric of excess (i.e. their concentration only upon the communicator and the delivery of a speech). In a later dialogue, *Phaedrus*, Plato states what is necessary for the establishment of a truly good theory of rhetoric – it should be aimed at truth rather than victory (cf. Ehninger 1965:165).

Some people regard Aristotle's *Rhetoric* as an answer to Plato's criticism of the rhetoric of the day. Aristotle's contributions are regarded today as the most influential in speech communication.

Aristotle (384–322 BC) was a student of Plato in Athens. In *Rhetoric* (consisting of three books which comprised a philosophy of rhetoric rather than a theory of rhetoric) he concentrates mainly on the art of persuasive speech communication (cf. Corbett (ed) 1984). Of the five classical canons of rhetoric which were developed later during the Roman period – namely **invention** (i.e. selection of proofs), **disposition** (i.e. the arrangements of these proofs), **style** of the **language, memory** and **delivery** of the message – Aristotle discussed invention, disposition and style, but only mentioned delivery and made no mention at all of memory. This may be because two works by Aristotle were never found, namely *Theodectea* (this reportedly dealt with style and the organisation of speeches – the same as Book III of *Rhetoric*) and *Gryllus* (which dealt with the history of rhetoric).

Aristotle regarded speech and reason (*logos*) as sufficiently powerful to create great benefits when correctly used, but maintained that speech and reason could be harmful when used incorrectly. (See Bredenkamp 1996 for a discussion of Aristotle's contributions with regard to the three kinds of speeches, artistic and non-artistic proofs, the syllogism and enthymeme.)

The Roman period

Roman writings on speechification elaborate, refine and systematise the works of the Greek writers. It was during this period that the Roman writers first clearly divided a speech into five tasks or canons (cf. Ehninger 1965:169).

The first extant Latin work on rhetoric was written about 82 BC and was called *Rhetorica ad herennium*. Unlike Aristotle's work *Rhetoric, Rhetorica ad herennium* gave practical hints to speakers. This book made virtually no impact when it was written, but was widely used during the latter Middle Ages and the Renaissance.

During the Roman period, Rome's leading speaker was Cicero (cf. Ehninger 1965:170). According to Cicero, any speaker should have extensive knowledge of many subjects in order to develop arguments.

Fabius Quintilianus was the first teacher of rhetoric to be hired by the Roman government. He produced a collective work on the training of the speaker which consisted of twelve books – the *Institutio oratoria*. Like Cicero, Quintilianus also emphasised the broad liberal arts education required by a student in order to become a good speaker.

One of the factors that made speech so important during the existence of the Greek city-states and the Roman Empire, was the nature of the political systems of the day. These political systems were a breeding ground for speech communication. They were open systems in the sense that governments existed where citizens and representatives of citizens debated topical issues. These systems also created an environment where teachers and schools of speech communication could emerge. After the decline of first the Greek city-states and then the Roman Empire, came the curbing of free institutions (cf. Ehninger 1965:170). Subsequent political systems did not have the same degree of openness which could assure the growth of speech communication. For this reason, no significant works on public speaking emerged for centuries after the decline of the Greek city-states and the Roman Empire.

Third century AD to the Renaissance

The only noteworthy teacher of speech communication during this period was Augustine. His works included *Confessions* and *De doctrina Christiana,* of which book IV is, according to McCroskey (1978:296), probably the best work on preaching that has ever been written.

The Renaissance

During the Renaissance, knowledge of many subjects was also considered important. This belief made Cicero's influence during this period greater than Aristotle's. Dominant works during this period, for example the works of Petrus Ramus, viewed speech communication and logic separately. Speech communication was regarded as the study of **style and delivery** only, while **invention** (discovery and analysis of subject matter and proof) and **disposition** (structure and arrangement of a speech) were assigned to **logic**. The above sentence refers to four of the five classical canons of rhetoric (i.e. persuasive speech communication) which are primarily concerned with the encoding process of communication. The fifth canon of classical rhetoric is **memory** – the ability of the speaker to be in command of the whole speech (cf. McCroskey 1978; De Wet 1991:29).

The first book on speech communication to be published in the English language was by Leonard Cox and entitled *The arte or crafte of rhetoryke*. Another work from England was Thomas Wilson's *Arte of rhetorique* (cf. McCroskey 1978). Both books concentrated on the classical tradition of rhetoric showing that the influence of the Ramistic approach had become less significant. It was during the late seventeenth century at the end of the Renaissance that parliamentary speaking was cultivated, particularly in the British Parliament and the French Revolutionary Assembly, laying the foundation for modern views on speech communication (cf. Ehninger 1965:172).

The colonial period

Fénelon, a French rhetorician, did not agree with the Ramistic approach of rhetoric and emphasised the close relationship between rhetoric and logic; he also advocated naturalness in style and delivery. A group of theorists known as the *Elocutionary Movement* (referring to *elocutio* or style – one of the five classical canons of rhetoric) developed a body of theory representing the antithesis to the naturalness in style and delivery.

The founders of the Elocutionary Movement were Thomas Sheridan (*Lectures on elocution* 1756), Joshua Steele (*Prosodia rationalis* 1775), John Walker (*Elements of elocution* 1781) and James Burg (*The art of speaking* 1761) (cf. McCroskey 1978). This group was influential during the late eighteenth and early nineteenth centuries. The Elocutionists produced highly artificial systems in their research methods when they observed speakers' voices and manners and then codified what kind of responses were produced when speakers verified their verbal and nonverbal communication.

Other influential writers during the colonial period were the British and their theories restated, clarified and extended the classical theories of the Greek and Roman writers. These writers included George Campbell (*Philosophy of rhetoric* 1776) who regarded the audience rather than the speech itself as the major element in a speech. Hugh Blair (*Lectures on rhetoric and belles lettres* 1783) concentrated on style and taste. Richard Whatley (*Elements of rhetoric* 1828) developed concepts originally used by Aristotle such as probability, burden of proof and ethos. Whatley also distinguished between reasoning from example versus reasoning from analogy (cf. McCroskey 1978:299–300).

The modern period

James Winans introduced psychology of **attention** as the basis for a system of public address in his book *Public speaking* (1915). Charles Woolbert was the first to approach rhetoric as a behavioural science and Herbert Wichelns the first to make a clear distinction between rhetorical criticism and literary criticism (cf. McCroskey 1978). I A Richards – in his *Philosophy of Rhetoric* (1936) – showed how language (in any kind of discourse) works in order to identify the causes of misunderstanding and to produce understanding in an audience. Kenneth Burke made his primary contribution to the theory of rhetoric in *A rhetoric of motives* (1969) in which he suggested that speakers wishing to persuade an audience should identify themselves with the audience, or become *consubstantial* with the audience (cf. McCroskey 1978:300; Ehninger 1965:177).

This examination of the origins of the fundamental concepts and principles of speech communication shows that much of our current knowledge and understanding of this subject is derived from these early periods.

WHAT IS SPEECH COMMUNICATION?

Key terms to understand and remember

boomerang effect
inoculated audience
speech communication
speeches for special occasions

informative speaking
sleeper effect
speeches to persuade

Speech communication is an intentional interaction between a speaker and an audience where the speaker purposefully, through premeditated verbal and nonverbal messages, informs and/or persuades and/or entertains an audience within a specific communication environment. Direct feedback from the audience is mainly nonverbal, or in some instances, for example when the speaker is speaking on radio or television, almost nonexistent (cf. Du Plooy 1991:11–12, 66).

Speech communication is **intentional** and **purposeful**, which means that it is a planned communication activity in which the speaker wants to transfer specific meaning to the audience.

First the speaker must establish the general purpose of the speech – to inform and/or persuade and/or entertain an audience, depending on the nature of the occasion. Then the speaker analyses the **audience** he or she is going to address within a specific **communication environment,** for example the mass-communication environment of radio and television. The message is **premeditated**, which means that it is selected for a particular purpose, researched and planned. It also means that the speech content is organised, substantiated with supporting material, consists of sound arguments, begins with a good introduction and ends with a conclusion, is illustrated by means of visual aids, and is written in a conversational style using well-chosen words.

Thereafter the speaker delivers the speech and considers both the method **and** nonverbal aspects of delivery. To improve on the preparation and presentation of a speech, we must be able to evaluate a speech. This is done by means of theoretical models that apply to speech communication.

To elaborate on the definition of speech communication, the **types of speech** which a speaker can deliver are discussed below. These types are related to the purpose and the nature of the speech occasion, which can be to *inform* and/or to *persuade* an audience or it can be a speech prepared for a *special occasion* (cf. Osborn & Osborn 1988; DeVito 1990; Gronbeck, German, Ehninger & Monroe 1992). We deal with each of the various types of speech in the section below.

Informative speaking

A speech is informative if the **main purpose** is to share knowledge and to create understanding. Most of the time this knowledge refers to information which the audience did not know or was not aware of previously. Therefore new information or understanding is provided for the audience, and at no time is the audience asked to **change** their beliefs or behaviour. An informative speech can shape perceptions and should present all relevant material on a topic to the audience in order to reveal and clarify the audience's options for action. For example, two speakers may speak on study methods, but each may advise the audience to follow a different approach. This gives the audience the opportunity to form an idea of which of the two methods will ensure the highest success rate.

Forms of informative speeches

The form of an informative speech is dependent on the topic of the speech, the level of knowledge possessed by the audience and on the abilities of the speaker. We distinguish between the following forms of informative speeches.

Speech of demonstration and instruction: A *speech of demonstration* shows or tells an audience how something is done or how something functions so that they can understand or apply the knowledge. Generally, *instructions* explain complex processes verbally and *demonstrations* explain **and** illustrate such processes verbally and nonverbally. These speeches require clarity and should be simple enough to enable an audience to repeat or reproduce the required steps after the speech has been delivered.

During such a speech, it is helpful first to present a broad overview and then to present a step-by-step sequence on how the task is to be performed. Visual aids, for example displaying the ingredients of a cake when demonstrating how to bake a cake, can play an important role in showing the steps of the process in sequence.

Speech of description: A *speech of description* describes an object, person, event or process. After such a speech the audience should have a clear picture of the subject. Selecting a specific *speech design* may assist the speaker in describing something. Although audiovisual aids can be a valuable tool during speeches of description, such speeches are frequently used on radio. On radio a speaker cannot show the listeners anything and must instead describe each object or image under discussion using a variety of descriptive phrases relating to colour, size, weight, mood, length, time, how rich/poor and the who? what? when? where? why? and how? often used by journalists to describe an event.

Speech of definition: A *speech of definition* explains the meaning or significance of an unfamiliar or unknown concept or process to the audience. This is done in order to define significant concepts which may be of relevance to the audience. For example, a speech of definition may be used to introduce the Internet to an audience which has never heard of the Internet before. After defining the Internet, the speaker may demonstrate to the audience how to use it. In this example, two types of informative speeches are used, namely a speech of definition and a speech of demonstration.

Oral reports: An *oral report* is a speech that assembles, arranges and interprets information after investigation, in response to a request made or a goal set by a group. Committee reports, academic reports and executive reports are examples of oral reports. Research findings on, for example, housing shortages or privatisation are normally presented to the people who requested the information by means of oral reports.

Speech of explanation: A *speech of explanation* informs the audience about concepts, ideas and beliefs. These concepts are more abstract than those dealt with in speeches of description or demonstration. The purpose of such a speech is to increase the understanding or appreciation of a particular field of knowledge or activity. Lectures on concepts used in a research process are an example of a speech of explanation.

Different **forms** of informative speeches can be included in a speech. For example, we can define **and** describe an object in one speech. However, an informative speech has a definite purpose and a speaker must decide which form of informative speech is necessary to present the specific information.

When giving an informative speech, the following principles must be considered:

▶ Limit the amount of information, but provide enough examples, illustrations and descriptions.

▶ Avoid overloading the audience with too much information without any amplification.

▶ Present information at the **appropriate level** so that the audience is neither bored nor confused.

▶ Relate new information to old to improve clarity and understanding.

▶ Package or cluster ideas together in groups of, for example, three, five and seven, because the audience can usually only remember between three and seven ideas at a time. Relate the different ideas to one another by stating the coherence between them.

▶ Motivate the audience by providing information which is relevant and useful to their needs and interests.

▶ Present information through several **senses** (i.e. let the audience see, smell, taste and feel the topic where applicable and possible during a speech).

▶ Hold the attention of the audience by making use of repetition; new or unusual phrases; contrast in volume, pitch of voice, rate of speaking and contrast of words and phrases. For example, the speech of Martin Luther King, Junior, delivered at the Lincoln Memorial, Washington, DC on 28 August 1963, in which he repeated the phrases "Now is the time" and "I have a dream", is a good example of how repetition can hold the attention of the audience. Another example is the speech delivered by John F Kennedy at the Presidential Inauguration Ceremony on 20 January 1961 in which he used the phrase: "... ask not what your country can do for you – ask what you can do for your country".

Persuasive speeches

The general purpose of a persuasive speech is to reinforce or change the attitudes, beliefs and behaviour of the audience – to convince the audience that they should support or reject a certain proposition. Speakers who deliver informative speeches are satisfied if the audience understands and remembers what they say. Conversely, speakers delivering persuasive speeches want the audience to agree with them and attempt to achieve this aim by reinforcing or changing the audience's attitudes, beliefs or behaviour and even by getting the audience to act on the message, if that is the purpose of the speech.

According to Bredenkamp (1996:1–38), persuasion is a complex process within which success or failure is difficult to measure. The theories of attitude change, the learning theories, the consistency theories, the social judgement and involvement theory and theories of mass-media effects are all applicable to persuasive speeches. These theories can help a speaker to know **what** persuades an audience and **why** and **how** an audience is persuaded, so that a speaker can reinforce or change attitudes and/or beliefs and/or behaviour. Speakers can anticipate certain attitudes, beliefs and behaviour from an audience when they have knowledge of theories that try to explain **how** persuasion works.

Forms of persuasive speeches

The following two forms of persuasive speeches can be distinguished.

Speeches to strengthen or change attitudes and beliefs: Most of the time religious and political speeches try to strengthen attitudes and beliefs. Changing attitudes and beliefs is difficult. First the speaker must estimate the current state of the audience's attitudes and beliefs. For example, if an audience is in agreement with the speaker, objectives can be stated early in the speech. (The theories of attitude change are relevant in this example.)

If, however, the audience disagrees with a speaker, the speaker must first cover those issues which are not controversial and then reserve the objectives of the speech until the audience has been provided with sound arguments which will be both respected and accepted. A multisided presentation, where a speaker first acknowledges and then refutes the opposition's arguments, thereafter discussing the advantages of a conflicting view, will enhance trustworthiness because the speaker will be shown to know and respect the opposition.

If a speaker demonstrates credibility, seeks change gradually and shows the audience how the attitudes and beliefs which the speaker holds relate to their own motives, the speaker's chances of succeeding will increase. (The consistency theories are relevant in this example.)

Speeches urging action: Urging a group or an individual to action goes beyond the changing of attitude and belief. When urging a **group** to action, a speaker ought to reinforce group identity by using inclusive pronouns (we, our, us) and by emphasising group goals, motives and achievements. When urging **individuals** to action, the speaker must first make the audience members see the value of action in personal terms by appealing to each member's self-interest. The consequences of action or inaction must be clearly spelled out, as in any action there is some degree of risk involved.

The audience must see the advantages of such action for themselves, what the speaker wants them to do must be realistic and the speaker must demonstrate a willingness to do the same.

A persuasive speech may perform both functions of urging action and strengthening or changing attitudes and beliefs, but usually one will be dominant.

To differentiate further between **informative** and **persuasive** speeches, we contrast the characteristics of both types of speech:

▶ **Persuasive** speaking aims at making the audience choose from a number of options by eliminating alternatives until only one choice remains. **Informative** speaking will only reveal and clarify these options.

▶ **Persuasive** speaking asks for more commitment than **informative** speaking.

▶ A **persuasive** speech entails greater responsibilities and ethical obligations on the part of the speaker than does an **informative** speech as the audience may be asked to believe or to do something which involves taking a risk.

▶ **Persuasive** speakers act more as leaders while **informative** speakers act more as teachers.

▶ **Persuasive** speaking depends more on logos and pathos while **informative** speaking depends more on understanding.

▶ As **persuasive** speaking often requires group action or group agreement, it frequently appeals to groups, in contrast to **informative** speaking which usually addresses the audience as individuals.

Rank's model of persuasion, the AIDA principle and Monroe's motivated sequence may all apply to persuasive speaking (cf. Bredenkamp 1996:21–26 for a discussion of the latter). However, for the purpose of this unit we discuss twelve steps that are specifically applicable to a **persuasive speech**.

The following twelve steps, grouped into four categories, may be necessary for the successful transmission of a persuasive message by means of **speech** communication.

Reception

Reception refers to the messages which are received by the audience. Reception includes:

1   **Exposure** – The audience must hear what the speaker has to say.

2   **Attention** – The speaker must grab the attention of the audience by means of a good introduction, and then hold the audience's attention by means of a good delivery.

3   **Involvement** – The speaker must motivate the audience by addressing their needs and interests so that the audience becomes involved in the speech and keeps listening. (Maslow's [1954] hierarchy of needs and Packard's [1960] theory of needs are relevant in this step.)

Orientation

Orientation concerns how the audience is geared to persuasion. Orientation includes:

4   **Comprehension** – A clear speech structure, simple language and a demonstration of complex terms and ideas are necessary to enable the audience to understand the speaker's message.

5   **Information** – The content of the speech must be credible; this can be achieved by the presentation of sound arguments which give the audience good reason to believe the speaker.

➡

---

6 **Providing skills** – If a speaker wants an audience to do something, guidelines and skills must be provided to enable the audience to put the plan into effect.

Acceptance

Acceptance may range from small concessions to total commitment. The following are necessary for acceptance:

7 **Agreement** – There are degrees of agreement. When a speaker's proposal involves risk and the audience has to deviate from previously held convictions, a lesser degree of agreement can be regarded as successful. (The consistency theories are relevant to this step in a persuasive speech.)

8 **Retention** – By means of examples, narratives and visual aids such as slides or models, a speaker can ensure that the audience not only agrees but also remembers what is said.

9 **Remembering agreement** – The audience must remember their commitment to a speech and the reasons for this commitment: signing a petition, urging the audience to write letters or to participate in a march may commit the audience to their agreement.

Integration

Audiences must integrate the content of the speech with their own beliefs, attitudes and behaviour. The following steps are involved:

10 **Utilisation** – The persuasive speech must help the audience to understand and interpret the **benefits** of adopting some attitude or course of action that the speaker proposes.

11 **Demonstration** – An audience may agree with a speaker but not demonstrate this in their behaviour. A series of persuasive speeches aims to secure long-lasting changes in attitude and belief, but especially behaviour.

12 **Consolidation** – A reinforcement of attitudes, beliefs and behaviour can be achieved by means of one speech; however, the transformation of an audience's attitudes, beliefs and behaviour can rarely be achieved by one speech only. In order to have an effect, the first persuasive speech must be part of a series of powerful persuasive appeals heard over a period of time. Attitudes, beliefs and behaviours are rarely formed in one day or as a result of one specific event: an appeal to one small change may therefore prove to be more successful than trying to change an audience's whole belief system.

The principles of a persuasive speech

When using the above twelve steps in a persuasive speech a speaker's success in persuading an audience will largely depend on the use of the principles of persuasive speeches. The following seven principles of a persuasive speech can be distinguished.

▶ A speaker who is regarded as credible will prove to be more persuasive. To be credible a speaker must come across as knowledgeable, dynamic and of good character.

▶ Listeners who **participate** actively in a speech are more likely to be persuaded than listeners who receive the message passively. Asking an audience to summarise the arguments for themselves is an example of active participation.

▶ A speaker can expect to gain little ground in persuading an *inoculated audience* (i.e. an audience which has previously been exposed to different opinions on the subject and which therefore can provide counterarguments to what the speaker has to say). It is usually easier to persuade an *uninoculated audience* which may not be familiar with any counterarguments on the subject. A speaker can strengthen an audience's beliefs by providing counterarguments and then refuting those arguments. This will create an inoculated audience which immunises itself against future attacks on these beliefs and values.

▶ An audience is best persuaded if a speaker appeals to their **needs.** If a speaker relates the attitudes and behaviours required of the audience to motives such as love, status, independence and freedom, the speaker will be more persuasive.

▶ More conclusive evidence is required if the decision the audience is asked to make is an important one (for example, the financial implications of buying a home versus those involved in selecting a pair of shoes).

▶ People **change gradually** over a long period of time. Persuasion will therefore be more effective if the speaker aims to bring about small changes over a period of time. If too much change is advocated, a speaker may create a *boomerang effect,* which makes the audience react more strongly than before to the speaker's opinion or position.

▶ After a persuasive speech, a speaker may experience a **delayed reaction** or *sleeper effect* from the audience. A sleeper effect refers to the situation where change occurs only after a period of time while the audience integrates the change into its own belief system. Even if the speech fails to change prevailing attitudes or beliefs, it may have served a consciousness-raising function, sensitising the listeners to the issue which may make them more receptive to persuasion on that particular subject in the future.

Case 1.1

Speech given by Minister Jay Naidoo at the Dr Knak Primary School, Alexandra, on World Water Day, 22 March 1996

(With acknowledgement to *South African Communication Service*)

Today is World Water Day and I have come here to your school to tell you about what the government is doing to ensure that there is enough water in the future not only for your parents and you as our children, but also for our factories and farmers.

➡

Despite the good rains we have had over the past few months, experts say that in the long term, water is scarce and so saving water is very important, not only for government, but also for each and every one of us.

Our country is very short of water and every drop must be made to count! We should be learning to use water wisely.

If we throw rubbish into our rivers, we reduce the amount of clean water available. We must work hard to clean up the Jukskei River which runs through Alex.

If we leave taps dripping, we take away drinking water from other people. We must not waste water in any way.

So what can you do? Every day, you can think about ways you use water and ways you can save it. For example, switching off the tap while you brush your teeth, or flushing the toilet less often or putting the plug in the sink or bath and using the water more than once.

The 2020 Vision of Water in South Africa is also running a competition to find the school in South Africa which can put on the best "Celebration of Water" activities.

The winning school will get a prize of R5 000 worth of conservation-related materials. I challenge you to be the school that wins the prize.

I want to hear from you about what you are doing and how you are progressing with your goal to learn more about saving water and how you are making a difference in this area.

To remind you of my challenge and of the importance of saving water, I have brought you a poster showing the cycle of water use and how it is wasted.

I hope that you will take this programme seriously and work toward making water conservation a way of life for everyone in this area.

I want each of you to be an organiser. Talk to your parents, your brothers and your sisters. Talk to students in other schools.

Let us build a better Alexandra – an Alexandra that we can be proud of, one that is clean and healthy, with trees and which is safe for all. Where everyone has clean water, in their homes, in the schools and in the clinics.

I am depending on you all.

ACTIVITY

Answer the following questions:

1 What form/s of informative and/or persuasive speech is/are found in Case 1.1?

2 Does this speech follow the twelve steps necessary for the successful transmission of a persuasive message?

Speeches for special occasions

The third type of speech takes place during special occasions or ceremonies. The purpose of a ceremonial speech includes sharing aims, beliefs and aspirations, which makes it possible for such a speech to be used as a foundation for an informative or a persuasive speech. Therefore, these speeches are in part informative, entertaining **and** persuasive. Occasions or ceremonies are usually characterised by a ritual involving a group of people who regard themselves as bonded together. This bond is more the result of a psychological state than of physical closeness. Speeches delivered during such occasions normally include that group's beliefs, values and attitudes, with the emphasis on ritualised tradition and a common heritage, rather than on change.

Forms of speeches for special occasions

Four forms of speeches usually delivered during special occasions can be distinguished.

Speech of introduction: During a *speech of introduction* a speaker usually introduces another speaker or a series of speakers and the specific subject under discussion.

Speeches of introduction are brief; they serve simply to introduce the speaker and do not cover the main speaker's subject, but only introduce the audience to the subject and its significance. Such speeches should serve to strengthen the ethos of the speaker and motivate the audience to listen to him/her. A few sentences outlining a speaker's past accomplishments and standing in the relevant field should be adequate – the audience came to listen to the main speaker and not to the introduction. The introduction of a panel of speakers on *Focus,* a discussion programme broadcast by the SABC, is a good example of a speech of introduction.

Speech of tribute: A *speech of tribute* recognises and celebrates the accomplishments of persons or the significance of events. These accomplishments could have taken place decades ago or just yesterday. For example, on *Youth Day,* 16 June each year, speakers pay tribute to the role that the youth played in the development of a democratic South Africa. Such tributes will inevitably contain references to the clashes in Soweto between police and schoolchildren in 1976.

Speeches of tribute are occasions of pride and appreciation and should illustrate both the relevant achievements and their consequences. Tributes should not be exaggerated so that the content becomes unbelievable; speakers must focus on the subject of tribute and not on themselves.

Speech of presentation: A *speech of presentation* usually honours or recognises a person or event by means of an award. During such a speech, the speaker should give the occasion an air of dignity and status by referring, for example, to the standing of the award and to previous recipients. The speaker must also state the reason for the presentation. Depending on how much the audience knows about the recipient of the award, the speaker can briefly sketch a background of the recipient's achievement/s. A short, concise and well-planned presentation will ensure that the speaker is not long-winded and uninteresting.

Speech of acceptance: Normally when a speaker, or the group or organisation which he/she represents, receives an award or honour, it is acknowledged by means of a *speech of acceptance*. If a speaker accepts the award on behalf of an organisation, the groups or individuals involved should also be thanked. The importance of the award and the activity being recognised should also be acknowledged. Clichés should be avoided during such speeches.

In this section of the unit we discussed the nature and purpose of speech communication. This discussion leads us to the next section which focuses on **how to prepare** a speech.

1.3 PREPARING A SPEECH

Key terms to understand and remember

argumentation	analogy
audience analysis	attitudes
beliefs	communication environment
conclusion	deductive reasoning
demographics	evidence
fixed beliefs	inductive reasoning
introduction	language
oral language	preliminary tuning effect
proposition	psychographics
purpose	reasoning
sociographics	speech atmosphere
speech design	speech material
speech outline	statistics
style	supporting material
testimony	thematic statement
topic	transition
values	variable beliefs
visual aids	warrants
written language	

A well-prepared speech makes presentation much easier because the speaker knows what he/she is about to say. A well-planned speech also means that the speaker is more likely to interest the audience.

The steps to be followed when planning a speech may differ according to circumstances – the importance of certain steps will be determined by the actual situation. If the speaker is not asked to talk about a specific subject, an audience analysis must be done even before selecting a topic. This will ensure that the speaker remains on the right track from the start and will prevent the speaker from having to change the context or structure of the speech after ascertaining the type of audience to be faced.

Analysing the audience and the speech environment

In speech communication an *audience* can be defined as a group of individuals gathered together to hear a speech. Such a speech usually takes place in a face-to-face situation. However, when someone speaks on radio or television it is not in a face-to-face situation and the individuals in the audience may be all over the country – or even all over the world – in front of their television sets or listening to the radio (cf. DeVito 1990:9, 113). The common factor with regard to the individuals who comprise these audiences is that they are listening to a speech. The concept **individuals** emphasises the uniqueness of the persons making up an audience, which means that audience members generally differ in terms of *psychographics, demographics* and *sociographics.*

The purpose of an *audience analysis* is to identify those characteristics which are common to the majority of the members. However, on a particular occasion a speaker may only be interested in the characteristics of a segment of the audience, for example only the graduates (and not the parents, press and academics who are also present in the audience) at a graduation ceremony (cf. Clevenger 1966:32–33). When speakers identify these shared characteristics they may make some generalisations about the audience, but these generalisations must not be used as stereotypes.

In order to identify these characteristics, prior to planning a speech, a speaker may interview a few members of the intended audience or speak to those who know the audience better than he or she does, for example the organiser who invites the speaker to speak. After a speech has been delivered, a speaker may again ask for feedback from the members of the audience.

When preparing a speech, the speaker should take into account the *psychographics, demographics* and *sociographics* of the audience and the *communication environment.* These four factors determine the nature of the information and how it is to be presented to a specific audience, irrespective of whether the speaker wants to inform, persuade or entertain the audience. In other areas of communication, such as public relations and advertising, audiences may also be defined by their geographic position, behaviour or needs.

Psychographics

Psychographics are definitions of the fundamental *values, beliefs,* and *attitudes* of an audience. Psychographic definitions group people "into homogeneous segments on the basis of their psychological makeup" (Arens & Bovée 1994:145). These values, beliefs and attitudes are interdependent and may reinforce or weaken each other (cf. Gronbeck et al. 1992:69–70, 75).

Values: Values are the basic constructs organising our orientation to life, providing the standards which we use to judge the relative positive or negative worth of a person, object or action. How we should behave (e.g. being honest, loving and responsible) and what the ideal state of existence for us should be (e.g. equality, freedom, a world at peace and a comfortable life) are determined by our values (cf. Gronbeck et al. 1992:75–76; DeVito 1990:114; Osborn & Osborn 1988:135).

Values are central to a person's self-concept and are resistant to change (cf. Osborn & Osborn 1988:135). Because values represent broad categories of our orientation to life, values are more basic than beliefs and attitudes and serve as their foundation. For example, if we hold a certain value such as *Nature conservation is vital for human existence,* our attitude towards national parks or ecotourism will be positive, and we may believe that *nature conservation may improve our quality of life.* If a speaker is able to highlight values which are shared with a specific audience, it will be easier for the audience to identify with the speaker.

Beliefs: Beliefs are convictions regarding what is true or false. Beliefs are held with varying degrees of certainty and include facts and opinions. Facts are beliefs supported by strong external evidence such as found in this message: *Smoking is harmful to your health*. Opinions are strong personal beliefs that may or may not be supported by strong external evidence, for example: *Job creation is more important than building houses*.

If opinions are widely held by an audience they may be regarded as facts. Facts and opinions may depend on the context in which they are held. Although South Africans may believe that democracy is the best form of government, people in some socialist countries may *know for a fact* that democracy is not the best form of government (an opinion). In the latter case it may be more important to know with what degree of certainty the audience believes in something than it is to know whether they regard it as fact or opinion. That is why we differentiate between *fixed* and *variable beliefs*.

Fixed beliefs are central to our thinking and are highly resistant to change. They can even develop into stereotypes. According to Gronbeck et al. (1992:71), people get more fixed in their minds as they grow older; for example, it is more likely that young voters will change their affiliation to a particular political party than will older voters. *Variable beliefs* are less fixed and may change as a result of experience and/or because of evidence we read or hear from authorities. In other words, if a speaker prepares a speech on a specific topic, it is important to ascertain whether the audience has fixed or variable beliefs regarding the topic.

Attitudes: Attitudes are emotionally weighted, positive or negative responses towards people, objects or ideas. Attitudes express an individual's beliefs and values such as: *South Africa is a beautiful country*, *I like dancing* and *Violence is wrong*.

Because attitudinal statements express values and beliefs, including preferences and feelings, such statements often control people's behaviour, as people normally do things they like and avoid things they dislike.

Speakers must be aware of an audience's **attitude towards them as speakers,** which is based on their reputation as speakers, the content of the speech and the speakers' presentation skills. Speakers should also consider the audience's **attitude towards the subject,** which may be influenced by interest and expectations. An audience which is more or less familiar with the subject of a speech will be likely to have preconceived expectations which can result in **listening barriers** (i.e. interferences with the communication process). It may be necessary to adapt to these expectations or to motivate the audience by means of a well-planned introduction.

An audience also has **attitudes towards the purpose of the speech.** The purpose of the speech may be to entertain, to persuade or to inform. Voters, for example, know that politicians want to persuade them to vote for a particular party; a politician's approach will therefore be different in a region hostile to the party than in a region where the party enjoys huge support.

Although values, beliefs and attitudes are important aspects of audience analysis, Osborn and Osborn (1988:130) regard **motivation** as vital when analysing an audience, because motivation is the drive that directs behaviour towards a specific goal. Motivation can be achieved by making people aware of a need and then by showing them how to satisfy that need. Abraham Maslow's (1954) hierarchy of needs and Vance Packard's (1960) theory of needs can for example, be effectively used by a speaker to motivate an audience to act after a persuasive speech.

Demographics

Demographics describes the physical attributes of the audience. Demographic variables include age, gender, home language, education and sociocultural background. Certain demographic characteristics, such as gender and approximate age, are easy to observe in an audience. However, other demographic characteristics, such as educational background, are rarely observable characteristics (especially in an adult audience), and may only be obtained by means of research. A speaker should take into account the following demographic characteristics (cf. Osborn & Osborn 1988; DeVito 1990; Gronbeck et al. 1992).

Age: Different age groups differ in their goals, interests, day-to-day concerns, respect for tradition and peer groups, and everyday life experiences. Accordingly, it is obvious that different age groups will have different values, beliefs and attitudes.

Younger people are more flexible in their beliefs because they are still seeking their identity. As we grow older, we tend to become more conservative, probably because we have more to lose and are therefore less open to change. Maximum receptiveness to persuasion occurs between the ages of nine and twelve and declines as we grow older.

Gender: A biological woman may assume a masculine sex role and a biological man may assume a feminine role. We know, for example, that black women in certain rural areas in South Africa play a significant role in farming the land, whereas it is mainly white men who farm the land in other rural areas. It would therefore be wrong to assume that only men should attend a meeting on farming methods in rural areas.

Any speaker must avoid **sexual stereotyping** (e.g. making broad generalisations about a gender group) and **sexist language** (e.g. making use of masculine or feminine nouns or pronouns where the gender is unknown or irrelevant).

Language: South Africa has eleven official languages. English is the language most widely spoken because of its international status. However, English is still the second or third language of many South Africans which means that a speaker should keep the language simple and understandable. As some South African politicians have shown, a speaker will certainly earn an audience's respect by addressing listeners in their first language, even if only for a few sentences.

Education: The higher an audience's level of education, the more informed they are and the broader the range of interests they tend to have. Such an audience also tends to be better trained to analyse what they hear and to be more critical listeners than those who are less educated. It is important to use everyday language when explaining technical terms to a less educated audience. It may be necessary to give more background information regarding the topic, to relate the topic to the immediate environment and to draw conclusions more explicitly.

Sociocultural background: A wide variety of sociocultural backgrounds exist in South Africa. Every language spoken in South Africa represents a specific culture including the Greek, Portuguese, Italian, German and Indian cultures. There are also differences in culture within a language group. For example, Xhosa-speaking Gauteng residents may differ in culture from Xhosa people living in the rural areas of Transkei. Afrikaans-speaking residents of the Western Cape can also differ from Afrikaans-speaking farmers in the Northern Province. Despite racial differences, many sociocultural characteristics of different racial groups may be similar, because they may come from a similar background and area of residence.

Sociographics

Sociographic definitions describe audiences in terms of group affiliations. Group affiliations can be useful predictors of the interests and the knowledge of an audience. Voluntary affiliation to groups is usually an indicator that the members share more or less the same values, beliefs and attitudes. The following group affiliations may be important when a speaker analyses an audience.

Occupational groups: Occupational groups may include people working for the same employer, for example *Spoornet*, or people in the same profession, such as nurses who are members of a trade union. Other occupational groups may be related to the level of employment, where income and status will determine group affiliation. Occupational groups may therefore give us insight into what the audience knows about a specific topic. The interests, time limitations, long-range planning, goals, job security and occupational pride of lower-status workers will be different from higher-status workers because they have a different working environment. It is important for a speaker to take the above factors into consideration, especially if both status groups are members of the audience.

Religious groups: Religious education is an important means of instilling values into people. Different religious groups may be more liberal or conservative than others in terms of religious, social and political attitudes, although there may be differences between members of the same religion. It may also be important to bear in mind that some audience members may consider themselves agnostic.

Political groups: Members of political parties tend to express relatively consistent opinions across a wide range of political issues. Such members are normally interested in policies and community issues. In South Africa some members of political parties are very hostile towards members of opposition political parties. Speakers may help to tone down these hostile attitudes by naming some common ground that exists between political parties, for example people wanting peace and better living conditions.

Social groups: People usually join social groups because of shared interests. Students interested in communication may join the Communication Student Association, hikers may join a hikers' club and nature lovers may join the Wildlife Society of South Africa. A speech delivered to a press club on the topic of environmental issues could give a speaker the opportunity of focusing on the role that newspapers can play in making South Africans more environmentally conscious.

All characteristics relating to an audience may not be relevant to a certain speech topic. A speaker therefore may only take into consideration those characteristics which will have a profound effect on the subject matter of the speech. For example, when a speaker addresses primary school children, age and education may be the most important demographic characteristics to consider; the speaker will have to use a simpler vocabulary and adapt to shorter attention spans. In other words, the more information speakers can gather about an anticipated audience, the better they should be able to plan their message.

The communication environment

The *communication environment* includes external factors that may have an effect on a speech. Such an environment includes the variables described below.

Time: During an early-morning speech some members of the audience may still be half asleep, in the afternoon it may be very hot in summer months, and in the evening members of the audience may be anxious to get home. Therefore, when the time may cause some inconvenience to the audience, a bit more humour, lively examples or a more forceful presentation may be necessary.

Physical conditions: Physical conditions may also influence the presentation of a speech. If the audience has to stand, a speaker should deliver a shorter speech than when the audience is sitting. There may also be more distractions when the speech is delivered outdoors and not indoors. When it is too hot or too cold, a speaker may also be compelled to take the length of the speech into consideration. A speaker will be compelled to adapt the presentation if there is no public-address system or if good audiovisual facilities are not available. The availability of electricity should also be considered in remote areas of South Africa where meetings are still commonly held on an open patch of land or in a huge tent.

Size of the audience: The larger the audience, the more differences there may be in terms of demographic, psychographic and sociographic characteristics. It may be necessary to speak more slowly and more loudly and to enunciate words more carefully if the audience is large and diverse. By selecting representative segments of the audience, the speaker should be able to remain in contact with the listeners, as individual eye contact with each audience member may be impossible. With a small audience speakers may be more casual and informal and their **facial expressions** may be picked up by the audience. This will not necessarily be the case with a larger audience, where **gestures** may be more effective.

Nature and purpose of the speech occasion: The topic, language, design and supporting material of a speech may all be influenced by the nature and purpose of the speech occasion. Therefore, the reason why an audience comes together, and what they expect of the speech occasion should be considered. When a speech is covered by the mass media, the speaker should not only consider the immediate audience but also the media audience (i.e. readers, listeners or viewers who are going to read about the speech in a newspaper, listen to it on radio or watch an insert thereof on television).

Context: Recent speeches and events may have an influence on a speech. At an occasion where different speeches are delivered by various speakers, the speeches which the audience has heard previously may have a *preliminary tuning effect* – a tendency by the audience to expect speakers who follow to respond to the speakers who went before. Previous speeches may have created a certain mood in the audience and it may be necessary to change the mood before a speaker can start with his or her speech. Such speeches may even contradict what the subsequent speakers are about to say. In such a case, speakers should bring to the attention of the audience that what the audience has heard from the previous speakers is not the total picture, but that there is another side to the topic as well.

Recent events that are applicable to a topic should be included in a speech. Relating a subject to topical events can make a speaker's arguments more credible and the speech more interesting and meaningful to the audience. For example, speaking on methods to improve South Africa as a tourist destination without considering the effect violent crime has on tourism, will weaken the speaker's credibility.

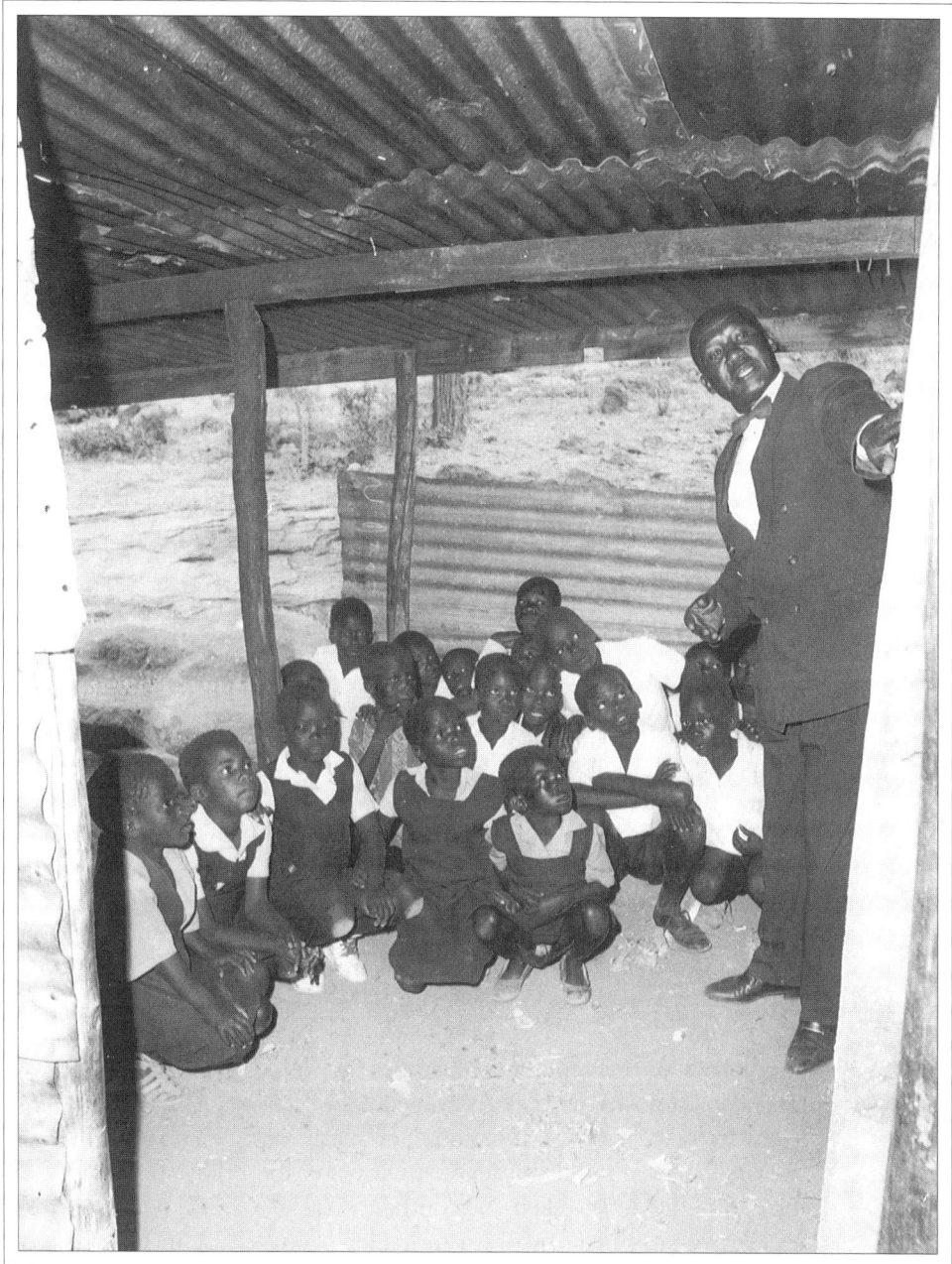

Figure 1.1 **A speech situation speakers may encounter**

(Reproduced with the kind permission of *Beeld*)

ACTIVITY

Analyse Figure 1.1. Which demographic, psychographic and sociographic characteristics of the audience, as well as factors determining the communication environment, do you think this speaker must take into consideration?

Once a speaker has analysed the demographic, sociographic and psychographic characteristics of the audience, as well as the communication environment, the next steps of the planning process of a speech can be followed, taking into account the information gathered from the audience analysis.

Selecting a topic or analysing a proposition

1

A *topic* in a speech is the subject which a speaker selects or about which a speaker is asked to speak. In argumentation, for example in a television debate, the point which a speaker is (or speakers are) asked to discuss is called a *proposition*. A proposition is one central idea stated positively in unemotional terms; it is not just a topic a speaker can speak about, but is rather a statement (idea). For example, *South Africa must keep pornography legalised* is a proposition of policy which the speaker or speakers must affirm or reject.

Selecting a topic

Sometimes a speaker is asked to speak about a specific, well-defined *topic,* for example on a radio programme. The speaker can then start to gather information on the topic. It may happen that a speaker is asked to speak about a general subject, for example *Transformation*; the task will then be to narrow down the subject and focus on what the speaker thinks the audience wants to know. At other times only the occasion is mentioned and the speaker must then decide what topic will interest the audience. In the latter two instances the speaker should select and/or narrow down the subject.

A good speech topic is one which is both important and interesting to the speaker personally. It should also be a topic which the speaker has mastered, or which allows the speaker enough time for research, so that the speech can be delivered with authority. At the same time, the speaker should know what will interest the audience and, with this as a point of departure, discuss a topic which will be both useful and thought-provoking to the audience and relevant to the occasion.

Analysing a given proposition

In a debate, for example on television, it is important to analyse the kind of proposition or propositions that are relevant, so that speakers know if they must argue about facts, values or policy. Too often speakers speak about the same topic but one speaker focuses, for example, on policy and the other on values. Consequently, at the end of the debate each speaker has addressed a different aspect of the topic and no progress has been made in terms of a solution or in furthering the audience's understanding of the topic.

Types of propositions

The following types of propositions are applicable in a debate or any kind of speech where speakers have to affirm or reject the proposition (cf. Lee & Lee 1989:47–56; Schutte 1990:1–5; Freeley 1993:46–49):

Proposition of fact: A proposition of fact asks the audience to affirm or reject a particular state of affairs. At times propositions of facts are debated before propositions of value or policy, since it is necessary first to establish facts before speakers can discuss values and policies.

It is difficult to establish what is a fact, as facts may consist only of possibilities. Therefore, when a proposition of fact is debated, speakers have to show by means of proof that the proposition is true – a fact – or not true. When speakers discuss a proposition of fact they have to describe it and state the cause or occurrence of such a proposition.

As certain facts may be very complex, research may simply show that a certain proposition of fact is only a possibility and it will be up to the speaker to convince the audience that the proposition is such a strong possibility that it can be regarded as a fact. For example, the statement *Democracy improves the quality of people's lives* may be a fact for some people, a possibility for others and untrue to a third group of people. The proposition *Province A has a better educational system than province B* is a proposition of value, as we have to compare the value of each educational system.

Proposition of value: With a proposition of value, speakers have to show that a certain belief, value or fact is **justified** or **unjustified**. When speakers argue on values they deal with evaluations of what can be considered good and bad, fair and unfair, right and wrong, ugly and beautiful, moral and immoral, and so forth. In many cases a proposition of value may be more or less the same as a proposition of fact. When speakers have to make more use of their own subjective convictions and proof – as opposed to external objective criteria – in order to support or reject a proposition, such a proposition will tend to be a proposition of value.

When debating a proposition, such as *South Africans ought to value traditional leaders*, speakers have to consider policy and make use of factual material as well in order to affirm or reject the proposition of value. In the case of a proposition of fact, the audience has to **cognitively** believe the speakers (i.e. using the mind), but when a proposition of value is debated the audience has to **affectively** believe the speakers (i.e. using the emotions).

Proposition of policy: When debating a proposition of policy, speakers ask the audience to affirm or reject an existing or future plan of action, for example *City councils in South Africa should be obliged by law to recycle waste*. Judging policies of the past is an evaluation and therefore a proposition of value. As is the case with other propositions, facts and values may also be relevant in a proposition of policy, although the final objective of such a proposition is to **decide on the correct plan of action**.

Determining the purpose of the speech

The general *purpose* of a speech may be to inform, to entertain or to persuade an audience. The response which a speaker seeks from an audience may be to understand, enjoy, feel, believe or act on what the speaker says. After deciding on the general purpose/s of a speech, the speaker determines the **specific purpose/s**, which concern(s) the actual **goals** to be achieved in the speech.

Examples of specific purposes can be:

1 *To explain to the audience what transformation in an organisation is* (to understand).

2 *To tell the audience in a humorous fashion what some people think transformation is all about* (enjoyment).

3 *To reduce the audience's levels of anxiety about transformation* (feelings).

4 *To persuade the audience that transformation is necessary* (beliefs).

5 *To persuade the audience to participate in a transformation process* (action).

After determining the specific purpose/s of a speech, the speaker formulates a *thematic statement* which captures the essence of the message developed to accomplish the specific purpose. The essence of the speech is built around the thematic statement.

An example of a thematic statement derived from the first above-mentioned specific purpose (to understand) is:

> *Transformation is the ongoing ability of an organisation to adapt to a changing external and internal environment.*

An example of a thematic statement derived from the fourth above-mentioned specific purpose (beliefs) is:

> *When a society changes, organisations within the society should adapt to accommodate new values, beliefs and attitudes to survive as institutions.*

Once the topic or proposition, purpose and thematic statement of the speech have been determined, the speaker can start collecting speech material.

Gathering speech material

With some effort it should not be a problem to gather enough quality information for a speech. In the first place, a speaker should not overlook personal experience and first-hand knowledge about the topic, as this can add credibility and freshness to a speech and is normally a good starting point. Interviewing experts on a subject or asking them where to find reference material can also provide a good point of departure.

Libraries today offer a wide variety of sources such as books, periodicals, government publications and computerised resources such as CD-ROM and the Internet. Other institutions such as the Human Sciences Research Council (HSRC), the South African Bureau of Standards (SABS), the Council for Scientific and Industrial Research (CSIR), the South African Advertising Research Foundation (SAARF), other research organisations, government departments and private institutions are also valuable sources of information, as are radio and television broadcasts.

There is no excuse for a speaker whose information is not reliable or trustworthy, thorough, topical and relevant to the topic/proposition, environment and the audience, as this information is readily available to members of the public.

Selecting the supporting material or evidence for the speech

If a speaker wants to come across as credible and trustworthy, all claims and statements made must be substantiated by *supporting material* or *evidence*. The concept used – supporting material or evidence – depends on the purpose of the speech.

Supporting material includes examples, statistics and testimony that speakers use to **clarify, amplify** and **show the relevance** of ideas. Evidence includes examples, statistics and testimony that speakers use to **prove** statements and/or premises so that the speaker can reach a conclusion with which the audience will agree.

According to Freeley (1993:101), evidence is the raw material of argumentation. Evidence may be classified into direct or circumstantial (indirect) evidence. Direct evidence shows the existence of the fact in question without the need of proof of any other fact. Circumstantial evidence shows the existence of the fact in issue, by first proving another fact or other facts from which the fact in question may be inferred.

Tests of audience acceptability

When a speaker presents evidence, it may happen that while the evidence is generally regarded as highly credible, it may not be acceptable to a specific audience. The following tests can serve as guidelines when selecting evidence (cf. Freeley 1993:136–140):

▶ The evidence should be **consistent** with the beliefs of the audience, as listeners will interpret evidence from the point of view of their own beliefs. For example, if a political candidate states that he or she is a member of a certain religious group this may serve as evidence that the candidate's beliefs are the same as those members of the audience who also belong to that religious group. However, this may be counterproductive if the candidate uses the same argument when addressing an audience belonging to a different religious group.

▶ The source of the evidence should be **acceptable** to the audience. For example, the view (testimony) of a respected elderly person in a rural community may be more acceptable to an audience in that community than research statistics relevant to the case in point.

▶ The evidence should suit the audience's level of education. When presenting evidence, there is no point in quoting from a prestigious academic journal using highly technical terms which the audience is unable to understand. In such a case the evidence should be explained to the audience or the speaker should present other evidence which the listeners will understand.

▶ The evidence should be consistent with the audience's attitudes and values. For example, when the legalisation of abortion is advocated, well-grounded evidence regarding the advantages of abortion may in some cases be dismissed by an audience on the simple basis of their religious values and beliefs.

▶ The evidence should be consistent with the audience's norms. For example, an audience consisting of scientists will impose much more rigorous norms on evidence than will a lay audience. Lawyers, accountants, physicians and politicians usually impose specific standards for evaluating the acceptability of evidence and it is important that a speakers should know these norms.

▶ The evidence should be **documented** for the audience: evidence must be verifiable. Every time that speakers use evidence in a speech they should state the author, credentials, publication and year.

It is not always possible to obtain evidence that the audience will accept. In such a case the speaker must use the available evidence because, if the evidence is credible, the arguments put forward will be more acceptable than would be the case if no evidence was presented at all.

Before supporting material or evidence is included in a speech, the speaker must also ensure that this material is credible. The following are forms of supporting material or evidence, and the related criteria to ensure credibility, which a speaker can use in a speech or argument (cf. Gronbeck et al. 1992; Ayres & Miller 1994).

Examples

Examples, and especially extended examples, are useful in clarifying ideas when presented in narrative form. Examples may be real or hypothetical, and can be presented by means of an illustration, a short specific instance, narratives or anecdotes. The speaker must ensure that there are sufficient examples and that the examples quoted are relevant.

Statistics

Statistics are examples translated into numbers which show relationships between phenomena. These relationships are analysed and presented in totals, fractions, percentages, proportions and ratios. Statistics clarify the nature of a situation by reducing large masses of information into generalised categories.

According to Freeley (1993:127), because of the criteria statistics have to meet, this type of evidence should be used only if a speaker cannot make a point without statistical references. Before a speaker makes use of statistics, information should be obtained regarding the source to ensure that the statistics meet the following criteria (cf. Freeley 1993:128–134):

▶ Are the statistics which have been collected **accurate?** That is, are the people interviewed in the research representative of the population or relevant to the point being made?

▶ Have the statistics been accurately **classified?** If a source states that 80 per cent of South Africans have access to electricity and to running water, but the necessary research was only undertaken in metropolitan areas, we know that the classification *South Africans* is not accurate because people living in rural areas have been excluded.

▶ Were the **units of analysis** in the research **properly defined**, so that all the respondents attached the same meaning to the same unit?

▶ Were the questions asked in the research **unbiased**?

▶ Does the research cover a **sufficient number** of cases to allow for a general conclusion?

▶ Is the **time frame** of the statistics relevant to the point being made?

▶ Was the research **properly conducted** by a reliable and objective source?

▶ Does the visual presentation of the statistics report the data **fairly**?

When speakers present statistics they should:

▶ Round off complicated numbers: say *nearly 200 000* rather than *198 763*.

▶ Use visual materials to add interest and to clarify complicated statistical summaries.

▶ Translate difficult-to-comprehend numbers into understandable terms.

▶ State the date and the source of the statistics.

Testimony

When making use of *testimony,* a speaker cites the opinions or conclusions of others in the exact words (quotation) or in a close restatement thereof (paraphrase). In both cases the speaker must acknowledge the source of the material. A testimony may add to a speaker's credibility if it is pertinent and if the source is regarded by the audience as an authoritative person. To ensure that the testimony will be accepted by the audience, the speaker must make sure that the testimony:

▶ has been obtained from a person who is well qualified and experienced in the field under discussion.

▶ has been obtained from a person who has first-hand knowledge of the topic or situation in question.

▶ has been obtained from a person with no ulterior motive in holding such an opinion.

▶ has been stated correctly, thoroughly, and in context; if applicable and possible, an explanation must be given **why** the opinion or conclusion has been reached.

▶ has not been presented as a fact when it is an opinion.

Formulating arguments in a speech

Once sufficient supporting material or proof has been collected, the speaker can start to build up arguments on the basis of this material.

Argumentation concerns the **giving of reasons** (premises) in communicative situations when the purpose of the speech is to justify acts, beliefs, attitudes and values. A reason justifies a statement that affirms or rejects a proposition. A good reason is psychologically compelling for an audience and creates the impression that further enquiry is both unnecessary and redundant (cf. Freeley 1993:2). According to Toulmin, Rieke and Janik (1979:13), reasoning is the presenting of ideas to support a claim (i.e. a conclusion). Although reasoning is for the most part a continuous process whereby **ideas are critically tested,** a speaker may also **arrive at new ideas.**

Arguments are *valid* in a speech if the premises imply the conclusion, and are *invalid* if the premises do not imply the conclusion. Although one of the premises in a valid argument may not be true, the fact that the premises imply the conclusion may still result in the argument being regarded as valid. An argument is *sound* only if we know the premises to be true. Arguments are sound if the premises (reasons) verify (not *imply* as in the case of a valid argument) the conclusion. Arguments are *fallacious* if the premises (reasons) do not verify the *propositions* (cf. Davis 1986:31; Schwartz 1994:55–57).

Major types and tests of reasoning

The most basic distinction we can make in reasoning is between *deductive* and *inductive reasoning*. Traditionally, deductive reasoning was regarded as reasoning from the general to the specific and inductive reasoning from the specific to the general. The current interpretation in speech communication is that in deductive reasoning the premises prove (establish the certainty of) the conclusion, and in inductive reasoning the premises support the conclusion with probability only (cf. Terrell 1967:10).

The objective of reasoning is to come to a conclusion (affirming or rejecting a proposition) after stating various premises. In a speech the speaker will use previously established premises that the audience accepts as well grounded, and through sound reasoning establish something new – a conclusion the speaker wants the audience to accept.

The following types and tests of reasoning can be identified (cf. Freeley 1993: 163–177; Schutte 1990:46–56). The symbols used in the examples – (G), (Q), (W), (C), (B) and (R) – are from the Toulmin model, which is discussed below in Section 1.5: *Systems of evaluation*. In the Toulmin model, *reasoning* is labelled *warrants*.

Reasoning by example: When a speaker *reasons by example,* the statements inferred from the examples are the same as the final claim inferred from a different example of the same kind. Reasoning from example involves cause and/or sign reasoning, as the speaker tries to show that the examples are a cause or a sign of the conclusion reached. Reasoning by example also involves generalisation, as the speaker will have to show that representative examples of one kind will also be true of additional examples of the same kind. As in many cases it will be impractical to consider all examples, therefore qualifying the final claim will be important when reasoning by example.

The following is an example of this type of reasoning:

> The 1994 general election and the 1995 community elections in South Africa were successful (G); therefore, unless violence prevents them from taking place (R), the community elections in 1996 in KwaZulu/Natal and in the Western Cape will probably (Q) also be successful (C), because the same electoral commission is responsible for all elections (W), and disputes regarding the KwaZulu/Natal and Western Cape elections have been settled between the different political parties involved (B).

The following questions are tests of reasoning by example:

▶ Are the examples relevant to the claim being made?

▶ Are there sufficient examples to justify the claim?

▶ Are the examples typical – are they representative of the claim being made and not exceptions?

Reasoning by analogy: *Reasoning by analogy* involves comparing two similar cases, in the knowledge that the two cases are the same in all relevant aspects and that they will therefore also be the same in an aspect that is known/evident of the one case but not known/evident of the other. Reasoning by analogy may be *literal* or *figurative*. **Literal analogy** compares cases from the same classification: for example, East London and Pietersburg if we compare cities. **Figurative analogy** compares cases from different classifications, for example when we compare a computer with the human brain. Figurative analogy has no logical proof but may make a point clear and understandable to the audience.

The following is an example of this type of reasoning:

> Atlanta hosted the Olympic Games in 1996 (G) successfully, so Cape Town will probably (Q) also be successful in hosting the Olympic Games (C) in 2004, because Cape Town will have more or less the same infrastructure in 2004 that Atlanta has today (B). The South African team bidding for the Olympic Games in 2004 can draw experience from the way Atlanta organised the Olympic Games in 1996 (W), unless there is not enough money available to host the Olympic Games in Cape Town in 2004 (R).

The following questions are tests of reasoning by analogy:

▶ Are there significant points of similarity between the cases compared?

▶ Are these points of similarity critical to the comparison?

▶ There will always be points of difference between two cases compared, but are these points of difference noncritical?

Causal reasoning: When a speaker makes use of *causal reasoning* it is inferred that a certain factor (a cause) is a force that will produce something else (an effect). A speaker may also reverse the process and infer what factor causes a known effect, thus reasoning from cause to effect or effect to cause. This type of reasoning is evident during weather reports where, for example, high or low pressure systems (cause) may result in wind, cold or rain (effect) and in economic analysis when economists predict the interest rates (effects) from inter alia the consumer price index, inflation rate and growth in money. Causal relationships are complicated because there are at times unknown causes and/or effects.

The following is an example of this type of reasoning:

> The good rains in the 1996 season (G) will, in comparison with the drier 1995 season, certainly (Q) result in an increased production of maize (C), unless farmers plant less maize (R). Good rains is a contributing factor to increased production of maize (W). The good rains in the 1978 season resulted in an increased production of maize in comparison with the drier 1977 season (B).

The following questions are tests of causal reasoning:

▶ Is the alleged cause relevant to the specific effect?

▶ Is the cause the only or distinguished causal factor – is the speaker oversimplifying the causal reasoning?

▶ Is there a possible counteracting cause that may occur in future and result in a different effect?

▶ Is there reasonable probability that no undesirable effect will result from the particular cause?

▶ Is the cause backed by other evidence?

Sign reasoning: When a speaker *reasons by sign,* it is inferred that relationships or correlations exist between two variables (of the same or from different phenomena) and that the presence or absence of one variable may be a sign of the presence or absence of the other variable. The nature of the relationship can be *natural* or *conceptual.* The correlation is **natural** when, for example, a high fever is taken as a sign that a person is sick. The correlation is **conceptual** when, for example, someone who owns many houses is regarded as rich.

The relationship can also be *reciprocal* or *nonreciprocal.* The relationship is **reciprocal** if each variable can be taken as a sign of the other; for example, when leaves are falling from a tree it is a sign that it is winter and it is inferred that it is winter when we see deciduous trees without leaves. The relationship is **nonreciprocal** when one variable may be taken as a sign of the other, but the other variable is not a reliable sign of the first. For example, if a person has a driver's licence, it is a sign that the person is older than eighteen years; however, the fact that a person is older than eighteen years is not a reliable sign that the person has a driver's licence.

The following is an example of this type of reasoning:

> The unemployment rate has dropped and more companies have been registered than was the case the previous year (G), therefore the economy is probably (Q) growing (C).

The following questions are tests of sign reasoning:

▶ Is there a sign relationship between the two variables?

▶ Is there more than one sign relationship to support the conclusion?

▶ Is there a counterfactor that will disrupt the relationship?

The above four types of reasoning – namely reasoning by example, reasoning by analogy, causal reasoning and sign reasoning – are those most frequently used in arguments. Each of these types may merge into the other; for example, a particular argument may be an example of both causal and sign reasoning. But these arguments and the general content of a speech must be ordered in a logical way so that the audience can easily grasp and remember the substance of the speech. This ordering is done by means of a speech design.

Ordering the information in the speech according to a speech design

A speech design helps the speaker to provide a full and balanced coverage of the speech content. The purpose of any design is to order ideas in a logical pattern that outlines their relationship towards each other. A speaker can combine different designs to suit the purpose of the speech. The following speech designs can be used (cf. Osborn & Osborn 1988; Gronbeck et al. 1992).

Spatial design

In a *spatial design* the speaker organises the main points of the speech in terms of their physical proximity to or direction from each other; these points are then described in a systematic way. In a discussion of the stadiums where the different soccer matches of the African Cup of Nations have been played, a speaker can arrange the stadiums from north to south, starting with the FNB stadium in Soweto and then moving southwards towards Bloemfontein, Durban and then East London.

Chronological design

In a *chronological design* the speaker arranges the ideas or events of a speech in a time sequence. Beginning at a specific point in time, a speaker can systematically move forwards or backwards. For example, when describing the evolution of a democratic South Africa, a speaker could select any date to start with and then take certain events following a particular time sequence which is considered to be important, concluding the speech with the present or with a specific date in the past.

Topical design

Some familiar topics are best organised in terms of their natural or standardised divisions. A *topical design* helps the speaker to reduce and organise information so that it does not overwhelm the audience. For example, when speaking on which trees to plant in a garden, a speaker could divide the topic – trees – into large and small trees, deciduous and evergreen trees, trees hardy and tender to frost and indigenous and exotic trees.

Sequential design

In a *sequential design* the speaker outlines the relevant steps to be followed in the process being discussed or demonstrated. For example, a speaker may describe possible steps to be taken when analysing a television programme or may discuss the steps to be followed while at the same time demonstrating how to build a brick wall. In this design the speaker can also make use of elimination. For example, a speaker could state all the options available when raising money to build a swimming pool at a school, and then eliminate options – some may not be practical, some may be too costly or may take too long to implement – until the most suitable option remains.

Problem-solving design

During the initial stages of a persuasive speech, the speaker must convince the listeners that they have a *problem* and then show them how to deal with that problem by providing – if possible – a specific *solution*. The solution can advocate action or changing beliefs or attitudes. It may be necessary to paint a mental picture of the results in the minds of the listeners and to state the benefits that they will receive if taking such action. In an informative speech a speaker would first establish that a problem exists and then simply suggest possible solutions.

Refutative design

In a *refutative design* a speaker will try to raise doubts concerning an opposing position or argument and disprove an opponent's viewpoint by pointing out inconsistencies, invalid proofs and/or absurdities. To refute the opposition successfully, a speaker should be familiar with the opposition's arguments and evidence. A refutative design will prove more successful in influencing doubtful or uncommitted listeners than would be the case with hardline supporters of the opposition who may thereby become embittered and more opposed to the speaker. South African politicians are eager to use this design before elections, but sometimes do so by destructively using personal references and attacks to discredit their opponents. Any refutation must be supported by competent and credible evidence.

The following principles should be applied when preparing a speech design (cf. Ayres & Miller 1994:98–103).

- ▶ Range from the known to the unknown.
- ▶ Range from the general to the specific.
- ▶ Organise from first to last.
- ▶ Present comparisons positively.
- ▶ Proceed from top to bottom, rather than from bottom to top.
- ▶ Devote a similar amount of time to each main point, especially those which are regarded as equally important, as one main point which is developed less fully than the others may create the impression in the audience that that particular point is less important.
- ▶ Devote a good deal of attention to the first and last points as it is these points that the listeners are most likely to retain.

Once a speaker knows what to say, attention must be given to the language and style of a speech.

Attending to the language and style of a speech

Well-chosen words can make listeners see the world as the speaker sees it, awaken emotions, encourage action, create group identity, focus feelings, deflect attention and even excuse behaviour. The *language* chosen by a speaker can greatly influence how the audience perceives the speaker and the purpose of the speech.

The speaker must ensure that the words chosen are accurate, simple, appropriate and vivid (cf. Gronbeck et al. 1992; DeVito 1990; Ayres & Miller 1994).

Accurate

Because of the connotative meanings which words can have, the choice of *accurate* words is important. For example, the word *democracy* may mean to affluent residents in cities economic freedom and a small, efficient public sector, while to rural residents it may mean the supply of electricity and running water. Choosing words accurately can also avoid vagueness. Saying that an object shines may not be a precise description of it – the object can blaze, glitter, flicker or beam.

Words can also reveal a speaker's feelings about ideas, objects and persons. A speaker must choose accurate words that will convey more or less the same attitude as the audience holds. For example, words like *freedom fighter, combatant* or *terrorist* and *previous government, apartheid government* or *apartheid regime* may all refer to the same persons or objects, but each conveys a different feeling.

Simple

Simple words mean short, direct words that convey concrete meanings. Because of the mass media such as radio and television, the speaker may at times be dealing with a media audience. Keeping language simple will guarantee that most of the members of the direct and media audience will understand a speech. For example, use words like *learn* and *help* rather than *ascertain* and *facilitate*.

Appropriate

Appropriate means to exercise good taste. Vulgar and improper language and intolerant remarks about any person or groups are inappropriate. The language must also be appropriate to the nature of the occasion. Serious or formal occasions require a more dignified and refined style of speech, while a lively, light and perhaps humorous style would be appropriate during a speech at an informal occasion.

Vivid

To create energetic, compelling and rousing words a speaker must:

▶ use active verbs, for example *she stands in the crowd* rather than *she is/was/will be in the crowd*;

▶ use imagery to make the audience see, hear, taste, smell and feel the subject matter of the speech;

▶ create immediacy by using personal pronouns such as *I, we, us, our*; this will help a speaker to speak **with** rather than **at** the audience;

▶ use figures of speech such as alliteration, antithesis, hyperbole, metaphor, personification, rhetorical questions and similes.

Examples of these figures of speech are (cf. Tulloch 1993):

alliteration – *John is cool, calm and collected.*

antithesis – *The past was dark, the future is bright.*

hyperbole – *That boxer is bigger than a house.*   ➡

metaphor – *The opposition made a glaring error.*

personification – *The new constitution will live for ever.*

rhetorical question – *Is this the way we want to build a community?*

simile – *She is as brave as a lion.*

Oral language versus written language

When writing a speech a speaker concentrates on *oral language* which differs from *written language* in the way the language is produced and received. Oral language, in contrast with written language

▶ is often less formal (using *we* and *you*);

▶ is more fragmentary, using shorter, simpler and more familiar words in shorter sentences;

▶ has a more spontaneous quality;

▶ must be simpler in construction;

▶ makes use of guide phrases such as *next, therefore, in contrast, in conclusion, furthermore,* and *similarly* that help listeners to follow the speaker's thoughts;

▶ uses more repetition to ensure understanding as the audience cannot go back and reread a speech.

There is no perfect or ideal style of speech delivery, but in oral language a speaker should adopt a conversational style (in formal and informal settings) when delivering a speech. This will help the speaker to speak with and not at the audience. A conversational style is more personable, uses more understandable language and prevents the speaker from being too dramatic or too formal. It also helps the speaker to be natural and prevents a forced change in style of speech or image just because an audience is being addressed.

The humorous style

The *speech atmosphere* (i.e. the mental attitude of the audience or the one which the speaker is attempting to create, the speaking situation and the speech purpose) at a specific speech occasion sometimes dictates what type of style to use. *Humour* is an important element in public speaking, but it is effective only in some situations, with some speakers and with some audiences. Therefore humour is not always a desirable or a necessary element in speeches, informal occasions included.

To be effective, humour must be appropriate to the audience and the occasion, relevant to the topic and purpose of the speech, and it must be brief, spontaneous and tasteful rather than sarcastic or vulgar. In this way humour can help a speaker to gain attention and maintain interest, for example during the introduction of a speech or when making the audience recall something important which has been said. Humour can also break up the mood and lighten the tone of a long and sombre speech and can help a speaker to gain confidence when used effectively.

A speaker will have a better idea of how to begin and end a speech once the body of the speech has been written and the main points and arguments have been identified. That is why the introduction and conclusion of a speech are normally written after the completion of the body of the speech.

Writing the introduction and the conclusion

Although an *introduction* and *conclusion* consist of only a few sentences in a speech, their functions are crucial. By following a few principles, a speaker can ensure that the introduction and conclusion strengthen rather than weaken the content of the speech.

Introduction

An audience will most certainly have a preconceived opinion of the speaker and the speech topic prior to the delivery of the speech. Just as first impressions are important in social settings, so will the first impression created by a speaker by means of an introduction have an influence on the opinions of the audience. In order to create a good impression and to sustain it, when preparing the introduction the speaker should follow the guidelines which are outlined below (cf. Osborn & Osborn 1988; DeVito 1990; Gronbeck et al. 1992; Ayres & Miller 1994).

First of all, a speaker must **gain the audience's attention**. This can be achieved by asking rhetorical questions, beginning with a quotation, telling a story, making use of humour, shocking the audience, involving the listeners by relating the topic to them, relating the topic to a personal experience or referring to the audience and/or the occasion.

Secondly, a speaker must **establish his/her credibility** This can be done by briefly stating his/her qualifications (without bragging) to speak on the topic, especially if the chairperson did not do so. It may be necessary for a speaker to prepare two introductions, depending on what the chairperson has to say when introducing the speaker. In addition, a speaker must establish common ground with the audience and express pleasure in speaking with them to establish goodwill and feelings of trust among the listeners.

Once a speaker has gained the audience's attention and established credibility, **the audience** should be **oriented** towards the topic. To do this the speaker should introduce the audience to the topic and stress its importance, state the objective/s of the speech and give the audience a preview of the main points.

A speaker should avoid the following during the introduction:

▶ Do not apologise or pretend to be what you are not.

▶ Do not promise something in the speech which cannot be delivered.

▶ Do not preface the introduction with, for example, "I just want to say …".

The following is an example of the introduction to a speech delivered by President Nelson Mandela at a *pitso* – a tribal meeting – in Maseru on 13 July 1995 (with acknowledgement to *South African Communication Service*):

> Khotso! (i.e. *Peace!*)
>
> Pula! (i.e. *Rain!*)
>
> Nala! (*i.e. Abundance!*)
>
> My visit to the Kingdom of Lesotho would be incomplete without an opportunity to join you, the people, in such a gathering.

ACTIVITY

How do you think does this introduction to a speech delivered at a tribal meeting meets the criteria of a good introduction?

Conclusion

When a speaker concludes a speech, the attention of the audience should be focused by means of a summary of the importance of the topic, the objectives and the main points. The speaker should also establish a closing mood by means of a motivation, an appeal or a challenge. During the last part of the conclusion the speaker can make use of a quotation, ask rhetorical questions, tell a short story, state a personal intention or refer to the introduction.

A speaker should bear in mind the following during the conclusion:

▶ In most cases it is best not to apologise for any inadequacies, in terms of content or presentation, as this can dilute the speaker's position.

▶ Do not present new material in the conclusion.

▶ Do not drag out the conclusion.

The following is an example of the conclusion of a speech delivered by President Nelson Mandela at a football banquet held in Pretoria on 1 March 1996 (with acknowledgement to *South African Communication Service*):

> Let all of us dedicate ourselves to make sport truly accessible to all our people, inspired by your achievements and by the warmth with which all the people of South Africa have taken you into their hearts.
>
> May I once more humbly say:
>
> Congratulations to Africa's Champions!
>
> Congratulations to South Africa!
>
> I thank you.

ACTIVITY

How successful is the closing mood which the speaker tries to establish in the conclusion of the above example?

Once the speech has been written, the speaker should make a summary using a speech outline.

Prepare a speech outline

A *speech outline* is the visual presentation of a speech which can be used as *speaking notes* (i.e. the notes a speaker uses when delivering a speech). As speaking notes differ from speaker to speaker, the speech outline may also differ; the requirements of a good outline **form** are the following (cf. Gronbeck et al. 1992:134–136).

▶ Limit each unit in the outline to one idea only.

▶ Rank subordinate ideas below main ideas.

▶ Use indentation to show the logical relatedness between units of the outline.

▶ Use a consistent set of symbols throughout the outline.

As the purpose of an informative speech differs from that of a persuasive speech, the concepts used to describe the sections in the speech outlines of these two types of speech will also differ. In an informative speech a speaker makes use mostly of "subheadings" and "supporting material" and in a persuasive speech or debate use is mostly made of "supporting arguments" and "proof".

The following is an example of a speech outline (cf. De Wet & Rensburg 1989:47):

INTRODUCTION (often written out in full)

PURPOSE STATEMENT (with the topic or proposition kept in mind)

1 **Main point** (crisp and clear, rather than lengthy and vague)
   1.1 Supporting arguments/Subheading
      1.1.1 Proof/Supporting material
   1.2 Supporting arguments/Subheading
      1.2.1 Proof/Supporting material

2 **Main point**
   2.1 Supporting arguments/Subheading
      2.1.1 Proof/Supporting material
   2.2 Supporting arguments/Subheading
      2.2.1 Proof/Supporting material
      2.2.2 Proof/Supporting material

3 **Main point**
   3.1 Supporting arguments/Subheading
      3.1.1 Proof/Supporting material

CONCLUSION (usually written out in full)

Deciding on visual, audiovisual and or audio aids

The correct use of *visual*, *audiovisual* and or *audio aids* (hereafter *visual aids*) has many advantages for both the speaker and the audience. According to Ayres and Miller (1994:154), one study showed that using visual aids enhances understanding and comprehension of lecture material by the audience, and another that speakers using visual aids are perceived as more credible and persuasive than speakers who do not make use of visual aids. Visual aids also add clarity and variety and reinforce the message because the audience can both hear **and** see the same message.

Numerous types of visual aids can be used, for example: the speaker (using his or her body to demonstrate self-defence); the actual object under discussion; blackboard; handouts (distribute only before or after the speech); models; charts, sketches; maps; graphs; photographs; overhead and slide projectors; films; video tapes; audiotapes and computer-generated visual materials. It is possible to make use of visual aids in nearly every type of speech.

The speaker should bear in mind the following when looking for or designing visual aids.

▶ Make use of information gathered from the audience analysis – first consider the audience and occasion and what the audience already knows about the topic.

▶ Choose the visual aid/s which will best communicate the particular kind of information contained in the speech.

▶ Visual aids must be easy to see (also the lettering, if applicable) by all the members of the audience without straining.

▶ Visual aids must be simple and clear with not too much detail.

▶ Visual aids must be relevant to the message and should reinforce the message.

▶ Visual aids must be as attractive as possible.

▶ Test the visual aids for clarity and workability.

▶ The speaker must be familiar with the electronic equipment which is being used and ensure that it is in good working order.

When presenting a speech the speaker should:

▶ integrate verbal and visual material effectively.

▶ use the visual aid only when it is relevant.

▶ not talk to the visual aids but to the audience.

▶ not let the visual aids interfere with the flow and the rhythm of the speech and so distract the audience. Thorough preparation and practice can avoid distraction.

Now that the speech has been thoroughly prepared, the speaker must determine how it is going to be presented.

Key terms to understand and remember

articulation	extemporaneous speaking
impromptu speaking	manuscript speaking
memorised speaking	nonverbal aspects
pronunciation	

It is clear that a lot of planning, research and preparation go into (or should go into) a speech before it is presented. All the preparation is a great advantage because when the speech is finally presented the speaker will not have to concentrate so much on **what** to say but rather on **how** to say it. Good preparation will increase self-confidence so that the speaker can then be enthusiastic and dynamic when delivering the speech. Good preparation also gives a speaker the opportunity to rethink the content of the speech.

Before delivering the speech, the speaker should practise using the speech outline in order to sound natural when speaking before a large audience with unfamiliar faces. When practising the speaker should read through the speech several times and first memorise the main points and thereafter the supporting material. Memorising the introduction and conclusion in any type of delivery is particularly important to enable the speaker to concentrate on how to begin and end the speech without consulting the notes; in this way the speaker remains in contact with the audience and thus maximises the impact. Practising before a friend or the mirror may help a speaker to gain valuable feedback.

Methods of delivery

The *method of delivery* will differ according the speaker's strengths and weaknesses, the purpose of the speech and the occasion; each method has its own advantages and disadvantages. Although *extemporaneous* speaking is the ideal method of delivery, speakers must decide for themselves which method of delivery they are the most comfortable with. The various methods of delivery are as follows.

Impromptu speaking

In the case of *impromptu speaking* the speaker has little or no time for preparation and must rely on previous experience and knowledge to get through the speech. If the speaker has a few minutes in hand, it may be possible to write down a short speech outline with a few main ideas to quickly structure thoughts and supporting material. Such a speech outline will prevent unnecessary repetition or the omission of relevant ideas. Impromptu speaking usually occurs at a relatively informal occasion.

Figure 1.2 illustrates that the ability to think on our feet is vital during impromptu speaking, especially if we do not have time to write down a short speech outline.

Figure 1.2 **Impromptu speaking**
(Reproduced with the kind permission of *Beeld*)

The **advantages** of impromptu speaking are:

▶ Spontaneity, speakers practise thinking on their feet and a great deal of preparation time is saved.

The **disadvantages** of impromptu speaking are:

▶ A lack of experience or self-confidence may cause speakers to panic, speak in a disorganised way or say something they will regret later on. There is also not enough time to do research.

Memorised speaking

In the case of *memorised speaking* a speaker delivers a speech after memorising every sentence and even the word order in the speech. If a speaker does not want to use note cards during a specific speech occasion, or when exact timing and wording are important, use can be made of memorised speaking. The speaker should write a memorised speech in an informal, conversational style so that the speech does not sound like a written essay when it is delivered. Although a speaker normally memorises the introduction, conclusion and important phrases in the speech, trying to memorise the entire speech should be avoided.

The **advantages** of memorised speaking are:

▶ The speaker can review each word, sentence or phrase to eliminate any potential problems.

▶ The speaker can maintain eye contact with the listeners and practise the delivery thoroughly.

The **disadvantages** of memorised speaking are:

▶ A speaker may forget what he/she was going to say.

▶ The speaker cannot easily adjust the speech to amplify points when responding to the feedback of the audience.

▶ When preparing the speech it may be difficult to write in an oral style.

▶ The memorised speech involves additional time for memorisation.

Manuscript speaking

When delivering a *manuscript speech* the speaker writes out the speech beforehand and then reads it from a manuscript to the audience. This method of speech is used when the wording and the timing of the speech are extremely important, for example when making an important finding public or when making announcements. Manuscript speaking involves the same skills as memorised speaking as the speech should not sound as if the speaker is simply reading something from a manuscript. When reading a speech it is important to practise beforehand so that the speaker sounds as if he/she is talking and not reading.

The **advantages** of manuscript speaking are:

▶ The speaker can control timing.

▶ There is no danger of forgetting or of struggling to find the right word.

▶ The speaker can devote a lot of attention and practice to the exact wording and style.

▶ The speaker can distribute copies of the speech and thus avoid being wrongly quoted.

The **disadvantages** of manuscript speaking are:

▶ Without sufficient practice, the speaker will have very little or no eye contact with the audience.

▶ It is time-consuming to write out the whole speech.

▶ The speaker cannot react spontaneously to feedback.

▶ The speech limits movements and gestures as the speaker is bound to the manuscript.

▶ If the speaker cannot read in a conversational style, the speech may sound prefabricated and can become impersonal.

Extemporaneous speaking

In the case of *extemporaneous speaking* the speaker carefully prepares, organises and rehearses the speech, but only uses speaking notes for the introduction, the main points, quotations, figures and the conclusion. The wording is created as the speaker delivers the speech. The speaker's speech outline may consist only of key words and is normally much more streamlined that the complete formal speech outline which was initially prepared.

The **advantages** of extemporaneous speaking are:

▶ The speech is largely spontaneous and natural as no attempt is being made to memorise the exact wording.

▶ Having to hold only a few notes means that the speaker is free to make use of movements and gestures.

▶ It is easy to present the speech in a conversational style.

▶ The speaker can react to feedback from the audience by explaining a point, adding examples or cutting out a main point.

The **disadvantages** of extemporaneous speaking are:

▶ An inexperienced speaker may search for words and use language that is not precise.

▶ Without proper preparation and practice, a speaker may overuse notes or appear to be giving an impromptu speech.

▶ Some variations may occur when repeating the speech.

▶ It may be difficult to stick to a specific time frame as the length of the speech may vary according to the occasion and the type of audience.

Extemporaneous speaking combines the best characteristics of the other methods of delivery. This method is based on thorough preparation, but not on memory, and there is seldom a need for speakers to think on their feet (except when reacting to feedback from the audience). It is thus the ideal method of delivery.

Nonverbal aspects of delivery

Just as writing a speech requires research, planning and practice to produce good content, so too does the delivery of a speech necessitate the practice and planning of *nonverbal aspects* to ensure that these aspects support what the speaker says. (Although nonverbal communication has been discussed in *Course book 1* [Steinberg 1994] and *Course book 4* [Rensburg 1996], the nonverbal aspects covered by this unit apply specifically to **speech** communication.)

When delivering a speech, the following **vocal aspects** are important. Vocal aspects are especially important when speaking on radio, as the audience can only listen to speakers and is not able to see them.

Pitch

Pitch refers to the relative highness or lowness of a voice. Persons speaking in public should employ a broader pitch range: their *highs* must become higher and their *lows* must become lower. The reason for this is the distance between the speaker and the audience in a face-to-face situation and the length of time the speaker has to talk. Speakers thus have to exaggerate their range of sounds during a speech, as a narrow pitch range may sound boring to the audience. On the other hand, a very wide pitch range may sound artificial. Generally speaking, a higher pitch communicates excitement and a lower pitch a sense of control or solemnity; a speaker will thus have to vary the pitch to fit the emotion to be conveyed. Variation is important – some speakers end each sentence on the same pitch level which can become boring after a time.

Volume

Volume refers to the relative intensity of a voice, and *loudness* to the perception of that relative intensity (cf. DeVito 1990:414). A speaker should speak loudly enough for everyone in the audience to hear in a face-to-face situation. Variations in the volume of a voice help to emphasise, to create a sense of expectation and to keep the interest of the audience.

Rate

Rate concerns how fast or slow one speaks. Listeners prefer a speech rate of about three words a second – that is, between 160 and 180 words per minute. Just as is the case with pitch and volume, the speech rate of a speaker should vary from time to time in order to maintain the interest of the audience, to change the mood if necessary, and to present the content of the speech in an interesting manner. The bigger the audience in a face-to-face situation and the more complex and serious the content of the topic, the slower the rate of speech should be – between 120 and 150 words per minute.

Pauses

Pauses can be filled or unfilled. A speaker should avoid filled pauses such as *uh, well, um, you know,* et cetera. Unfilled pauses are silent pauses lasting a few seconds which interrupt the normal flow of a speech. Pauses break words and sentences into meaningful units, vary the rate and emphasise ideas. These pauses can be very effective, providing that a speaker pauses:

▶ at transitional points;

▶ after asking a rhetorical question;

▶ before an important idea/announcement;

▶ after an important idea/announcement.

Articulation and pronunciation

Proper *articulation* and *pronunciation* help the audience to hear every word a speaker says. In South Africa, where English is the second language of most of its speakers, the same word may be articulated and pronounced in different ways. Although some speakers may have an accent when speaking English, a problem only arises when the audience finds it difficult to follow the speech because of poor articulation and/or pronunciation. A speaker should therefore practise the articulation and pronunciation of sounds and words to avoid being perceived as uneducated.

1

Write down a few English words that you think you do not articulate or pronounce properly. Consult an appropriate dictionary and practise these words to make sure that you articulate and pronounce them correctly.

Articulation refers to the formation of consonant and vowel sounds. When not articulating sounds well, a speaker may

omit sounds:

gov-a-ment	**instead of**	gov-ern-ment
comp-ny	**instead of**	com-pa-ny

substitute sounds:

dese	**instead of**	these
bedder	**instead of**	better
feory	**instead of**	theory

add sounds:

filim	**instead of**	film
countery	**instead of**	country

Pronunciation includes the use of correct sounds and the proper accent on syllables. When words are not pronounced correctly, it may result in errors of

accent:

democracy	**instead of**	democracy
orator	**instead of**	orator

pronouncing silent sounds:

almond	**instead of**	amond for almond
honour	**instead of**	onour for honour

Other **nonverbal aspects** of a speech are also important. How can a speaker, for example, urge an audience to take action while remaining motionless with an expressionless face? A speaker can use the following nonverbal aspects to support the vocal aspects and the content of a speech.

Posture

A speaker's posture should fit the speaking occasion. Standing to speak is a form of emphasis, although sitting on the front edge of a table may be effective in an informal speech occasion. However, at any formal occasion where speakers want to address the audience in a serious manner, they should stand up straight on both feet, without looking sloppy or moving visibly from one foot to the other, without their hands in their pockets and without leaning on the desk or podium. Leaning slightly forward may indicate interest in the audience: a stance which is too stiff and erect will make a speaker appear tense and afraid.

Figure 1.3 **Nonverbal aspects of delivery support the content of a speech**
(Reproduced with the kind permission of *Beeld*)

Figure 1.3 illustrates that leaning slightly forward may help a speaker to emphasise a point and it may indicate interest in the audience.

Facial expression

Facial expression has a great emotional impact on face-to-face communication as listeners usually study speakers' faces when they are addressing the audience. If speakers are relaxed they can more easily use their faces to express and support what they say.

Eye contact

Eye contact reveals that a speaker is honest and sincere towards the audience, as well as being self-assured. When speaking in front of a large audience, the speaker must maintain eye contact with groups of people all over the audience (left, right, front, middle and back), as individual eye contact with each audience member will not be possible. Eye contact serves as a visual bonding between a speaker and the audience and, if a speaker is too dependent on notes, this bond with the audience may be lost.

Gestures

Gestures are movements of the arms, hands, head and shoulders of a speaker. Gestures attract attention and should therefore be purposeful. In general, gestures should be larger for larger audiences in a face-to-face situation. A speaker should also vary gestures in a natural and spontaneous way without using the same gesture over and over again, as these mannerisms may distract the audience from the message.

Figure 1.4 **Speaking without making use of gestures**
(Reproduced with the kind permission of *Beeld*)

Figure 1.5 **Speaking while making use of gestures**
(Reproduced with the kind permission of *Beeld*)

▶ Compare Figure 1.4 with Figure 1.5 – in what way do the two figures differ?

▶ Ask friends and colleagues if you are making effective use of gestures in your speeches.

Movement

A speaker can use movement to the front, back or side in a face-to-face situation to stress an idea or to indicate a change in topic as the movement helps keep the attention of the audience. As is the case with all other nonverbal aspects associated with a speech, movement should be purposeful. At times movement is the message, for example when demonstrating to athletes how to jump over a hurdle.

Personal appearance

The clothing and general appearance of a speaker should fit the occasion and not be so extreme that the audience is distracted from the message. The speaker's appearance is the first impression the audience receives and however formal or informal the speaker wishes to look to suit the occasion, the general appearance must be neat.

1.5   SYSTEMS OF EVALUATION

Key terms to understand and remember

acceptance	act
agency	agent
analysis	artistic standard
backing	Berlo's process system
claims	concepts of hierarchy
data	dramatic pentad
dramatistic system	evaluation
fallacies	guilt
identification	interpretation
neo-Aristotelian system	observation
purification	purpose
qualifications	rebuttals
redemption	rejection
scene	SMMA system
Toulmin model	warrants

To be able to criticise any speech the critic must follow four steps, namely: *observation, analysis, interpretation* and *evaluation* (cf. Cathcart 1988:22–26).

During the first step of **observation** the critic must have a credible copy in the form of a manuscript or an audio or video recording of the speech. First of all the critic undertakes an **intrinsic investigation** of the text which includes observation of the introduction and conclusion, the use of arguments, the supporting material and evidence, the speech design, the nonverbal aspects, language and style, method of delivery and the theme (i.e. thematic statement) of the speech in terms of the medium used (i.e. face-to-face communication or a speech on radio or television). This intrinsic investigation must also consider what the message omits and what it includes. Secondly, the critic must do an **extrinsic investigation** which includes observation of the audience and the speech environment.

During the second step, the critic **analyses** what was observed during the first step. The critic questions **why** specific arguments, a specific speech design, nonverbal aspects, language and style, method of delivery and theme were used for the particular audience and speech environment in terms of the medium.

During the third step, the critic **interprets** what has been observed and analysed. When a critic interprets a message, he or she finds out **how** the different variables interact in the speech process, for example how the evidence is selected for the specific audience; how the radio medium is used specifically to reach audiences in remote areas; how the speech design contributes to the persuasiveness of the speech; whether the content of the speech influences the immediate audience differently from the media audience and how the speech environment influenced the content of the speech.

The fourth and last step of the critical method is **evaluation**. During this step the critic arrives at a judgement of the speech and he or she must also be able to defend the judgement. To evaluate a speech a critic must have criteria by which to arrive at a judgement.

Although the critic's personal beliefs, values and attitudes influence the evaluation of a speech, systems of evaluation are used as criteria in this evaluation. Different systems of evaluation exist to explain how speech communication functions. Each system has its own merits and it is up to the critic to decide which system will best evaluate a speech. Evaluation gives speakers valuable feedback so that they can improve on the preparation and delivery of a speech. Evaluation also helps speakers to understand speech communication better.

The SMMA system

The *SMMA system* (an acronym for **Speaker**, **Message**, **Medium** and **Audience**) helps the critic to evaluate a speech on: results (i.e. judging the speech on how effectively the speaker informs, persuades and/or entertains the audience), and truth (i.e. judging the speech on whether the message is true and clarifies, upholds and reveals the truth), and ethics (i.e. judging the speech on the motives, character and personality of the speaker).

The SMMA system is based on the *neo-Aristotelian system* and *Berlo's process system* of communication. The SMMA system provides an artistic standard in terms of which the critic can evaluate a speech; this means that all elements and variables in a speech are judged according to principles of speech communication which are derived from tested theory (e.g. theories that apply to persuasive communication) and from the best speeches made in the past. This enables one to set principles for speech communication. The purpose of the first sections in this unit is to introduce the principles of speech communication, that is, what principles must be taken into account when one prepares and delivers a speech.

David Berlo (1960:30–38) proposed a process system of communication consisting of the communication source who encodes the message, the message itself, the channel and the communication receiver who decodes the message. Today this system is known as the SMCR system (this is an acronym for the elements of communication, namely the **Source**, **Message**, **Channel** and **Receiver**). Berlo's process system provides a system comprising all these elements, each with its own variables, in speech communication.

This system enables us to see how and why the variables of the elements influence each other and to determine whether all variables of the elements have been considered in a speech. These variables can be studied either as **dependent** or **independent** variables. For example, how does the communication environment and medium (independent variables) affect the message or how will the audience respond if a certain language and style are used in the speech. The Berlo system therefore also has a predictive function. Probable communication outcomes may be predicted which will enable the speaker to plan strategies likely to result in the predicted effect (cf. Miller 1972:62–65).

The variables in the neo-Aristotelian system are derived from Aristotle's classical treatise in his book *Rhetoric*. These variables are applied to modern speech communication. The neo-Aristotelian system determines to what degree a particular speech represents effective or ineffective persuasion (cf. Cathcart 1988:83).

According to the neo-Aristotelian system, people are essentially rational beings. People seek truth and then act in accordance with their understanding of that truth. In speech communication knowing the truth occurs through social agreement regarding what is probable in a given situation. Therefore this truth in a persuasive speech is probable rather than certain; the truth may change, or may be understood differently in different situations by different audiences. If speakers want audiences to agree with them, there must be a free marketplace in which speakers can compete so that audiences can choose the ideas and proposals which are the most true and useful.

In the neo-Aristotelian system it is assumed that certain variables make speech communication work. The variables referred to are the classical canons of speech communication developed by the ancient Greeks. These canons include the selection of proofs (i.e. artistic and nonartistic proofs), the arrangement of the proofs, the style of the language and the delivery of the message.

In order to persuade an audience, these variables must be constructed in a logical way that fits the demands of the speaker, the message, the medium and the audience within a specific speech environment. According to Cathcart (1988:84), the audience is compelled to act on that which is made to appear logical and reasonable.

The SMMA system combines the Berlo process system and the neo-Aristotelian system, but also tries to add variables where the other two systems fall short. Figure 1.6 gives an outline of the SMMA system with the four elements – each with its own variables.

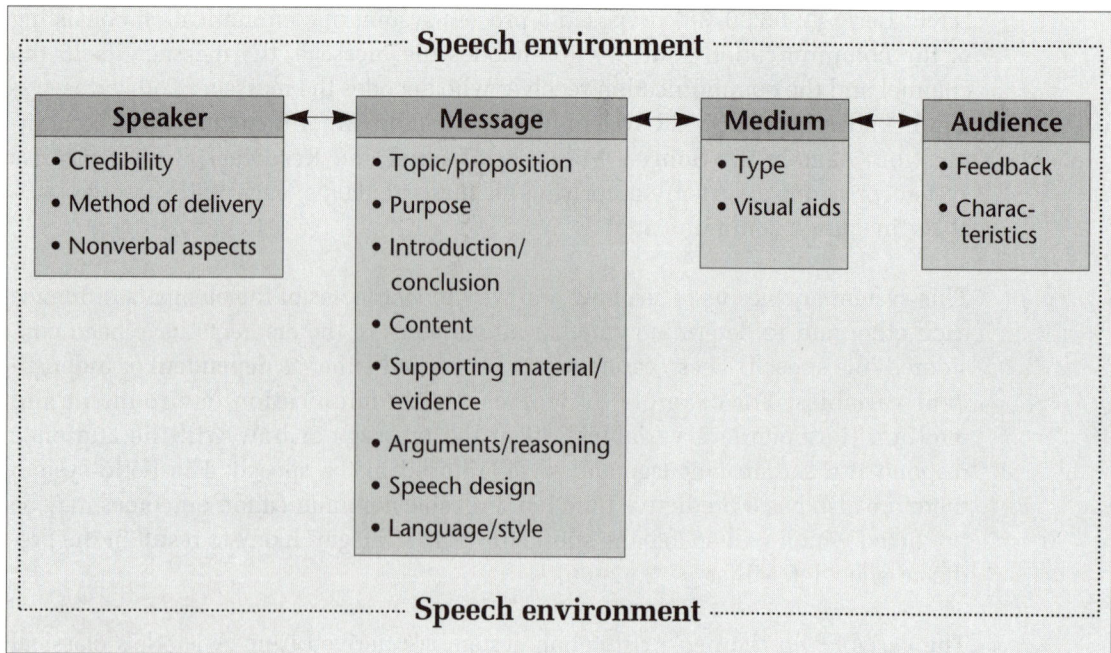

Figure 1.6 **The SMMA speech evaluation system**

We can use the following check list of the SMMA system to evaluate a speech.

Speaker

Credibility: Does the speaker know the topic he or she is talking about – is the speaker trustworthy and what image does the speaker project during the presentation? What the audience knows about the speaker prior to the presentation should also be considered when we evaluate the speaker. Here we have to bear in mind that some speakers, and in particular politicians, have several speech writers, which means that in some cases it may be difficult to assess whether the speaker is delivering a speech that really conveys what he or she wants to say.

Method of delivery: Does the method of delivery suit the speech occasion and is the speech properly delivered in accordance with the method?

Nonverbal aspects: Does the speaker make effective use of all the nonverbal aspects relevant to a speech? Does the speaker verify his or her nonverbal communication? Do the nonverbal aspects effectively support the message? Does the speaker employ the nonverbal aspects effectively for the specific medium (i.e. face-to-face communication, radio or television)?

Message

Topic/proposition: Is the speaker a suitable person to speak about the topic; does the topic suit the audience and the speech occasion? Is the speaker conversant with the proposition of the speech/debate and does the speaker know which type of proposition/s he or she is speaking about?

Purpose: Is the purpose of the speech to inform, and/or to persuade and/or to entertain and is/are the specific purpose/s clearly evident in the speech?

Introduction and conclusion: Does the introduction gain the attention of the audience, establish the credibility of the speaker and orient the audience towards the speech topic/proposition? Does the conclusion summarise the importance of the subject, the purpose and the proposition/s of the speech? Does the speaker establish a concluding mood by means of a motivation, an appeal or a challenge?

Content: Is the information or content of the speech accurate, thorough, topical and relevant to the topic/proposition and the purpose of the speech?

Supporting material/evidence: Is the supporting material/evidence relevant and sufficient and is there a variety of supporting material/evidence to support the arguments? Does the supporting material/evidence also meet those criteria which relate to examples, testimonies and statistics?

Arguments/reasoning: Are the arguments sound and the reasoning logical, without any fallacies?

Speech design: Does the speech design order the contents of the speech in such a way that points follow logically and does it provide a full and balanced coverage of the speech content?

Language/style: Is the language accurate, simple, vivid and are the language and style appropriate to the purpose of the speech and the speech occasion?

Medium

Type: Does the speaker use the medium effectively? The medium is the speaker's voice in a face-to-face situation, the radio or television. Does the speech delivery meet the criteria for speaking on a radio or television interview?

Visual aids: Does the speaker make effective use of visual aids in the speech?

Audience

Feedback: Does the audience respond according to the intended purpose/s of the speech? Does the speaker know if the audience was informed and/or persuaded and/or entertained? Is the feedback mainly verbal or nonverbal in a face-to-face situation – why? Is any feedback (for example phone calls, letters or articles in newspapers) received after a speech on radio or television?

Characteristics: Does the message of the speech take into account the demographics, psychographics and sociographics of the audience? Bear in mind that, although a small audience may be present during the delivery of a speech, the audience that the speaker may have in mind is the one that listens to the speech on radio and/or watches it on television.

The speech environment

Does the speaker take into account the time, the physical conditions, the size of the audience, and especially the nature and purpose of the occasion and the context in which the speech is delivered?

The dramatistic system of criticism

Critics use Kenneth Burke's (1969) *dramatistic approach* when they consider human motives as if analysing drama. In this drama, language and thought together function as modes of action where individuals are viewed as acting out their purposes on a life stage. Selecting certain symbols (e.g. certain language) over other symbols is meaningful because people's (i.e. the speaker's and the audience's) motives, attitudes and feelings can be derived from the symbols that they have selected.

The fundamental assumption of the dramatistic system is that when one person in any way (by sensations, concepts, images, ideas, attitudes, property and even by belief only) *identifies* him or herself with another, that person is substantially one with the other person, although each person is unique. Therefore persons may be both separate and joined, at once a distinct substance and consubstantial with one another (cf. Burke 1969:21). These persons use symbols to produce an **identification** that lets them act together in some ordered way (cf. Cathcart 1988:87). The opposite of identification is division. Division and guilt are the primary motives for communication so that identification can be reached. Communication between the speaker and the audience will be more successful if the identification is greater than the division. So identification with the audience may increase or decrease by the action of the speaker (cf. Littlejohn 1992:180).

Identification is the key term in Burke's *A rhetoric of motives* (1969). Only through language symbols can people induce understanding and co-operation in an otherwise divided world.

Burke (1969:55) quotes from Aristotle's *Rhetoric*: "It is not hard to praise Athenians among Athenians" and says

> You persuade a man only in so far as you can talk his language by speech, gesture, tonality, order, image, attitude, idea, *identifying* your ways with his.

Therefore speech communication includes all symbolic resources that function to promote social cohesion and, in Burke's view, these symbolic resources can be any act, event or object that is capable of producing identification. Thus, according to Burke, speech communication and its evaluation are not limited to speeches only (cf. Cathcart 1988:87).

Because the nature of society is to co-ordinate and to seek order, all symbolic acts are related to (1) *concepts of hierarchy* (people structure society in hierarchies), (2) *acceptance* and *rejection*, and (3) *guilt, purification* and *redemption*. Competitions and divisions result among classes and groups in the hierarchy and result in guilt because of the acceptance or rejection of the hierarchy.

For Burke, **guilt** is the primary motive behind all action and communication. We communicate to purge our guilt. In the broadest sense, speech communication functions as a means of inducing co-operation through acceptance or rejection of the established hierarchy. Speech communication, then, also produces the means of adjusting the guilt resulting from the acceptance or rejection of the hierarchy (or from the breaking of rules in language), through purification and redemption (cf. Littlejohn 1992:179). For example, when we support free primary health care, we may experience guilt because we do not know if there is enough money for such a scheme. However, if we do not support free primary health care we also may experience guilt because of the fact that some people cannot afford health care at all. People are sensitive to failings and therefore also experience guilt when they imagine (through language) a state of perfection which they cannot reach.

Every act of speech communication has an ethical dimension and such acts can be evaluated as a contribution to identification and co-operation (cf. Cathcart 1988:88).

The dramatistic system is different from the SMMA system as the critic does not evaluate speech communication in terms of the interaction between the speaker, message, medium and audience within a speech environment. Instead, the critic evaluates the *dramatic pentad* (i.e. a group of five) which characterises all speech communication acts. This dramatic pentad consists of the *act, scene, agent, agency* and *purpose*.

The **act** tells us what took place or what was accomplished in thought and deed and the **scene** tells us more about the speech environment within which the act (in this case a speech) occurred. The **agent** is the person who performs the act. The agent uses an **agency**, that is, the means or vehicle used to reach reason for the act – the **purpose**. The dramatic pentad helps us to evaluate a speech in the following way: when we evaluate the **act** we must know what speech has been delivered. To evaluate the **scene** we must know when and where the speech was delivered. We also evaluate the speaker and the audience, all that is known about them, their history and personalities – that is, the **agents** in the dramatic pentad. We evaluate how the speaker delivered the speech – that is the **agency** – and why the speech was delivered – that is, the **purpose**.

Evaluating these five variables of the dramatic pentad helps us to understand the functioning of speech communication in relation to the whole social drama. In the dramatic pentad the speaker and the audience are not considered separate entities, while both of them detect and interpret symbols, co-operate in creating meaning and agree on concerted action.

Therefore, an act of speech communication is a response to hierarchy by rejection or acceptance (for example, feminists who reject male dominance) and produces the means by which we deal with guilt through purification and redemption. Thus, when we criticise a speech by means of the dramatistic system, we ask how symbolic forms are acting in the dramatic pentad so that we can discover recurrent strategies of identification in humans who act together (cf. Cathcart 1988:89).

A system of reasoning: The Toulmin model

While the SMMA and the dramatistic system help the critic to evaluate most or all the elements and variables in a speech situation, the Toulmin model serves only as a system to evaluate arguments within a speech. Aristotle's syllogism and enthymeme were the primary methods of analysing arguments for centuries until Stephen E Toulmin, an English logician, proposed a model for argumentation in his book, *The uses of argument* (1958). According to Toulmin (1958:96), since the time of Aristotle the structure of an argument has been divided into minor premises, major premises and a conclusion; in some cases this was too simple a strategy to explain sophisticated arguments.

ACTIVITY

In a few short sentences give an example of how you would present an argument to an audience.

According to the Toulmin model, an argument consists of the following six elements (cf. Toulmin 1958:97–107; Toulmin, Rieke & Janik 1979:25–101; Freeley 1993:158–161). Examples of how these elements are structured in an argument can be found under the heading *Formulating arguments in a speech.*

Claims (C): The *claim* is the conclusion which the speaker wants to reach and which will be generally accepted in public.

Data (D): The *data* or grounds are the facts in the argument, evidence such as examples, explanations, statistics and testimony, which speakers use to clarify and establish the truth of their claim.

Warrants (W) (reasoning): *Warrants* are statements **indicating the general ways of arguing** being applied in each particular case (Toulmin et al. 1979:43). Warrants serve as a bridge between the data and claim and in a sense legitimise the steps taken in the argument from the data to the claim. Warrants are explanatory and are at times not necessary when the claim to be reached is a well-known fact. Warrants are an active reasoning process.

Backing (B): The *backing* is expressed in categorical statements of facts and should lend authority and trustworthiness to the reasoning (warrant).

Qualifications (Q): *Qualifiers* qualify the claim and indicate the **strength** or degree of reliance the warrants render to the argument. Qualifiers include adverbs such as certainly (i.e. an absolute truth), probably (i.e. a high degree of likelihood), plausibly (i.e. a lesser degree of likelihood) and possibly (i.e. a very low degree of likelihood) which indicate the degree to which the claim can be regarded as true.

Rebuttals (R): *Rebuttals* indicate the circumstances in which the authority of the warrant will have to be set aside – when the warrant cannot be true. If the data (evidence) and the warrant can provide absolute certainty that the claim is true in all circumstances, then rebuttals will not be necessary.

The following outline gives an example of how the six elements can be used in an argument:

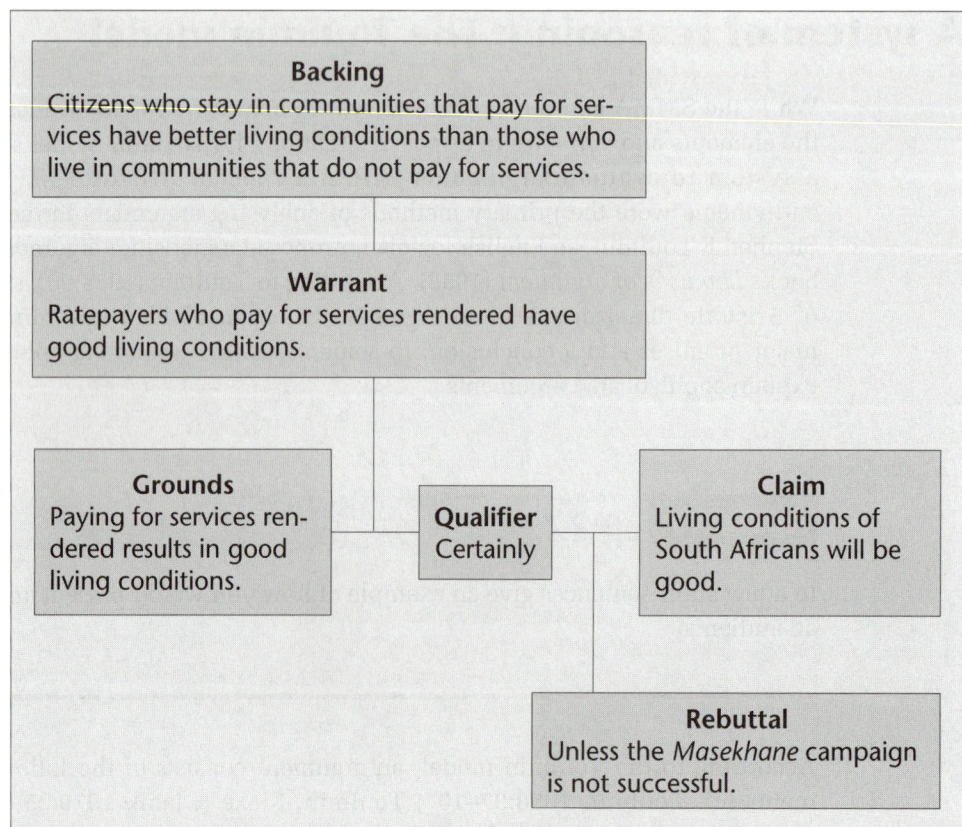

Backing
Citizens who stay in communities that pay for services have better living conditions than those who live in communities that do not pay for services.

Warrant
Ratepayers who pay for services rendered have good living conditions.

Grounds
Paying for services rendered results in good living conditions.

Qualifier
Certainly

Claim
Living conditions of South Africans will be good.

Rebuttal
Unless the *Masekhane* campaign is not successful.

Figure 1.7 **The Toulmin model** (cf. Freeley 1993:152–157)

Structure the argument used in the previous activity according to the Toulmin model. Does this model help you to structure a better argument?

The following questions should be asked when testing any type of reasoning to ensure that it is sound (cf. Freeley 1993:162–163):

▶ Is the evidence reliable enough to establish solid grounds?

▶ Does the warrant justify the movement from the grounds to the claim?

▶ Is the backing adequate, especially if the warrant or rebuttal is not sufficient to stand alone?

▶ As almost any argument is subject to rebuttal, has the rebuttal been properly evaluated?

▶ Has the degree of qualification (from certainty to possibility) been properly determined?

Fallacies of reasoning

When we evaluate a speech, we may identify unsound arguments. Unsound arguments are *fallacies*. In the Toulmin model these fallacious arguments imply the incorrect use of warrants and show that the steps taken in the argument from the data to the claim are not legitimate.

These fallacies may be accidental because of an error in logic or a mistaken or false belief. Fallacies are the result of the unacceptability of a premise, the irrelevance of a premise or the inadequacy of the grounds (the combined premises) of an argument to establish its conclusion (cf. Damer 1987:9).

The following are the fallacies which are most commonly used in speeches and which must be avoided (cf. Damer 1987; Freeley 1993; Toulmin et al. 1979).

Fallacies of linguistic confusion: These fallacies result from the misuse of or confusion in the **meaning** of words, phrases or sentences (cf. Damer 1987:20). Such fallacies could be employed in the following manner:

1 When a speaker uses a word or phrase inconsistently in an argument.

   For example:

   > Pornography is a form of art and pornography is vulgar.

2 When a speaker implicitly suggests but does not assert the conclusion.

   For example:

   > I hope democracy will last in South Africa.

Begging-the-question fallacies: These fallacies smuggle the arguer's position on the claim at issue into the wording of one of the premises. The conclusion is not warranted by the evidence, therefore the audience is "begged" to accept the conclusion. Such fallacies could be employed in the following ways:

1 When a speaker adopts a premise for the argument that is the same as the conclusion to be proved.

   For example:

   > Democracy is the best form of government in South Africa because South Africans prefer democracy.

   This argument does not tell us why democracy is the best form of government.

2 When a speaker formulates a question in such a way that a specific answer is proposed.

   For example:

   > When is management going to sign the contract to approve the wage demands?

   Here the speaker assumes that management is going to sign the contract to approve the wage demands.

Unwarranted assumption fallacies: Arguments are fallacious because, although the arguments may employ popular assumptions, these assumptions are highly questionable. Such fallacies could be employed in the following manner:

1 When the speaker assumes that what is true of some of the parts is therefore true of the whole.

   For example:

   > Car X is not a reliable car, therefore all American cars are not reliable.

2 When a speaker assumes that what is true of the whole is therefore true of the parts of the whole.

   For example:

   > University Y is a good university, therefore all the academic departments in that university are good.

3 When a speaker assumes that a conclusion has only a few alternatives while at the same time assuming that one of the suggested alternatives must be true.

   For example:

   > If you do not have a diploma or a degree, you will fail in life.

4   When a speaker assumes that because something is now in practice it ought to be the universal practice or because something is not the practice it should never be the practice.

For example:

> No city council in South Africa recycles waste, so why should we recycle waste?

5   When a speaker wishes something to be true, that something is or will be true, or because the speaker wishes something not to be true, that something is not or will not be true.

For example:

> We know that a Volkstaat is not a practical option in South Africa at present, but in the future it will be, and therefore we are working towards that goal.

6   When a speaker assumes that a moderate or middle view between two extremes is the best option, simply because it is the middle view.

For example:

> Because the IFP wants international mediation to negotiate regional powers, and the ANC says South Africa can solve its own problems, national mediation will be the solution to the problem.

7   When a speaker assumes that a new policy, law, or action is good simply because it is new.

For example:

> "Under new management" signs imply that the new management is or will be good.

Fallacies of missing evidence: Reasoning is fallacious because a speaker uses too little evidence, biased evidence, no evidence at all or only the appearance of evidence. Such fallacies could be employed in the following ways:

1   When a speaker draws a conclusion from too few examples, from exceptional cases or from unrepresentative or biased data.

For example:

> South Africa is a violent country because there is regular violence in the rural areas of Natal and in the city of Johannesburg.

2   When a speaker claims that something is true because the opposite cannot be proven or there is no evidence that it is false.

For example:

> You cannot prove that sixteen-year-old children can drive well enough to earn a driver's licence; therefore eighteen years of age must remain the minimum age to obtain a driver's licence.

3   When a speaker uses an aphorism or cliché in place of evidence.

For example:

> All white South Africans are racists.

4   When a speaker ignores or minimises the importance of evidence unfavourable to the adopted position.

For example:

> A speaker refers only to the negative side of the new SABC, for example the scaling down of Afrikaans, but omits to mention in the same argument the fact that three other languages are being broadcast for the first time from 1996.

Causal fallacies: These fallacies infer causal explanations from premises that do not provide adequate support for such explanations. Such fallacies could be employed in the following manner:

1   When a speaker oversimplifies the causes of a specific event or series of events.

For example:

> Comparative advertising will result in brand bashing.

2   When a speaker assumes that A caused B simply because B follows A in time.

For example:

> Since Richard has become the new head of department (A) the student numbers have declined (B).

Fallacies of irrelevance: These fallacies employ premises that are logically irrelevant to their conclusions. Such fallacies could be employed in the following ways:

1   When a speaker reaches the wrong conclusion from the evidence provided, thereby missing the point.

For example:

> The students performed poorly because they have to study through distance education.

2   When a speaker makes personal and abusive attacks on an opponent as a means of ignoring or discrediting the opponent's argument.

For example:

> Only a person as stupid as you are will think that abortion should be legalised.

Irrelevant appeals: These fallacies make specific appeals to factors that are usually irrelevant to good reasoning. Such fallacies could be employed in the following manner:

1 When a speaker attempts to persuade others by appealing to their emotions or to popular sentiments, instead of providing evidence for his/her own view.

For example:

> Cuba helped the liberation movements of South Africa during the darkest days of apartheid; we should therefore not be critical of the Cuban government.

2 When a speaker attempts to persuade others to adopt a particular point of view by threatening them with an undesirable state of affairs, instead of by presenting evidence to prove the point.

For example:

> In the past, many white politicians regularly scared white voters into believing that Communism would overrun South Africa, thereby hoping to persuade voters to adopt their point of view. Today some politicians constantly refer voters to the past of the country in order to make a point, instead of providing evidence to support their arguments.

3 When a speaker appeals to people to accept or reject a position simply because the majority of people, or at least a great number of them, accept or reject the position.

For example:

> A speaker calls for the reinstatement of the death penalty in South Africa, on the grounds that the majority of South Africans want it.

Fallacies of diversion: Speakers use these fallacies to direct attention away from the actual point at issue in order to manoeuvre themselves into a more advantageous or less embarrassing position. Such fallacies could be employed in the following ways:

1 When a speaker attacks a less significant point in the opponent's argument saying:

For example:

> You oppose my arguments because you don't like me.

2 When a speaker makes use of humour or ridicule instead of evidence to cover up an inability or unwillingness to respond to the opposition's argument.

For example:

> A minister is asked what he is going to do about the air pollution caused by vehicles in the city, and his response is: "I think that people must start riding bicycles; this will not only reduce air pollution but keep them fit as well."

1

Listen to a debate on *Focus* or any other discussion programme broadcast on television in your country and see how many fallacious arguments you can recognise during the debate.

A knowledge of the different systems of evaluation will enable you to evaluate any speech more thoroughly, taking into account all the elements, variables and fallacies that may occur in arguments.

Case 1.2

President Nelson Mandela's first official speech as President of South Africa at his inauguration ceremony, Pretoria, 10 May 1994

(With acknowledgement to *South African Communication Service*)

Today, all of us do, by our presence here, and by our celebrations in other parts of our country and the world, confer glory and hope to newborn liberty.

Out of the experience of an extraordinary human disaster that lasted too long, must be born a society of which all humanity will be proud.

Our daily deeds as ordinary South Africans must produce an actual South African reality that will reinforce humanity's belief in justice, strengthen its confidence in the nobility of the human soul and sustain all our hopes for a glorious life for all.

All this we owe both to ourselves and to the people of the world who are so well represented here today. To my compatriots, I have no hesitation in saying that each one of us is as intimately attached to the soil of this beautiful country as are the famous jacaranda trees of Pretoria and the mimosa trees of the bushveld.

Each time one of us touches the soil of this land, we feel a sense of personal renewal. The national mood changes as the seasons change. We are moved by a sense of joy and exhilaration when the grass turns green and the flowers bloom.

That spiritual and physical oneness we all share with this common homeland explains the depth of the pain we all carried in our hearts as we saw our country tear apart in a terrible conflict, and as we saw it spurned, outlawed and isolated by the peoples of the world, precisely because it had become the universal base of pernicious ideology and practice of racism and racial oppression.

➡

We, the people of South Africa, feel fulfilled that humanity has taken us back into its bosom; that we, who were outlaws not so long ago, have today been given the rare privilege to be host to the nations of the world on our own soil.

We thank all our distinguished international guests for having come to take possession with the people of our country of what is, after all, a common victory for justice, for peace, for human dignity.

We trust that you will continue to stand by us as we tackle the challenges of building peace, prosperity, non-sexism, non-racialism and democracy.

We deeply appreciate the role that the masses of our people and their political, mass democratic, religious, women, youth, business, traditional and other leaders have played to bring about this conclusion. Not least among them is my Second Deputy President, the Honourable FW de Klerk.

We also like to pay tribute to our security forces, in all their ranks, for the distinguished role they have played in securing our first democratic elections and the transition to democracy, from blood-thirsty forces which still refuse to see the light.

The time for healing of the wounds has come. The moment to bridge the chasms that divide us has come. The time to build is upon us.

We have, at last, achieved our political emancipation. We pledge ourselves to liberate all our people from the continuing bondage of poverty, deprivation, suffering, and gender and other discrimination.

We have succeeded in taking our last steps to freedom in conditions of relative peace. We commit ourselves to the construction of a complete, just and lasting peace.

We have triumphed in the effort to implant hope in the breasts of the millions of our people. We enter into a covenant that we shall build a society in which all South Africans, both black and white, will be able to walk tall, without any fear in their hearts, assured of their inalienable right to human dignity – a rainbow nation at peace with itself and the world.

As a token of its commitment to the renewal of our country, the new Interim Government of National Unity will, as a matter of urgency, address the issue of amnesty for various categories of our people who are currently serving terms of imprisonment.

We dedicate this day to all the heroes and heroines in this country and the rest of the world who sacrificed in many ways and surrendered their lives so that we could be free. Their dreams have become reality. Freedom is their reward.

We are both humbled and elevated by the honour and privilege that you, the people of South Africa, have bestowed on us, as the first President of a united, democratic, non-racial and non-sexist South Africa, to lead our country out of the valley of darkness.

We understand that there is no easy road to freedom. We know it well that none of us acting alone can achieve success. We must therefore act

➡

together as a united people, for national reconciliation, for nation building, for the birth of a new world.

Let there be justice for all. Let there be peace for all. Let there be work, bread, water and salt for all. Let each know that for each the body, the mind and the soul have been freed to fulfil themselves.

Never, never and never again shall it be that this beautiful land will experience the oppression of one another and suffer the indignity of being the skunk of the world.

Let freedom reign. The sun shall never set on so glorious a human achievement. God bless Africa!

ACTIVITY

Evaluate the speech in Case 1.2 according to the dramatistic system of criticism.

The section that follows concentrates on how a speaker should speak during a radio and television interview.

1.6   SPEAKING IN A MASS-MEDIA INTERVIEW

Key words to understand and remember

emotional interview
informational interview
live interview
residual message

hard-exposure interview
interview
recorded interview

Every day on radio and television listeners and viewers are exposed to a wide variety of interviews. The word *interview* comes from the French and means "to exchange views". Interviews are one of the main techniques of radio and television to gather news and information, and to give the viewer or listener the opportunity to hear this news or information from the people who are making the news, or from people who can interpret the news.

If a speaker is asked to participate in an interview on television or radio, the interview may be in the form of a debate, where the other interviewee/s has/have opposing or different opinions on a specific topic, or where the speaker may be the only interviewee. But a speaker is not always asked to participate in an interview. A public relations officer may, for example, contact a regional radio station and ask for an interview to announce or to tell the public more about a forthcoming event. If there are good reasons why such an event is newsworthy and of interest to the public, the public relations officer may succeed in obtaining a chance to promote the event by means of an interview on radio or television (cf. Brown & Brandreth 1986:117–118).

An interview may be *live* or *recorded*. During a live interview, everything that the interviewees say is directly broadcast to the listeners or viewers, so there is no chance to correct anything that goes wrong. In the case of a recorded interview, five or ten minutes may be recorded but only ten or twenty seconds may be broadcast. This may result in comments being taken out of context, but it does allow the interviewee to correct possible mistakes made during the interview; for example, the interviewee may have a second chance to answer a specific question. No matter if the interview is live or recorded, the principles of an interview on television or radio stay the same.

This section of the unit concentrates on how the **interviewee** should speak in a radio or television interview.

Types of mass-media interviews

The type of interview depends on the information the interviewer wants and the circumstances of the interview. According to Boyd (1994:70–91), there are three basic types of mass-media interviews, each with its own specific function. These types of mass-media interviews are:

1   The purpose of a **hard-exposure interview** is to investigate a subject – to deal with important facts relating to a major topic and/or to investigate the cause of a major event. For example, a panel of economic experts could be interviewed to try to find out why the value of the Rand decreased so dramatically against the American dollar at the beginning of 1996.

2   The purpose of the **informative interview** is to put the audience in the picture. The interview gives background to events which are happening or about to happen. Sometimes the purpose may also be to entertain, to look at the lighter side of life and make the audience smile. Interviews conducted during magazine programmes on television frequently make use of informative interviews.

3   The purpose of an **emotional interview** is to reveal an interviewee's state of mind, providing, for example, a personality profile of a well-known person, which outlines what the person does, why the person does it, what motivates the person and what made them what they are today. The emotional interview may also attempt to lay bare the interviewee's feelings. For example, an interview with the South African soccer player Mark Fish could reveal what type of person he is off the soccer field and what motivates him to be a good soccer player.

Preparing for the interview

In order to be able to prepare adequately for an interview, the interviewee should first know what the task of the interviewer is (cf. Biagi 1992:57–58, 124–132; Hyde 1995:251–270; Koehler & Sisco 1981:171; O'Donnell, Hausman & Benoit 1987: 152–169).

The interviewer

The primary objective of the interviewer is to create an interview that will attract the interest and attention of the audience. The interviewer does research to obtain enough background information on a topic that is of interest or importance. The research is necessary so that the interviewer can ask informative and relevant questions and, if possible, establish each guest's background, accomplishments, and attitude and beliefs regarding the topic under discussion. The questions should preferably be short, single-idea questions that progress from point to point in such a manner that the audience will understand the discussion in the interview. The interviewer selects an interviewee or interviewees who are accessible, accountable and quotable – the interviewee must be well informed on the topic or proposition under discussion.

Just before the interview, the interviewer makes the interviewees familiar with the operation of an interview, in or outside a studio. The interviewer will also outline the interview without giving specific questions and will not discuss a specific aspect of the interview in detail.

During the interview, the interviewer emphasises the importance of the topic and establishes the interviewees' credentials to the viewers or listeners. The interviewer ends the interview by thanking the interviewees for their participation and concludes, if possible, with a short summary of the interview. The interviewer should control the interview and the interviewees should respect that by answering the interviewer's questions, and not try to deliver a speech on a different aspect of the topic.

The interviewee

Having been asked to participate in an interview, a speaker should first **orientate** him/herself towards the interview by obtaining the following information (cf. Hurst 1992:185–189; Rafe 1991:13):

▶ the topic and the type of interview;

▶ when, and on what programme the interview will take place;

▶ whether or not the interview is related to a specific news event;

▶ why he or she has been selected as speaker;

▶ whether other speakers are also being interviewed and who they are – rivals or supporters;

▶ whether an audience will be present who may be allowed to ask questions;

▶ whether the interview is live or recorded;

▶ who will conduct the interview;

▶ what areas of the specific topic under discussion will be covered;

▶ how long the interview will be, which may range from ten seconds to half an hour.

The speaker should thereafter work out the *residual message* (i.e. a lasting impression) which he/she wishes to leave with the radio or television audience (cf. Koehler & Sisco 1981:175–176). A residual message helps the speaker to focus on the single most important point to be made, as well as helping to concentrate on relevant information and to eliminate material that does not contribute to the residual message. It also helps the speaker to determine which information relates to and supports the basic message the speaker wants to put across to the audience. This residual message can be compared with the formulation of a thematic statement when a speaker prepares a speech.

Thirdly, a speaker should **anticipate** the interview. If a speaker watches or listens to the interviewer and the programme before being interviewed, the speaker may have a better idea of what to expect in terms of style and presentation. It is also advisable to work out expected questions in advance. A friend may ask the speaker probable questions to which the speaker can practise responding. Such preparation prior to an interview can be recorded on a tape recorder so that the speaker can listen to him or herself. This will give the speaker valuable feedback regarding the answers given and the use of his/her voice.

Bearing the residual message in mind, the speaker can make notes of a few main points to be made or anticipated during the interview. The time available should be kept in mind when these notes are being prepared.

The interview

An interviewee should look neat and tidy during an interview. Patterns on clothes, such as thin stripes or checks, create a blurred effect on the television screen and should be avoided.

The key to successful interviews is **saying what you mean and meaning what you say**. Although an interviewee has no control over the opening statement of the interview, an attempt should still be made to begin with a strong opening statement linked to the first question asked. No matter what questions are asked during an interview, a speaker can find a way to link the residual message to the question – but the questions should still be answered. As is the case with all types of speeches, a speaker should use language that the audience will understand. A speaker should not try to impress an audience with jargon, as the use of unfamiliar words will only confuse them. The interviewee's message is intended for the television and radio audience and not for the interviewer; the message therefore should focus on the interests of the audience (cf. Rafe 1991:15).

An interviewee should listen carefully to questions. Avoiding questions will cause the audience to lose confidence in the speaker. Answering all questions honestly will do much less damage than trying to hide something that comes out later. The use of sound arguments is important during an interview: no claims should be made without evidence. It is also important for a speaker to distinguish between facts and opinions during the interview. A speaker must also clarify whether the opinion is his/her own or that of the organisation or group that he/she represents.

Nonverbal aspects, as discussed in Section 1.4 of this unit, are also important during a radio or television interview. However, during a radio interview, speakers have only their voices to communicate with the audience. Therefore they should concentrate especially on how they pronounce and articulate their words and on the vocal aspects of their nonverbal communication. On television vocal aspects, pronunciation and articulation of words are also important, but speakers must in addition consider their posture, facial expressions, eye contact, gestures and personal appearance to convey a message. During the interview the interviewee looks at the interviewer and at the other interviewees, but not into the camera/s.

Just before the end of the interview, the interviewer may ask the interviewees if they have anything to add. This gives interviewees the opportunity to make a statement or say something that they regard as their final and most important opinion on the topic under discussion. The final statement should be linked to the residual message of the interview to ensure a lasting impression on the audience.

ACTIVITY

Describe in what ways the delivery of a speech differs from speaking in a mass-media interview.

During an interview it is not always possible to say what one wants to say, contrary to the position when delivering a speech. However, if a speaker concentrates on the residual message, the main idea or argument will come across to the audience.

Summary

In this unit we discussed speech communication. A short history of speech communication made us aware of previous contributions in speech communication that are still valid today. We then considered the types of speeches we can deliver, as well as audience analysis. Thereafter we paid attention to the preparation and delivery of a speech. We examined the ways in which a speech and arguments in a speech can be evaluated. We concluded this unit with the principles of speaking in a mass-media interview.

SUGGESTED READING

Burke, K. 1969. *A rhetoric of motives*. Berkeley, Calif: University of California Press.

Cathcart, R.S. 1988. *Post communication. Rhetorical analysis and evaluation*. 2nd edition. New York: Macmillan.

Corbett, E.P.J. (ed.) 1984. *The rhetoric and poetics of Aristotle*. New York: Random House.

Damer, T.E. 1987. *Attacking faulty reasoning*. 2nd edition. Belmont, Calif: Wadsworth.

De Wet, J.C. & Rensburg, R.S. 1989. *Evaluation of public speaking*. Cape Town: Juta.

Freeley, A.J. 1993. *Argumentation and debate. Critical thinking for reasoned decision making*. 8th edition. Belmont, Calif: Wadsworth.

Gronbeck, B.E., German, K., Ehninger, D. & Monroe, A.H. 1992. *Principles of speech communication*. 11th edition. New York: HarperCollins.

McCroskey, J.C. 1978. *An introduction to rhetorical communication.* 3rd edition. Englewood Cliffs, NJ: Prentice-Hall.

Rafe, S.C. 1991. *Mastering the news media interview: how to succeed at television, radio and print interviews.* New York: HarperBusiness.

Schutte, P.J. 1990. *Debattering en redevoering.* Pretoria: Academica.

Toulmin, S., Rieke, R. & Janik, A. 1979. *An introduction to reasoning.* New York: Macmillan.

Introduction to Public Relations

Christien Bredenkamp

Overview

This unit is an introduction to the study of public relations within the organisational context and focuses on the important role that it plays in modern society. In our study of public relations a historical overview of the development of public relations is provided and an indication is given as to why public relations needs to be studied within the social sciences and specifically within communication. We define public relations and highlight some of the problems that arise in various attempts to define it. We pay attention to various theoretical approaches in studying and practising public relations and introduce you to the planning of public relations. We conclude this unit by indicating the relevance of planning in public relations with reference to the public relations campaign and public relations programme.

Key terms to understand and remember

booming twenties
early American beginnings
seedbed years
1930s and thereafter

conceptual definition
descriptive definition
public relations

external publics
future publics
internal publics
marginal publics
opponent publics
proponent publics
public
primary publics
secondary publics
traditional publics
uncommitted publics

process approach
rhetorical/persuasive approach
symmetrical and asymmetrical approach
systems approach

planning
public relations campaign
public relations event
public relations programme
RAISE formula

Objectives

At the end of this unit you should be able to:

1   Describe the major developments in the history of public relations and explain the significance of each development.

2   Define *public relations* and distinguish between *conceptual definitions* and *descriptive definitions* of public relations.

3 Define *public* and distinguish between various categories of publics.

4 Describe the various *theoretical approaches* to public relations and indicate their relevance for the practice of public relations.

5 Distinguish between an *event*, a *public relations campaign* and a *public relations programme.*

6 Plan a public relations *campaign* according to the *RAISE formula.*

7 Plan a public relations *programme.*

INTRODUCTION

During the twentieth century it became essential for social scientists to study human communication, which includes the process and effects of human interaction. The conclusions that these scientists reached regarding communication are helpful as we try to bring about human understanding. Part and parcel of the process of human understanding are the misconceptions and conceptions concerning *public relations* in a democratic society. Public relations has often been misunderstood by the public at large, and yet it is indispensable to a modern democratic society. Reasons for this include first of all the fact that public relations operates according to the fundamental rights of freedom of speech and freedom of the press, which means that everyone has an equal right to be heard. Secondly, public relations is essential in modern democracies, as these are characterised by mass societies and mass communication. Public relations provides a way for all individuals, groups, organisations, governments, et cetera to communicate and deliver their messages by way of the mass media and to have a chance to be heard by others. Thirdly, public relations can only exist in democratic societies. As defined in this unit and by the public relations profession, public relations cannot exist in authoritarian and dictatorial states. Fourthly, public relations can only exist in a democracy because everyone has the right to his or her own view of the truth. Although we may all have different views of the truth, we have to convince the majority in a democracy of the view that should prevail. Therefore the "truth" could be described as the "will of the majority" in a democracy (cf. Hiebert 1988:2–3).

In a democratic society *public sentiment*, or as some authors refer to it, *public opinion* (cf. Seitel 1995; Baskin & Aronoff 1992; Cutlip, Center & Broom 1985) is of great importance and the public relations professional is the person who moulds public opinion. Public relations professionals are the people who work in the profession and who interpret the *publics* and public opinion to their clients, organisations and institutions and vice versa. To interpret the relevant publics and public opinion is, however, not as easy for an organisation as it may seem to be. Through the ages public relations has been practised as an intuitive art, but as the profession is coming of age we can study and practise it as part of the social sciences, and more specifically, as we endeavour to do in this unit, as part of communication science.

Professionals and academics have been describing, defining and studying public relations past and present. By testing their theories and remedies they all contribute to the *body of knowledge* which constitutes public relations as a profession. In our study of public relations we combine the work done in the social sciences, communication science and by professionals in the practice of public relations, with the aim of bringing about better understanding of public relations as a profession in modern democracies.

2

Throughout history, leaders in all civilisations were very aware of the importance of influencing public opinion. Examples cited to verify this awareness vary from the Babylonians of 1800 BC who made stone tablets of their messages to farmers so that the farmers could learn how to harvest, sow and irrigate in order to increase the wealth of the country; the sophists who were masters of rhetoric and verbal persuasion; the Romans, and more specifically Julius Caesar, who was a master at rallying support for his views; and even the Catholic Church which helped to "propagate the faith" in the 1600s by establishing a college of propaganda (cf. Seitel 1995:28). However, these examples focus on the development of communication techniques, whereas the persuasive abilities and the actual development of public relations is a fairly recent development.

Public relations as studied in this unit is less than 100 years old. Four factors are cited as reasons for the development of public relations during the twentieth century (cf. Seitel 1995:26–27).

▶ The first factor relates to the growth of big organisations and institutions in modern society. During the twentieth century we have seen the development of big organisations, for example, the development from local grocery stores to big chain stores and also the development of multinational organisations, which all need to communicate and interpret their messages to their relevant publics.

▶ A second factor is represented by the increase in change, conflict and confrontation in modern society. Governments and organisations in the twentieth century are constantly confronted with the fact that they need to better their communication towards their relevant publics, who are concerned with issues such as the environment, animal rights, gay rights, labour disputes, retrenchments and affirmative action.

▶ Technological inventions, as a third factor, have played a major part in the awareness of publics of more and better communication between themselves and their relevant organisations or institutions. Developments such as satellite television, video tapes, computers and facsimile machines serve as examples.

▶ Lastly, the establishment of democracies during the twentieth century in Latin America, Eastern Europe, the former Soviet Union and South Africa has increased people's awareness of the importance of public opinion and the effect the latter has on the development and operation of such democracies.

Although these factors played a major role in the evolution of public relations as we know it today, public relations originated in the United States of America where the power of public opinion and the competition for public acceptance and support is vast. We could claim that the development of public relations in the United States of America (USA) has determined its development in other countries, especially in South Africa, and therefore a brief overview of the history and development of public relations in the USA is necessary to determine the roots of public relations.

The early American beginnings

To understand public relations in the twentieth century we need to trace its steps from earlier activities that took place, and relate these to public relations during the seventeenth century. Examples of such activities include the following: the creation of publicity to raise funds, the promotion of causes, boosting commercial ventures and the building of box-office personalities in the USA (for a full discussion of publicity, see Units 3 and 4). Various authors (cf. Baskin & Aronoff 1992; Cutlip et al. 1985; Seitel 1995) mention the first systematic *fund-raising campaign* in the USA that was initiated by the Harvard College in 1641 as an identifiable example of a public relations activity. This campaign was accompanied by a fund-raising brochure entitled *New England first fruits* (cf. Baskin & Aronoff 1992:25), the first of its kind in history.

Most of public relations' history is reflected in the tools and techniques that have been used during major historical events associated with politics and war. The first example of what we could call a *public relations campaign* was initiated by Samuel Adams during the American Revolution War. He is renowned for his attempts at organising public opinion, which can be recognised in the following activities related to public relations (cf. Baskin & Aronoff 1992:25–26).

▶ The manner in which Adams and his fellow revolutionaries made use of symbols that were easily identifiable, for example the Liberty Tree.

▶ The use of slogans such as "Taxation without representation is tyranny".

▶ Organising and staging an event such as the Boston Tea Party (1773) to influence public opinion.

▶ Using all available media for staging such an event and making sure that their side of the story reached the public first.

The next landmark in the development of public relations is recognised in the publication of *The Federalist letters* written to newspapers during 1787–1788 by Alexander Hamilton, James Madison and John Jay (cf. Cutlip et al. 1985:25). The publication and dissemination of these letters led to the ratification of the constitution of the USA and is described as "history's first public relations job" (Baskin & Aronoff 1992:26).

Subsequently, we find the first indication of a public presidential campaign during the *1820s and 1830s* in the work done by Amos Kendall as a pollster, counsellor, ghostwriter and publicist for president Andrew Jackson. Kendall excelled in moulding public opinion and creating events on important issues during Jackson's period in office. He could be called the first presidential press secretary, as it is known today (cf. Endres 1976:5–12). During the 1830s another person's efforts need to be highlighted: those of Matthew St Clair Clarke (cf. Baskin & Aronoff 1992:39). In an effort to develop a politician to oppose Andrew Jackson, Matthew St Clair Clarke created the myths surrounding the historical figure Davy Crockett and launched the most extensive, though unsuccessful, public relations campaign up till then. Clarke saturated the media with releases, reports and pamphlets in an unsuccessful effort against the forces and efforts of Jackson and Kendall.

The *Industrial Revolution* during the last quarter of the nineteenth century had a profound effect on every aspect of society as we have come to know it. This era changed business and forced politics to change as well, thereby paving the way for some very shrewd public relations pioneers. Public relations entered the *pressagentry phase* which was characterised by press agents exploiting freaks to publicise circuses, inventing legends to promote politicians and in general telling lies, thereby providing popular entertainment but very little real news. The most successful *press agent* of the nineteenth century was P T Barnum. Phineas Taylor Barnum (1810–1891) is often referred to as a showman or even a huckster (cf. Seitel 1995:30). However, irrespective of this label, we can also label him a master *publicist*. He was successful in creating, promoting and exploiting the careers of many celebrities such as the midget General Tom Thumb and the original Siamese twins, Chang and Eng (cf. Newsom, Scott & VanSlyke Turk 1989:32). Although many of today's public relations professionals would criticise his **publicity** stunts as exploitive, manipulative and outrageous, we can deduce that he was a master in generating publicity for his travelling show that was also well known as the Barnum Circus. Much of the blame currently put on public relations practitioners for generating publicity by using manipulative techniques is attributed to the efforts of PT Barnum.

Public relations in the twentieth century

The development of public relations in the twentieth century can be traced in terms of the careers of important public relations pioneers, certain business practices, and the effects of two world wars.

The *seedbed years* (1900–1919), as they are called by Cutlip (1994:1–92), saw the establishment of the first *publicity agency* in the history of public relations. Early in the 1900s George VS Michaelis, Herbert Small and Thomas O Marvin established The Publicity Bureau in Boston (cf. Cutlip 1994:10). This "**publicity agency**" gathered factual information about its clients, such as the nation's railroads, for distribution to the newspapers. Other agencies were also established in Washington, DC, San Francisco, New York, Oklahoma City and Atlanta during the first few years of the nineteenth century.

The era mentioned above also saw the rise of someone who is sometimes referred to as **a father** of public relations, Ivy Ledbetter Lee (1877–1934). He was a Wall Street reporter who changed his vocation to become a political publicist and then became instrumental in forming the nation's third publicity bureau in 1904. It is well known that Ivy Lee was the first person to publish a *Declaration of principles* (cf. Seitel 1995:33) to all newspaper editors in an attempt to "open up" to the media on behalf of his client, George F Baer and Associates during an anthracite coal strike. This *Declaration of principles* had a profound influence on the development of press agentry, publicity, and thereafter public relations. Lee is also remembered for acting on behalf of quite a few important clients such as the Pennsylvania Railroad and the Rockefeller family (cf. Newsom et al. 1989:41; Cutlip 1994:37–72). Ivy Lee laid the groundwork for contemporary public relations by contributing many of the techniques and principles that public relations professionals follow today. In an epitaph to a speech he delivered in 1934 he wrote:

> Extensive experience in assisting large corporations to adjust themselves to the demands of public opinion in making their purposes and policies understood and in creating for themselves a favourable position in the public mind has shown that no amount of propaganda is any value unless the policy of an institution is in the first place sound and honest, and is responsive to the high demands of enlightened public sentiment (Cutlip 1994:153).

Even though Lee used publicity to describe his vocation, he had in fact arrived at what we call **public relations**. According to him, a **publicist** is someone who advises a client on which policy to pursue in the creation of favourable public reaction. Thereafter, it is also the publicist's function to draw up the information in order to keep the public informed (cf. Cutlip 1994:154).

However, Lee's contribution to the practice of public relations does not go without criticism. Olasky (1987:50–53) mentions the fact that Lee chose his words very carefully in his *Declaration of principles* and created an inaccurate impression of "opening up" to the media. In fact, Olasky claims Lee kept to the letter of the principle of accuracy (keeping to the facts) but not in the spirit of telling the truth. The coal strike in Colorado called the *Ludlow Massacre* is used as an example to verify Olasky's criticism of Lee's so-called "opening up" to the media (cf. Newsom et al. 1989:41; Olasky 1987:51). This strike was accompanied by considerable violence with the end result that two women and eleven children died. Lee was employed by Rockefeller, Junior, to repair the damage caused by the press coverage of the tragedy. Lee claimed that the women and children, while fleeing in panic from an uncontrolled Colorado State Militia, had overturned a stove and started a fire which caused them to die. Lee could therefore suggest that the women and children died because of their own carelessness. Many reporters pointed out that it would be foolish to expect people to watch their step when fleeing such a situation, but Lee could state with accuracy at that stage that he did not lie (cf. Olasky 1987:51). He later admitted that the "facts" he conveyed to the media were the facts as management saw them and that he had not checked them for accuracy (cf. Newsom et al. 1989:41). In reality, therefore, Lee had created dishonest impressions from factual statements. Lee was also severely criticised for working for the Nazi organisation and for his support of Soviet Russia and encouraging USA–Soviet relationships. However, Lee is not so much remembered for what he **did** during his career, but instead for what he **said** about the vocation, that we refer to as public relations.

Further highlights of the development of public relations during the *first quarter of the twentieth century* include the extensive use of *public relations consultants* by the railroads in the USA. Nonprofit organisations, such as churches, charity, health and welfare organisations and colleges, began to make use of extensive publicity efforts in order to raise funds for their causes. In the business sector the American Telephone and Telegraph Company's (AT & T) use of publicity and other public relations activities are noted as having an important influence on the development of public relations. The most notable effort was the one mounted by the United States in World War I. Never before had such a vast, multifaceted and co-ordinated programme been used to get support for the United States' effort during World War I (cf. Baskin & Aronoff 1992:35). This effort focused on **publicity to mobilise opinion**. George Creel, as head of the Committee on Public Information during World War I, used public relations techniques, such as creating publicity to increase the sales of Liberty Bonds, help build the Red Cross and promote food conservation (cf. Baskin & Aronoff 1992:35). His efforts proved the necessity of public relations activities during wartime and in the process trained many of the influential practitioners of this century.

Figure 2.1 **Edward L Bernays (1891–1995)**

The *booming twenties era* (1919–1930), as Cutlip (1994:105) calls it, saw the rise of **another father** of public relations, namely Edward L Bernays (1891–1995). Bernays, nephew of Sigmund Freud, started out as a publicist in 1913 but he is best known for publishing the first book on public relations, called *Crystallizing public opinion* (1923), in which he coined the term *public relations counsel* (cf. Bernays 1923:11). This is documented as the first time that any person practising public relations or performing such activities was called **public relations counsel.** The contribution of this book to public relations as a vocation is described by Goldman (1948) as the emphatic dissociation of public relations from either press agentry or mere publicity work. Goldman (1948) emphasises the fact that Bernays declared the primary function of public relations to be the changing of both public policy and public attitudes so as to bring about a relationship between the two. This means that the public relations counsel, as Bernays called it, helps to mould the actions taken by the client as well as to mould public opinion.

Bernays was truly a public relations scholar in every sense of the word, and taught the first course in public relations at New York University in 1923. By making use of market research (i.e. various research techniques used to study the market of a product or service), social surveys and public opinion polls, he was instrumental in a shift of interest in public relations. The focus turned from the **power** of public opinion, to the **nature** of public opinion and the **role of communication** in its formation.

Crystallizing public opinion was, however, the first of many books and articles published by Bernays during a period of some seventy years, which brought about understanding and acceptance of what he called public relations counsel. In 1955 Bernays published another significant book, namely *The engineering of consent*, which included principles for public relations but also gave rise to criticism levelled against Bernays for his approach towards public relations. The term *engineering of consent* (and by **consent**, public opinion is implied) was described by his critics as connoting various **negative** meanings to the practice of public relations. Negative meanings refer to the manipulation of the public which was not inherently what public relations practitioners felt they should endeavour to do. However, Bernays was instrumental in the search for *professional recognition* by public relations practitioners (and identifying the obstacles that prohibit this), as well as contributing to the **body of knowledge** which makes up such an essential part of any profession.

The **booming twenties** also saw public relations growing in scope and stature. Public relations practitioners considered themselves as being responsible for educating management in public opinion and for informing the mass media and public. During this period Arthur W Page was offered the vice presidency of AT & T and he insisted on having a say in shaping the corporate policy of the company. The reason for this prerequisite was that he realised the importance of public approval for the effective operation of any organisation. He insisted that a publicity department (as it was called) should be the interpreter between the public and the company and also gauge and utilise public opinion. Today, the stock of AT & T and its other diversified companies is held in high esteem by dealers on the stock exchange.

The *1930s and thereafter* are characterised by the influence of the Great Depression and World War II on society as a whole. The depression was instrumental in the change in public relations activities from occasional defensive efforts to continuous programmes. There was a realisation that persuasion and publicity are only effective when used in combination with responsible performance. The period just before World War II also saw the increased use of public opinion polls but in a more precise way, being more scientific in the application of measurement and assessment criteria.

World War II accelerated the development of public relations and the United States made use of a powerful and organised information campaign by the Office of War Information (cf. Baskin & Aronoff 1992:40). It was also the period in which paid advertising was first used as a tool of public relations (today referred to as *public relations advertising* or *institutional advertising*). These forms of advertising are discussed at length in Units 3 and 4.

The *postwar era* saw public relations gaining respectability and acceptance and striving for *professionalism*. As mentioned previously, public relations really grew as a result of the influence of four factors on society, namely (1) the growth of big organisations and institutions; (2) the increase in change, conflict and confrontation in modern society; (3) technological inventions; and (4) the establishment of democracies throughout the world. These factors influenced the *development of public relations* in the following ways.

1   The growth of big organisations and institutions created the need for public relations practitioners to interpret business for the public.

2   Change, conflict and confrontation are part and parcel of modern society and organisations are in constant need of public relations practitioners to interpret public opinion for the organisation and vice versa so that organisations can fulfil their social responsibility towards society.

3   Because of the advancement in technologies in society, publics have become segmented, specialised and sophisticated. Organisations have therefore had to adapt their communication to their relevant publics to enable the organisations to persuade, inform, influence or reach these publics.

4   The growth in democracies throughout the world has made it increasingly important for organisations to become aware of the significance of public opinion; this has resulted in the need for professionals to fulfil the function of acting on and moulding public opinion. In other words, a public relations professional has become essential.

Although the above-mentioned factors illustrate why a public relations professional is essential in an organisation, the growth of the profession and the development towards professional status in the 1950s resulted in a concern for control over the *ethics* of public relations professionals – a dilemma which still exists in the modern practice of public relations. This concern resulted in *codes of conduct* being enforced by professional organisations and in the improvement of the standards of professional performance by members of the professional organisations through certification, accreditation and various educational qualifications.

Currently *public relations associations* exist in more than seventy countries (cf. Rensburg, Mersham & Skinner 1995) and the international organisation that connects the majority of them is called the International Public Relations Association (IPRA), which was founded in London in 1955 (cf. Skinner & Von Essen 1995:21). In Africa, the Federation of African Public Relations Associations (FAPRA) was established nearly twenty years ago in Nairobi, and it functions as a federated organisation of national public relations associations (cf. Opukah 1993b:15–17). However, public relations as a profession seems to be in an emerging state in most countries in Africa.

The **development of public relations in South Africa** started with the establishment of an Information Bureau in 1937 with the aim of spreading official (governmental) information (cf. Skinner & Von Essen 1995:21). The Public Relations Institute of

Southern Africa (PRISA) governs the conduct of its members who practise public relations in South Africa. It was established in 1957 with approximately nineteen members. Currently PRISA consists of approximately 4 000 members. Following the trend throughout the world, South Africa is also witnessing a growth in the number of practitioners of public relations because the need and necessity for professionalism continues to increase.

Together with the increase in the number of professionals in public relations during the twentieth century comes the need to define **what public relations actually means.** This is due to the fact that organisations seem to give public relations practitioners (people who practise public relations) a variety of titles, for example public relations, external affairs, corporate communications, public affairs, corporate relations. In addition to the above concern is the fact that people practising public relations are increasingly subject to public scrutiny. It is therefore essential that we define public relations and determine what it actually means.

ACTIVITY

List the most important developments in the history of public relations and describe their significance for public relations as a profession.

2.3 THE COMMUNICATIVE NATURE OF PUBLIC RELATIONS

Throughout the history of public relations, the practice has been linked to the communication between an organisation and its *relevant publics* (the term **publics** is defined and explained later in this section). To illustrate the communicative nature of public relations, we can distinguish between four distinct *stages of development* of public relations in the USA. These correspond with particular periods in the history of the USA, and provide an indication of the communicative nature of public relations during specified periods in time.

Historical periods	Characteristics of public relations	Communicative nature
1600–1799 the early beginnings	publicists, press agents, promoters and propagandists	communicating/ initiating
1800–1899 civil war, industrial revolution	writers as spokespersons for special interests	reacting/responding
World War I, booming twenties, depression	public relations incorporated into management function	planning/preventing
1940 to the present World War II postwar era	attempts to control the development, education and practice of public relations	professionalism

Table 2.1 **Stages of development and communicative nature of public relations**

Public relations activities or practices are therefore highlighted during certain *historical periods* and provide a useful background to the problems we encounter when trying to explain the meaning of public relations. In Table 2.1 the development of public relations is explained by indicating that public relations activities were applied during the **era of press agentry and publicity** to **communicate and initiate** actions taken by the institutions concerned, for example in the government, in industry and in organisational contexts.

The second period, which spans the **civil war** and the **industrial revolution**, saw an increase in institutions using public relations practitioners as spokespersons, especially to **react** to exposed scandals associated with government and capitalism. The **third stage of development** of public relations, referred to as a period of **planning and preventing,** is the first indication of public relations being used as a systematic and planned effort in communicating with organisations' relevant publics. However, during this period very serious concerns regarding the profession arose. Society needed qualified and professional social scientists and counsellors and many public relations practitioners were not up to the task.

The **last period** in the development refers to public relations as it is practised today and is typified by a sense of **professionalism.** Public relations has become highly visible in organisations during the last quarter of the twentieth century and this has brought about increased criticism of the profession. Critics of the profession are concerned mainly with factors such as the credibility, accountability and responsibility of the practitioners of public relations and these factors will continue to play a role in the development of the profession.

Defining public relations

As is the case with any developing profession, public relations continues to change. Change is also the reason why **public relations** continues to elude a final definition. The history of public relations reveals valid reasons for both trusting and distrusting the profession. Criticism is levelled at the profession from social scientists who criticise some of its techniques, such as manipulating public opinion for personal or governmental gain. The Information Scandal in South Africa during 1978 and 1979 is an example of the latter. Various publics distrust the profession because individuals who refer to themselves as public relations professionals are not always accountable, credible or responsible in the performance of their duties.

We need, therefore, to bear the historical facts in mind when trying to formulate a definition of public relations. Searching for a definition of public relations became really important during the **professionalism stage.** As history shows, Edward Bernays was among the first to define public relations as a profession. He refined his original 1923 definition of public relations to a more condensed version in 1952, finally defining it as

1   information given to the public,

2   persuasion directed at the public to modify attitudes and actions, and

3   efforts to integrate attitudes and actions of an institution with its publics and of publics with that institution (Bernays 1952:3).

The verbs used in this definition, namely **to inform, to persuade** and **to integrate,** indicate that public relations is a link between two entities – an organisation and its relevant publics. His definition also indicates that the link does not consist of a one-way relationship, but rather a two-way relationship, which shows that public relations is an **active** process.

In 1975 a study was undertaken in the USA to search for a **universal definition** of public relations as a profession. This study was commissioned by the Foundation for Public Relations Research and Education, which appointed Rex F Harlow as co-ordinator and sixty-five public relations leaders in the profession to assist him. Their task was to develop a definition that would be clear-cut, viable, acceptable and useful to public relations professionals, but which would also be used in public relations education (cf. Harlow 1988:7–16). The aim of the study was to collect all definitions of public relations published up to that time, break them down and determine their basic, central ideas, and thereafter to condense these ideas into a final definition of public relations.

After having collected 472 definitions, the study came up with what they called a *working definition* of public relations and a *description definition* of public relations. According to Harlow (1988:9), the **working definition** of public relations reads as follows:

> Public relations is a distinctive management function which helps establish and maintain mutual lines of communication, understanding, acceptance and cooperation between an organization and its publics; involves the management of problems or issues; helps management to keep informed on and responsive to public opinion; defines and emphasizes the responsibility of management to serve the public interest; helps management keep abreast of and effectively utilize change, serving as an early warning system to help anticipate trends; and uses research and sound and ethical communication techniques as its principal tools.

To the definition above they added a **description definition** which includes descriptions of the public relations profession such as (cf. Harlow 1988:9–10):

1 it is a specialised body of knowledge, skills and methods;

2 a management function which deals with the relations between two or more organisations or publics;

3 public relations activities relate to a variety of organisations, for example, government, industry, education, finance, labour and education; and

4 public relations practitioners are aware of the influence of public opinion, and counsel and communicate in various ways.

Harlow (1988:13) concluded that time would tell if the definitions would change, as change is part and parcel of society – and change they did.

As a result of dissatisfaction with the above definitions, further attempts were made by public relations practitioners to define public relations. According to Cutlip et al. (1985), definitions of public relations can be divided into either *operational definitions* or *conceptual definitions*. **Operational definitions** (also called description definitions) tend to describe the type of activities, tasks and functions undertaken by public relations professionals. **Conceptual definitions,** on the other hand, attempt to unify the broad range of activities and purposes in the practice of public relations. Such definitions also specify what **is not** part of public relations. According to Cutlip et al. (1985:4), the **working definition** formulated by Harlow and his colleagues is both conceptual and operational. The problem with such a definition is that it is a very lengthy and extensive description of what takes place in practice.

Various **conceptual definitions** have been formulated by academics, professional bodies and practitioners in the profession (cf. Cutlip et al. 1985:4; Seitel 1995:7; Newsom et al. 1989:5; Baskin & Aronoff 1992:4). However, conceptual definitions often provide a limited scope and understanding of what the practice involves and therefore these definitions are usually accompanied by a **description definition** to overcome this problem.

Nevertheless, more and more definitions were formulated as the profession changed, and in 1987 the Public Relations Society of America (PRSA) launched two official attempts of providing a basis for consensus in terminology (cf. Lesly 1987). PRSA came up with two definitions which, in their view, establish a perception of the role of public relations, namely "Public relations helps an organisation and its publics adapt mutually to each other" and "Public relations is an organisation's effort to win the co-operation of groups of people" (Lesly 1987:5).

The above two definitions are clearly **conceptual definitions** which are not necessarily incorrect, but they fail to indicate **how** a public relations professional succeeds in getting an organisation and its publics to adapt to each other or **how** they succeed in getting the groups of people to co-operate.

In 1993 the Institute of Public Relations (IPR) in the USA recommended that a working party investigate a change to the accepted definition, as it was being criticised for its "lofty aspirations" and for being "broad, idealistic and not reflecting the real world of persuasive communication" (Newman 1993:12). No matter how good it may sound, no organisation wants to pay for a consultation on mutual understanding. They came to the conclusion that the profession needs three definitions: firstly, a definition that clearly states what is meant by the term *public relations*; secondly, a definition that defines public relations as a professional practice; and thirdly, an attempt to obtain an agreement on the words used as job titles (or descriptions) and consultancy services. Their recommendations were as follows.

▶ What is meant by public relations? "Public relations is reputation – the result of what you do, what you say and what others say about you" (Newman 1993:12).

▶ A definition that defines public relations as a professional practice reads as follows: "Public relations practice is the discipline concerned with the reputation of organisations (or products, services or individuals) with the aim of earning understanding and support" (Newman 1993:12). They do, however, add that some practitioners would prefer to see the phrase "with the aim of influencing behaviour or opinion" added to the end of the definition, but agree that this remains open to debate.

▶ That the term **public relations** is the best term to use because it encompasses the full range of activities which are involved in modern practice. Many practitioners would, however, prefer other phrases as defined in a list supplied by Newman (1993:15) because they are more appropriate to the specialist function which they perform within the profession.

The investigation mentioned above, and the recommendations that followed, constitute a serious attempt by the people who engage in public relations every day to debate their work. As Newman (1993:14) concludes, if public relations professionals claim to be able to establish mutual understanding, then this debate or process is an attempt to lead to such mutual understanding.

However, whether or not the debate continues, we still need to be able to practise the profession in South Africa according to an acceptable **conceptual definition.** The one accepted by the Public Relations Institute of Southern Africa (PRISA) reads as follows: public relations is *"the deliberate, planned and sustained effort to establish and maintain mutual understanding between the organisation and its publics, both internally and externally"* (Rensburg et al. 1995:11).

This definition highlights certain aspects of public relations that need further elaboration.

▶ **Deliberate, planned and sustained effort** refers to all activities in public relations having definite aims and publics to be reached. In order to achieve these aims and reach the various publics, public relations professionals need to plan their activities, strategies and emergencies according to certain steps. Being a planned effort also means that public relations is not a haphazard activity, but is systematically organised in order to reach predetermined goals. As a sustained effort, public relations involves both parties of the communication process: in this case, the organisation and its relevant publics. It is also a continuous activity because, for example, the publics of an organisation could change and the message would need to be adapted, changed, et cetera.

▶ **Publics** refers to the recipients of the organisation's message. A public could be described as a group of people with common interests exerting an influence on and affecting the organisation and its operations in some way (cf. Newsom et al. 1989:73). It is important to take note of the fact that a particular individual can be a member of different publics at the same time, and at different times. For instance, a Unisa student belongs to a group of Communication III students (a public), but at the same time the student can also be a member of a social, political or professional organisation, each of which constitutes a separate public. (Publics are further defined and explained below.)

▶ The words **establish** and **maintain** refer to the purpose of public relations. Public relations needs to be able to establish a relationship between an organisation and its relevant publics, and to maintain these relationships. In other words, "to establish and maintain relationships" refers to the sustained and continuous activity taking place between an organisation and its relevant publics.

▶ Public relations aims to make the organisation understood by others, and this could be done by **reaching mutual understanding**. Therefore both the organisation and its relevant publics need to understand each other and the message as it was intended. Only then can a positive relationship be established.

There are also critics of PRISA's definition. Their criticism correlates with Newman's 1993 study which was mentioned previously. However, PRISA's definition does serve as a point of departure for those studying public relations, and it encourages the practitioners in the profession to think about **what** they do, **why** they undertake particular activities and why they claim to be **special** (in the sense of being a profession).

ACTIVITY

1 Define public relations in your own words.

2 Given the search for and the dilemma surrounding a true definition of public relations, do you agree/disagree with PRISA's definition? Give reasons for your answer.

The publics of public relations

You will have noted that we frequently refer to the *publics* when describing public relations. Put differently, the **publics** in public relations are the recipients or audiences which are grouped together because of their common bond or interest in a particular matter (cf. Newsom et al. 1989:73). However, grouping and arranging recipients into certain groups does not imply that they are entirely separate. In other words, the demarcations or characteristics used to differentiate between two or more groups sometimes overlap. Therefore publics are categorised according to the needs of a particular organisation and will differ from one organisation to the next.

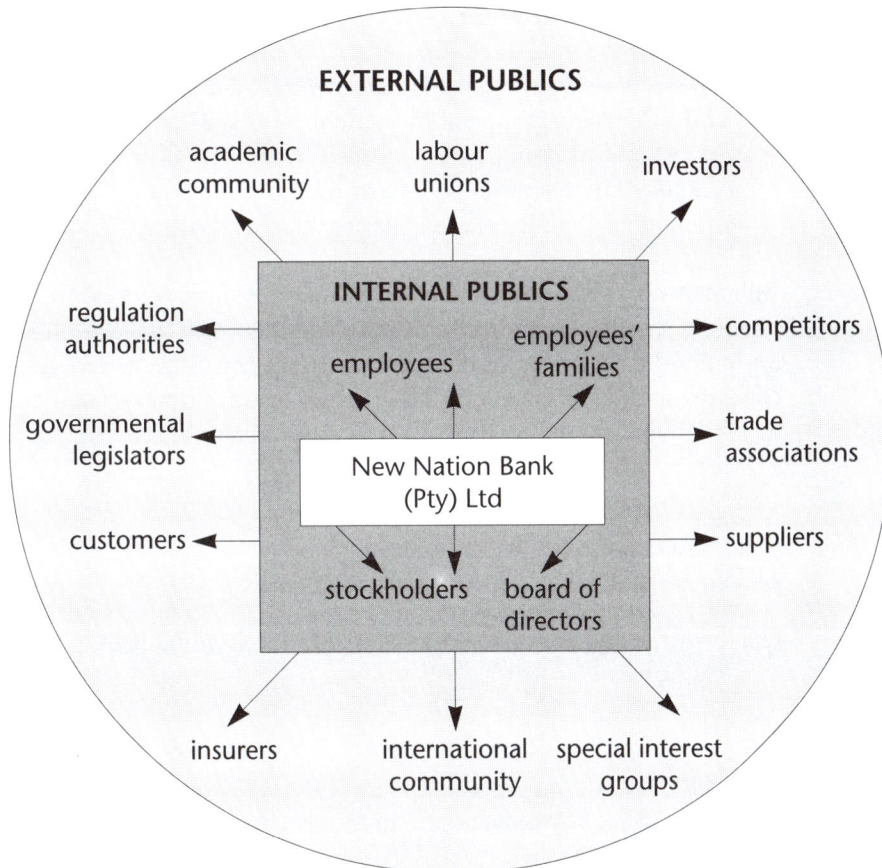

Figure 2.2 **The publics of New Nation Bank (Pty) Ltd**

As an example, Figure 2.2 distinguishes between the various publics of a fictitious multinational company based in South Africa called New Nation Bank (Pty) Ltd. The organisation will adapt its communication with each and every one of these relevant publics depending on which of these particular publics they want to address and reach at a certain point in time.

In order to distinguish between various publics, organisations categorise them according to one of the following sets of categories (cf. Seitel 1995:9–10).

▶ *Internal* and *external publics*. **Internal publics** are those groups of individuals who are members of an organisation, for example its employees, stockholders and the board of directors. **External publics** refer to those groups of individuals who are not directly connected with the organisation, and this will include the mass media, government, customers, community, et cetera.

► *Primary, secondary* and *marginal publics*. These categories of publics are classified according to their importance to the organisation concerned. In other words, **primary publics** are those groups of individuals who can especially encourage or inhibit the organisation's efforts, whereas **secondary publics** are less important, and **marginal publics** least important of all. For example, New Nation Bank (Pty) Ltd is awaiting a ruling on certain stipulations that govern the banking institutions in South Africa. In this example the Reserve Bank is categorised as its primary public, whereas legislators and other publics such as clients, the mass media, et cetera, are classified as its secondary publics.

► *Traditional* and *future publics.* Employees and current customers of New Nation Bank (Pty) Ltd are its **traditional publics.** Potential customers are classified as its **future publics.**

► *Proponents, opponents* and *uncommitted publics*. As the titles for these three publics indicate, groups of individuals are classified according to their degree of **support** and **opposition** to an organisation. The members of these publics continuously change and are determined by the issue, campaign or programme with which a public relations professional is dealing.

Although an organisation should be very sensitive and aware of all its relevant publics it should also endeavour to speak as one voice to the publics concerned. Bearing in mind that the groups of individuals who constitute different publics are forever changing and are very complex in nature, organisations should communicate with them frequently and directly, by way of effective public relations activities.

ACTIVITY

List the different publics to which you as an individual belong.

2.4 THEORETICAL APPROACHES TO PUBLIC RELATIONS

Public relations is rapidly developing within the realm of the *social sciences.* The development of a **body of theoretical knowledge** is central to this development and is essential for acknowledgement as a profession. This body of knowledge should differentiate public relations from other professions and contribute to the constant development and advancement of the profession as part of a scientific discipline.

For our purposes, we study public relations as a social science that originated academically within the schools of journalism and which is currently part of communication. As a social science the theories of public relations are grounded on the theories and research methodology of other social sciences. Communication theory and communication research methodology, in particular, act as a point of departure. It is only recently (during the 1980s) that public relations professionals have expressed the need for the development of public relations theories that are derived from public relations as a profession itself.

The practice of public relations leads to the development of theories in public relations, but in spite of the long history of public relations, theory development seems to have been limited to finding answers in "how to do it" and "how to do it better" public relations. With a few exceptions, this still seems to be the trend, and public relations has not yet succeeded in addressing the development of theory or the relationship of the practice of public relations to research and theory development (cf. Botan 1989:100).

In this section we provide an overview of the most outstanding *theoretical approaches* to public relations, and highlight only the most prominent theories or models within each approach. By **theoretical approach** we mean ways of thinking about and ways of practising public relations. Some of these approaches have been developed specifically as theories of public relations, whereas others have been identified as ways of practising public relations.

The process approach to public relations

The *process approach* suggests that public relations should be analysed and examined as a set of routinised activities which is an ongoing process and which is not limited to a specific time frame. Examples of such a **process-oriented approach** to public relations are found in the process model developed by Cutlip et al. (1985) and the management-by-objectives (MBO) model presented by Nager and Allen (1984). The MBO model is a goal-oriented approach where step-by-step procedures are provided in order to establish the success of the public relations efforts in terms of the results obtained and not in terms of the activities performed. However, by making the focus of public relations the mere attainment of a certain goal, limitations are imposed upon the communication process which is such an essential part of public relations.

The process model developed by Cutlip et al. (1985) describes public relations as a managed function which is part of an organisation's *problem-solving process*. By applying the **process approach** to public relations, practitioners explain and practise public relations according to four basic steps in order to solve problems (cf. Cutlip et al. 1985:200).

▶ The first step involves **defining the problem.** In other words, it relates to monitoring and determining the opinions, attitudes and behaviour of the relevant publics of the organisation by way of research and fact finding.

▶ **Planning and programming** is the second step in the process. This refers to decisions being made about objectives and procedures; the determination of the relevant publics, and the planning of strategies that need to be used in the problem-solving process.

▶ The third step involves **taking action and communicating**. This includes the implementation of the plans and programmes in order to achieve specific objectives.

▶ **Evaluation** is the fourth step and, for example in a public relations programme, involves determining the results of the specific programme, as well as assessing the effectiveness thereof. Adjustments can be made after evaluation to continue the programme, or the programme can be terminated.

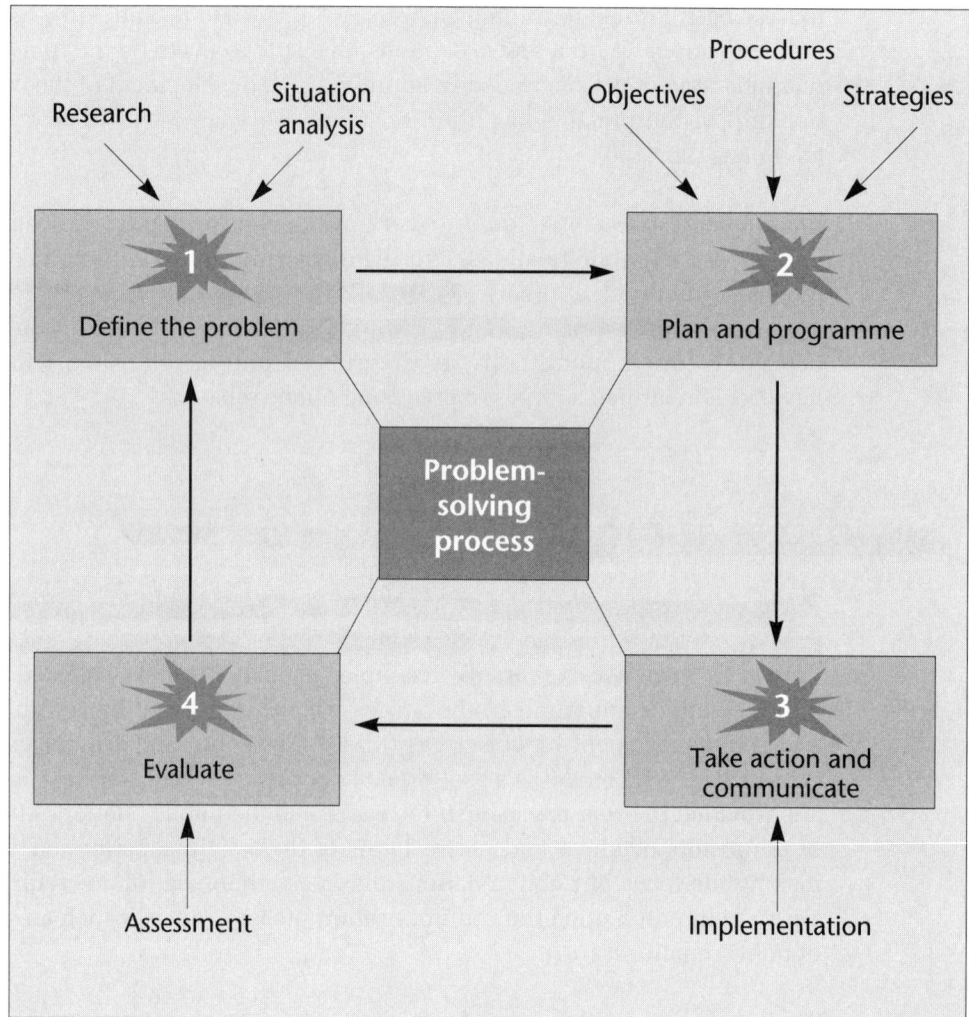

Figure 2.3 **Four-step problem-solving process of public relations**

As indicated in Figure 2.3, the problem-solving process starts off with the identification of the problem and each step thereafter is of equal importance. However, all these steps overlap and in practice it is not that easy to determine where one step ends and the other begins.

This approach may work very well in the practice of public relations where the aim is to solve problems and where the final evaluation is based on questioning whether all the preceding steps were followed. However, as we pointed out, public relations is not simply a simplistic four-step process and needs to be understood as a profession. In other words, public relations professionals need to be able to explain **what** they do, **why** they undertake particular activities and also **why they are the only professionals** who can perform these functions.

The systems approach to public relations

The *systems approach* is a multidisciplinary approach, which emphasises the importance of maintaining the *equilibrium, balance* and *interdependence* of the various systems and subsystems in society. Therefore all systems and subsystems, according to this approach, work together to maintain an **equilibrium** and **balance** (cf. Rensburg 1996:113–115 for a more detailed discussion on the systems approach to organisations).

The **systems approach** describes public relations as a series of events that contain the following (cf. Long & Hazelton 1987:5):

1   input from the environment and organisational policymakers to the system;

2   transforming these inputs into communication goals, objectives and programmes; and

3   output from the organisation to all the relevant publics and the environment which in turn results in reactions from the environment and publics and creates further input from them to the organisation.

Public relations therefore involves a series of inputs (internal and external) and outputs (actions and communication) which are designed to reduce conflicts and to build meaningful relationships between an organisation and its relevant publics. Figure 2.4 is a diagrammatical illustration as an overview of this process.

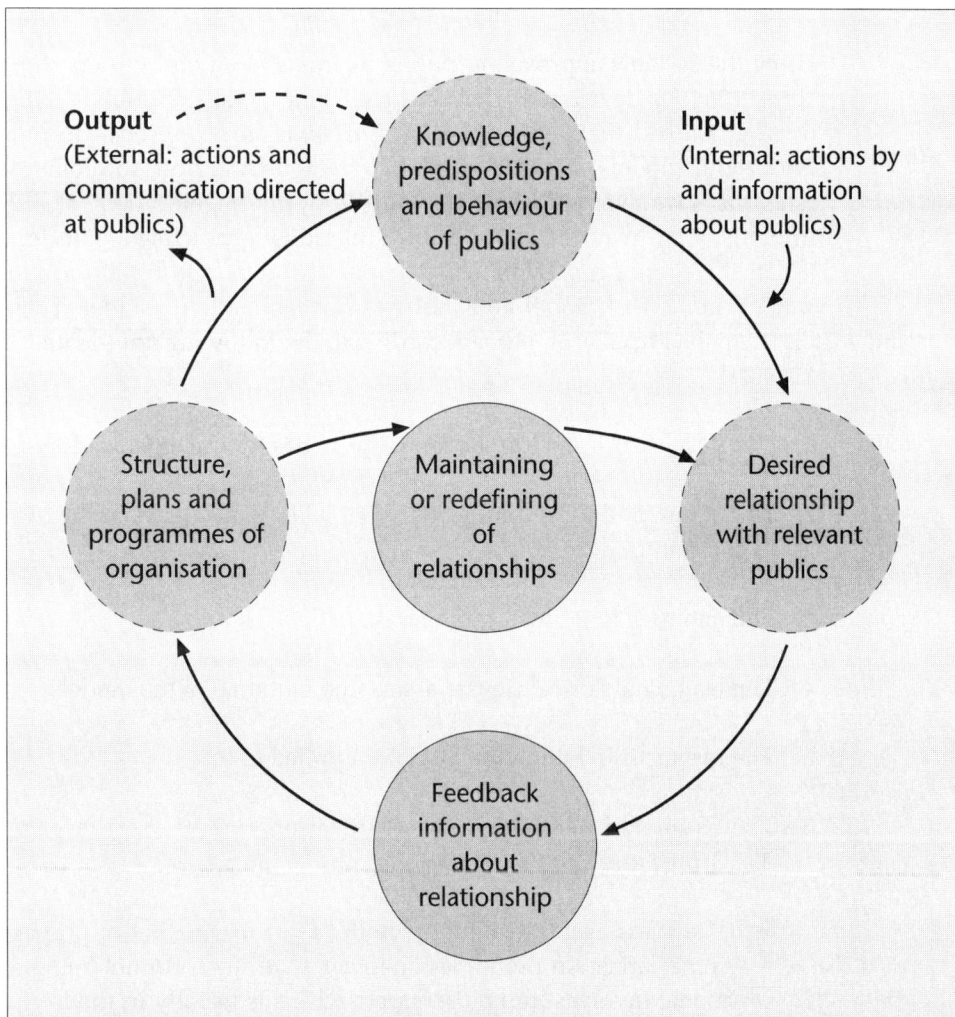

Figure 2.4 **An open systems model of public relations**

In addition to the importance of balance and equilibrium within an organisation as a system, we can also distinguish between *open* and *closed systems* in public relations. A **closed system** has an impermeable boundary in that it cannot exchange information with its environment. In contrast, an **open system** exchanges information. However, when referring to a social system as such, no system is completely open or completely closed. In terms of public relations it is exactly this degree of openness or closedness of an organisation that gives us an indication of the organisation's sensitivity to its environment and its relevant publics. The degree to which public relations practitioners obtain a balance between organisations, their relevant publics and the environment can be used as a yardstick for the success of the efforts of the practitioners.

Although the systems approach is most frequently used in an attempt to explain the meaning of public relations, it is probably also the most difficult approach for professionals actually to apply to everyday practice. Furthermore, this specific approach tends to focus only on the actions and communication of various systems in society and neglects to point out the extremely complicated process of human communication in which individuals play an essential part (cf. Rensburg et al. 1995:48).

The symmetrical and asymmetrical approach to public relations

Using the systems approach to public relations as a point of departure, Grunig and Hunt (1984:22) developed what they call "four models of public relations practice", or what we call the *symmetrical and asymmetrical approach* to public relations. These four models were developed to demonstrate how the four roles of public relations have evolved in history and how the development of public relations influences the way in which public relations is practised. The four models are called the *press agentry/publicity model*, the *public information model*, the *two-way asymmetrical model* and the *two-way symmetrical model*. These models are distinguished from each other according to the following criteria (cf. Grunig & Hunt 1984:22):

1   The purpose or function the model provides for the organisation.

2   The nature of the communication that takes place between the organisation and its relevant publics.

3   The nature of the research undertaken.

4   The leading historical figures associated with one of the models.

5   The instances in which the model is applied today.

6   The estimated percentage of organisations practising the particular model (i.e. Grunig and Hunt's estimates up until 1984).

   ▶ The **press agentry/publicity model**'s purpose is that of propaganda and the communication process is one-way, with the truth not being essential. This model involves limited research, which is usually in the form of press clippings. PT Barnum serves as a historical example and in modern public relations we find the model is applied in sports, theatre and product promotion. Grunig and Hunt estimate that 15 per cent of the market follows this model.

   ▶ The purpose of the **public information model** is to disseminate information by means of one-way communication, with truth also not being essential. Limited research is done, and it usually takes the form of readability tests and readership surveys. Ivy Lee is given as a historical example of this model. It is usually practised in government, nonprofit organisations and structured companies. It is estimated that 50 per cent of the market follows this model.

- ▶ The **two-way asymmetrical model** has persuasion as its purpose by way of two-way imbalanced communication (imbalanced because it favours the organisation). Formative research and the evaluation of attitudes are examples of research being done according to this model. Grunig and Hunt (1984:22) mention Edward Bernays as a historical example of this model and they conclude that it is usually practised in competitive business and agencies. They estimate that 20 per cent of the market follows this model.

- ▶ Mutual understanding is the purpose of the **two-way symmetrical model.** The nature of the communication is also two-way, but in a balanced manner (i.e. neither the organisation nor the publics are favoured in the communication). Research takes the form of formative research to learn how the publics perceive the organisation and to determine the consequences of the organisation's actions for the publics. Bernays is cited (cf. Grunig & Hunt 1984:22) as a historical example and current public relations educators are beginning to adopt this model which is usually practised in regulated business and in agencies (i.e. regulated by government). The estimated market share of this particular model is 15 per cent.

Although the two-way symmetrical model seems at the outset to be the ideal model for public relations practitioners, Grunig and Grunig (1989:31) admit that few organisations apply this model in practice because their world-view (i.e. way of thinking) of public relations does not correspond with the characteristics of this model, nor do most organisations have the required personnel and expertise to implement it (cf. Murphy 1991:120). Grunig and Grunig (1989) say that many organisations practise the two-way symmetrical model at times, but it is seldom the dominant or only model that is used. It is usually practised in combination with the two-way asymmetrical model (cf. Grunig 1989:30). This has led Grunig (1992) to refine and explain his theory in more detail in his book *Excellence in public relations and communication management* in an attempt to encourage public relations practitioners to follow the two-way symmetrical model.

The main criticism of the two-way symmetrical model comes from theorists such as G R Miller (cf. Miller 1989:45–66) who believe that public relations is intrinsically interwoven with effective persuasion and control over relevant publics and the environment. Therefore public relations must inevitably be a controlling instrument for the organisation and is a manipulating force per se (cf. Van der Meiden 1993:9)

The rhetorical/persuasive approach to public relations

It is commonly known that rhetoric or persuasion is vital to society. By way of persuasion, people (individually, as part of publics or on behalf of an organisation) influence opinions, understanding, judgement and actions. Mass society has increased the need for public relations professionals who make use of a vast amount of tactics, techniques and social-scientific methods to reach and influence their relevant publics. Therefore the *persuasive approach* to public relations **can** and **is** used to *put the organisation's best foot forward.*

A prominent theorist of modern-day public relations is Robert L Heath who advocates the **persuasive approach.** This approach was, however, practised as far back as the booming 1920s by Edward L Bernays. Bernays explains his *engineering of consent* approach in the sense of public relations practitioners having a myriad of choices to make and interests (those of the internal and external publics, group leaders, opinion leaders and the mass media) to take into account. Therefore *engineering of consent* deals with attitudes and actions of the organisation, with a close link to the public and private interests, and communication with the relevant publics in order to inform and persuade them (cf. Bernays 1955:3–4.) With the term *engineering* Bernays means **planning**. He sees careful planning as the essential factor that distinguishes public relations from hit-or-miss publicity and propaganda. Bernays developed eight methodical steps (cf. Bernays 1955:9–10) to *engineer the consent of the public* and stipulates them as follows:

1   define the objectives;

2   research the publics to find out whether the objectives are realistic and attainable;

3   modify the objectives to reach goals that the research has indicated as attainable;

4   determine the strategy to reach the goals;

5   plan the action, themes, symbols and appeals to the public;

6   plan the organisation to meet the goals;

7   time and plan the tactics to meet the goals;

8   carry out the tactics as planned.

As we have stipulated above, the *engineering of consent* concept appears to have picked up a very manipulative connotation since the 1920s. Bernays, however, kept on defending the concept by saying that public relations is not the application of common sense. Public relations is to adopt the engineering approach to the problem of gaining consent for a point of view, ideas or things (cf. Cutlip 1994:187).

In modern times the **persuasive approach** to public relations is used by public relations practitioners to achieve compliance, goodwill, understanding, appreciation and action, as well to create images and to manage reputations (cf. Heath 1992:18). In other words, public relations activities or techniques are essentially performed not only by means of communication but also by means of persuasion. For example, public relations professionals create identities for their organisations and products, and create publicity for special events. Words, logos, slogans, et cetera (the meaning of terms such as *corporate identity* and *corporate personality* are discussed and illustrated in Unit 3) are carefully researched, planned and selected to attract customers and investors or to create a corporate identity for the organisation. These are very often aimed at raising employees' pride and productivity for their organisation. Therefore public relations practitioners, in conjunction with other departments in an organisation, help form the publics' opinions about their purchase or use of certain products.

In order to form or influence the opinions of various publics, an organisation needs to negotiate its relationship with these publics. This is done by the public relations practitioner by deciding on the actions to be taken, setting limits, creating strategies and planning programmes which influence the relationship between the organisation and its relevant publics. However, **persuasion** does not only work for the organisation, it also works for the publics. Demands made by labour unions and environmental pressure groups (as publics) of a particular organisation serve as examples of how publics can use persuasion to influence the actions of an organisation (cf. Heath 1992:19).

It is important to note how the **influence** of public relations is studied when trying to evaluate the persuasive approach. Criticism of this approach will differ if critics believe that persuasion is used only by organisations (or public relations professionals) to dominate their publics, or to manipulate publics, or to control thought. Therefore we need to stipulate exactly what we mean by **persuasion** when criticising this approach (cf. Rensburg 1996:1–38 for a detailed discussion of the meaning of persuasion).

The variety of approaches and theories of public relations also indicates the confusion that exists in practice. In any profession, theory and practice are not separate entities. However, when we try to determine which theories of public relations do exist, we find such theories being criticised for being superficial. Furthermore, critics claim that the lack of a body of knowledge in public relations is partly due to its rapid and random growth and its lack of focus (i.e. public relations includes a variety of goals, processes and activities).

Based on the discussion in the above section, we therefore conclude that there is no conclusively right or wrong approach in the practice and theory of public relations. However, theorising about the profession – thereby developing a body of knowledge – contributes to the recognition of public relations as a profession.

ACTIVITY

1   Assume that you are the public relations professional of the Department of Health in South Africa responsible for educating the relevant publics about the prevention of AIDS. Which theoretical approach to public relations will you use as a point of departure? Give reasons for your answer.

2   Which theoretical approach to public relations do you prefer? Give reasons for your answer.

2.5 THE PUBLIC RELATIONS CAMPAIGN AND PROGRAMME

As history has shown (by way of prominent public relations practitioners such as Edward L Bernays) and from the way in which public relations has been practised in the second half of the twentieth century, it is clear that *planning* is an essential part of public relations. In fact, our definition of public relations indicates that public relations is the **planning of communication** and, within this realm of planning, the public relations practitioner plans the communication by way of a *public relations programme, public relations campaign* and/or a *public relations event* (cf. Hunt & Grunig 1994:23). Although the distinction between a programme, campaign or event may not be universally recognised, for the purposes of this unit we distinguish between them according to their various requirements.

An **event** is a once-off occurrence. It occurs at one point in time – it could last an hour, a day or perhaps even a week – and it has one prime purpose with reference to one or more relevant publics. The objective of an event is usually the dissemination of information to a public on a once-off basis. For example, if a managing director retires from an organisation and a banquet is held in his honour in conjunction with his retirement, this would be an event. If the president of South Africa were to visit an organisation, it would be called an event from which the organisation could generate publicity.

A **campaign** also has a specific beginning and end. However, a campaign could last for weeks or even months and can consist of various events. The objective is usually to get support for an issue, a candidate or an organisation and therefore influence or change the behaviour of the relevant publics. An election campaign serves as an example. Candidates for a political party organise various events (i.e. delivering speeches at political rallies, visiting hospitals and other welfare organisations, and planting trees on National Arbor Day) where they endeavour to make contact with all their relevant publics. Campaigns build up to a point – in our example the campaign builds up to an election or getting the publics to vote for the party's candidates on the election day. However, campaigns need not be a once-off effort. A cycle of campaigns – one campaign building on another and profiting from the previous ones – is also possible. Many organisations find a cycle of campaigns preferable to a continuing public relations programme because repeated revision, additions and different directions could be more effective, and the evaluation of one campaign can serve as the research phase of another (cf. Kendall 1992:9). Figure 2.5 is an illustration of the cyclical nature of public relations campaigns.

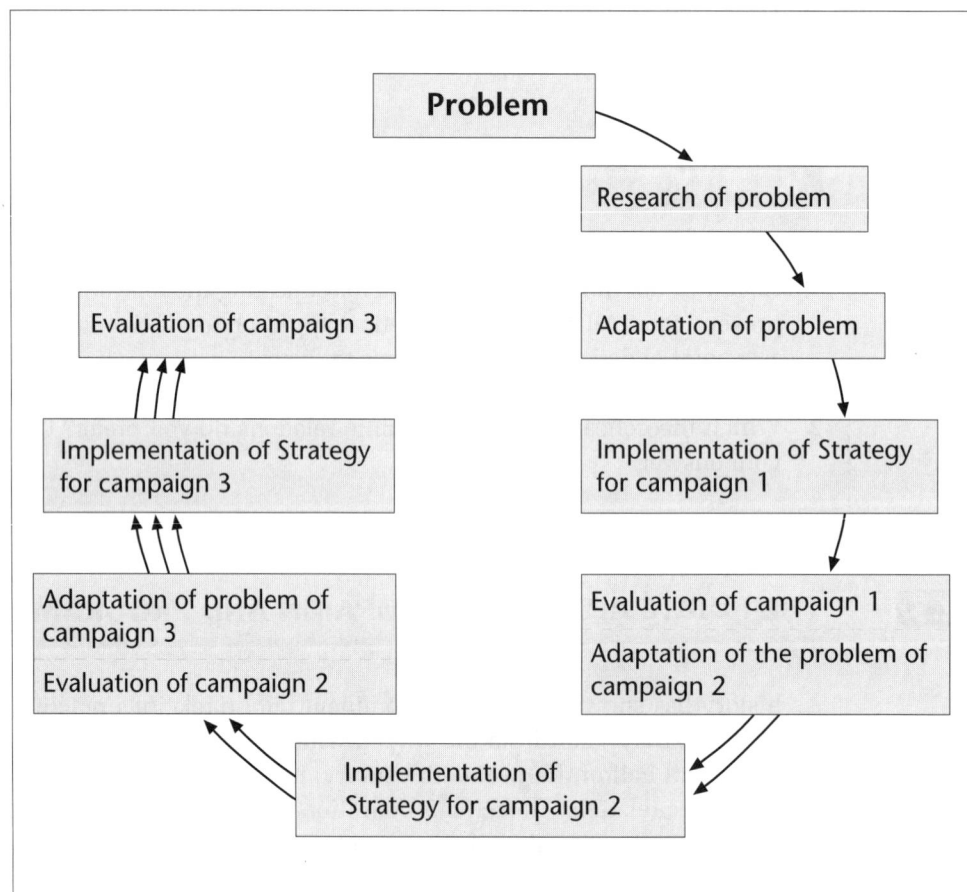

Figure 2.5 **Public relations campaign cycles**

A **programme** is similar to a campaign in that it also consists of various events but it differs from a campaign in that it has no preset end. A public relations programme is put in place because of an anticipated need by an organisation for continued dissemination of information to its relevant publics. The programme is reviewed periodically to determine whether its objectives are being met and the programme as a whole or parts thereof will be continued, providing that the need for more communication between an organisation and its relevant publics exists. The objectives of a programme are usually to create or maintain understanding between an organisation and its relevant publics. Examples of continuing public relations programmes include the following: road safety, blood donation, drug education, AIDS education and nature conservation programmes. These are continuing programmes because there will never be a complete solution to the problem and a constant need to be informed exists within the relevant publics.

Understanding the difference between a campaign and a programme is essential for public relations practitioners as it could influence their productivity in terms of time, money and the effectiveness of the organisation in communicating with its relevant publics.

ACTIVITY

Describe how you would distinguish between an event, a campaign and a programme with "water conservation" as a theme.

The public relations campaign

A **public relations campaign** is a planned, co-ordinated and purposeful effort that takes place over a certain period of time (cf. Newsom et al. 1989:294) and, as mentioned above, its objective is usually to change or maintain behaviour. Public relations campaigns are designed and developed to **address an issue, to solve a problem** or **to correct a situation**. For example, in the organisational context, a public relations campaign that deals with "smoking in the workplace" is addressing an **issue**. A public relations campaign concerned with "training the workers" in a specific organisation is an example of **problem solving**, and a campaign in which an organisation tries to rectify a situation created by one of its factories spilling toxic waste into a nearby river is an example of **correcting a situation**.

Public relations practitioners stipulate different steps that need to be taken into account when planning a public relations campaign (cf. Rensburg 1996:66–70 for the PRISA model when planning a public relations campaign). Nevertheless they all seem to agree on including **certain fundamental steps**. The formula most frequently adopted by public relations practitioners is the *RAISE formula* which is an alternative formula originating from the *RACE formula* devised by John Marston (1963:161–289). The **RAISE formula** stands for *research, adaptation, implementation of strategy* and *evaluation* (cf. Kendall 1992:8–11). A campaign need not, however, include all of the steps set out below, and these steps need not necessarily be taken or completed in the order stipulated. A public relations campaign briefly involves the following steps.

▶ **Research** – This step includes the process of discovering the facts to confirm the issue, situation or problem; making use of verifiable methodology to research the issue, situation or problem; identifying the issue, situation or problem and formulating it as a statement.

▶ **Adaptation** – The organisation must adapt to the identified problem. This is done by subdividing the problem into measurable objectives; distinguishing between various publics by way of priority (in terms of the problem); doing research and brainstorming to seek possible solutions; determining the resources and limitations of the campaign in terms of money, time and people, and developing a system of liaising with the organisation's management.

- **Implementation strategy** – A strategy must be selected from the possible solutions formulated above, according to the publics that need to be addressed. It is important to note that the objectives and relevant publics should dictate the strategy on the basis of the research that has been undertaken. A communication plan must be designed and dates attached. Furthermore, a budget needs to be tabled and justified to the management.

- **Evaluation** – This step involves the measurement of the degree of success of the campaign in terms of the objectives. Formative evaluation can be used during the campaign, and summative evaluation conducted after the completion of the campaign. The success or failure of the campaign needs to be spelled out and further recommendations must be made.

The following is an example of a public relations campaign that has been planned according to the *RAISE formula*. This is a hypothetical example, used for purposes of illustration.

Case 2.1

PUBLIC RELATIONS CAMPAIGN: Nuclear reactor threatens our lives!

Background

In 1990 an organisation called Nukefit (Pty) Ltd built a nuclear reactor in Gauteng, South Africa. Although Nukefit was able to prove at the time that the reactor posed no threat to its surroundings, a faulty valve was detected in September 1995. This valve at the reactor permitted radioactive steam to escape which resulted in questions being asked about how well the equipment was functioning, as well as the extent of the threat and danger to employees and to people living in the neighbourhood and surroundings (environment). The original decision to allow the reactor to be built is now also being questioned, as are the qualifications of the people operating the nuclear plant.

The public relations campaign

In order to **research** the situation that arose and to develop a campaign strategy to alleviate it, the public relations practitioner must determine what actually happened when the valve began to leak. Various research methods may be used, but this type of situation usually requires conducting personal interviews with the relevant people who are directly involved with the problem.

The **objectives** of this campaign could include the following: to inform all the relevant publics of the facts as they occurred; to rectify the situation by making sure that such a problem does not arise again and trying to minimise

➡

the damage done to the image of the organisation. The public relations practitioner must consider certain essential variables when deciding what to do about this problem, namely: **the proximity of the publics involved** (geographically and emotionally) and **the extent to which the relevant publics could be hurt, helped, rewarded or penalised**. In order to establish the **proximity** of the publics involved, the following must be considered:

▶ the employees on the job who are very close to the situation (both emotionally and geographically);

▶ the publics living close to the reactor;

▶ the managers and engineers of the reactor;

▶ the inspectors who approved the equipment, including the leaking valve;

▶ the supplier of the valve;

▶ environmentalists, licensing authorities, politicians and other lobby groups for or against the reactor.

Publics are also classified according to the variable of **timeliness**. Although in this instance there are various important publics, we need to know which publics need our attention **immediately,** which a **month later**, and which **next year**. In this situation involving an emergency, the employees and the immediate neighbours of the plant are publics that need immediate attention (must be researched immediately). Government and other important officials, for example, would be researched at a later stage because of the proximity and timeliness variables.

Planning the strategy to alleviate the problem is based on admitting that a mechanical problem has arisen and indicating that it will be corrected as soon as possible. (Only a brief outline of the actual campaign is provided in this example, because a problem such as the one we are illustrating would involve research into the implications of the threat in much greater depth.) After determining who the relevant publics are and their proximity to the problem, **communication is planned** according to those who warrant immediate communication, for example the employees and neighbours of the plant. Such communication is of high priority because of the safety factor. Also of a high priority are consumers of nuclear energy provided by the plant, as this will definitely have an influence on the image of the organisation. The mass media are also important and need to be informed immediately of the problem. Once the danger has decreased, other publics, such as the groups who oppose nuclear power, would be targeted. Consumers in other provinces, stockholders and associations would be of less importance in the immediate situation.

Communication differs according to the various publics concerned, the money available for the campaign, and the applicability of the media to the different publics. For instance, meetings could be called with employees to inform them of the facts as they occurred. This would also put a stop to rumours being spread and the resultant harm to the image of the organisation. E-mail or bulletin boards with notices could be used to inform employees of management's actions to ensure that a similar incident does not happen again. The mass media must be contacted and informed about the

◆

problem and solutions by way of a press conference with a press release. After the problem has been rectified, further advertising should be used to promote the organisation and its policy of "safety in the community". All these activities will be determined by the amount of money which management allocates for the campaign.

One way of **evaluating** whether the organisation has been successful in persuading the relevant publics that the problem has been solved is to monitor the mass media's news reportage. This means that Nukefit must monitor how frequently the media report on the incident and what they have to say about it. Other means of evaluation include surveys among the employees, the community and other relevant publics to determine the status of the image of the organisation. Such feedback can also determine whether the relevant publics believe that the organisation has satisfactorily rectified the problem. If it is found that the results of the surveys are unsatisfactory, recommendations must be made concerning a follow-up campaign.

ACTIVITY

Choose one of the themes reflected in Figure 2.6 and use one of the cues provided for that theme to plan a public relations campaign according to the *RAISE* formula.

POLITICS

A glimmer of hope – not a surefire fix

But give the imbizo a chance

DISASTER

LABOUR

THE LABOUR DEBATE

Flexibility is the key

FLOOD RELIEF.

HEALTH

Money wagered on a shaky bet

FIGHTING MALARIA

Workplace democracy could alleviate conflicts

Reserve Bank's new face

COMPANIES

Bruised but confident as earnings drop 20%

South Africa can't afford the square peg syndrome

It is very high risk to deal with companies who cannot guarantee ongoing research, development and updates in line with changes that are going on in the world

MD finds his silver lining

New business development

GOVERNMENTAL

Pension fund performance deceptive

Government housing

Gambling Bill takes the shine

KwaZulu Natal plans investment

SAFETY & SECURITY

WE'VE GOT SECURITY NAILED

THE ONLY PROTECTION YOUR LITTLE BOY WILL NEED CYCLING ALONE AFTER DARK

EDUCATION

UNIVERSITY OF SOUTH AFRICA

PROGRAMME IN
INDUSTRIAL PRODUCT MARKETING
(INCLUDING EXPORT MARKETING)

GAIN A COMPETITIVE ADVANTAGE THROUGH CREATIVE TRAINING!

Making home hunting easy

College of Property Management & Development

SPORT

SOCCER:

SA makes its mark among the world greats

Olympics

Last chance for two to come to Atlanta

Soccer

Offers hope of new era in SA

Figure 2.6 **Problems and issues in South Africa**

The public relations programme

Public relations programmes are not once-off activities that organisations plan as part of their communication with their relevant publics. Instead, a public relations programme is the actual planned and sustained effort (as stipulated in the definition of public relations) by organisations with the purpose of reaching mutual understanding between an organisation and its relevant publics. Therefore, no definite steps are supplied for planning the public relations programme, but instead certain **phases** are provided which public relations practitioners need to take into account. These phases are as follows: *research, planning, execution* and *evaluation* (cf. Hunt & Grunig 1994:28).

▶ **Research** – Informal and formal research are included in this phase because an organisation needs any type of information which could help it to identify its **relevant publics** and the **objectives** of the programme. Only thereafter can the organisation formulate an appropriate public relations **message**. As in the case of the campaign, it is also essential that the objectives of the programme correlate with the needs of the publics with whom the organisation wishes to communicate, and that they comply with the true nature of the organisation. For example, if an organisation claims that it wants to communicate a more "youthful" image to reach a younger public, the question arises whether this is a true representation of the character of the organisation, or whether it is in reality conservative, and should in fact aim its communication at a more middle-aged public.

Furthermore, the objectives of a public relations programme must also be realistic and attainable in terms of the publics that the organisation or institution wants to reach, and in terms of the nature of the organisation or institution. We therefore find that a programme will usually include short, medium and long-term objectives which must be evaluated on a continuous basis and changed if the public relations practitioner deems it necessary.

During this phase, the public relations practitioner must also determine the message which the organisation wishes to convey to its relevant publics by way of the public relations programme. The message of a public relations programme should be general enough to encompass all facets of the programme, but could also be divided into various secondary messages which are directed at a number of specific publics. For example, the general message of a "Drive Safely" programme could be that too many lives are lost because of motorcar accidents, whereas a secondary message, such as encouraging motorists to fasten their safety belts, could be used to support the general message.

▶ **Planning** – The planning phase involves the actual planning of the programme according to the publics that have been identified, the programme's objectives, and the message that was determined in the research phase. The public relations practitioner must write out the public relations programme. This usually takes the following format (cf. Cohen 1987:82–85):

TABLE OF CONTENTS

▶ **Executive summary:** A summary of the major categories addressed in the programme.

▶ **Introduction:** The general background to the programme under consideration.

▶ **Public relations objectives:** The objectives that are addressed in the programme.

▶ **Strategy (or methodology):** A general explanation of how the message is to be communicated (i.e. whether through an assortment of media, events, or activities, et cetera).

▶ **Programme implementation:** The actual "tools" or activities that will be used are explained in more detail. For example, if press activity is planned, explanations must be given of the following: the frequency and nature of press releases, news conferences, featured articles and other material directed at the mass media. In other words, all "tools" must be explained in terms of the budget and time frame of the programme.

▶ **Evaluation:** This is an explanation of how the evaluation of the programme will be done, how often evaluation will be undertaken, and what results are anticipated. The results influence the next phase of the programme.

▶ **Conclusion:** A final justification of the approach followed and the benefits of the programme.

▶ **Budget:** A detailed budget should indicate exactly the anticipated costs of all activities.

▶ **Evaluation** – Although the evaluation phase is mentioned as the last phase in this discussion, evaluation of a public relations programme is actually done on a continuous basis during its implementation and after completion of specified activities of the programme. Evaluation is done to justify the need to expand a programme beyond its present scope, to justify the money being spent, or to explain a need to shift the focus of the programme. The evaluation of the programme could therefore lead to a revised programme that follows exactly the same phases. Figure 2.7 is an illustration of how a public relations programme could be altered into a revised public relations programme.

▶ **Execution** – The third phase in the public relations programme is the execution. All activities, as set out in the planning phase, must now be implemented. If difficulties are encountered in achieving certain objectives, or if certain publics are not reached, this is the phase where adjustments must be made to the programme. While implementing the programme, a constant update of the budget will also be necessary, as unforeseen costs could arise.

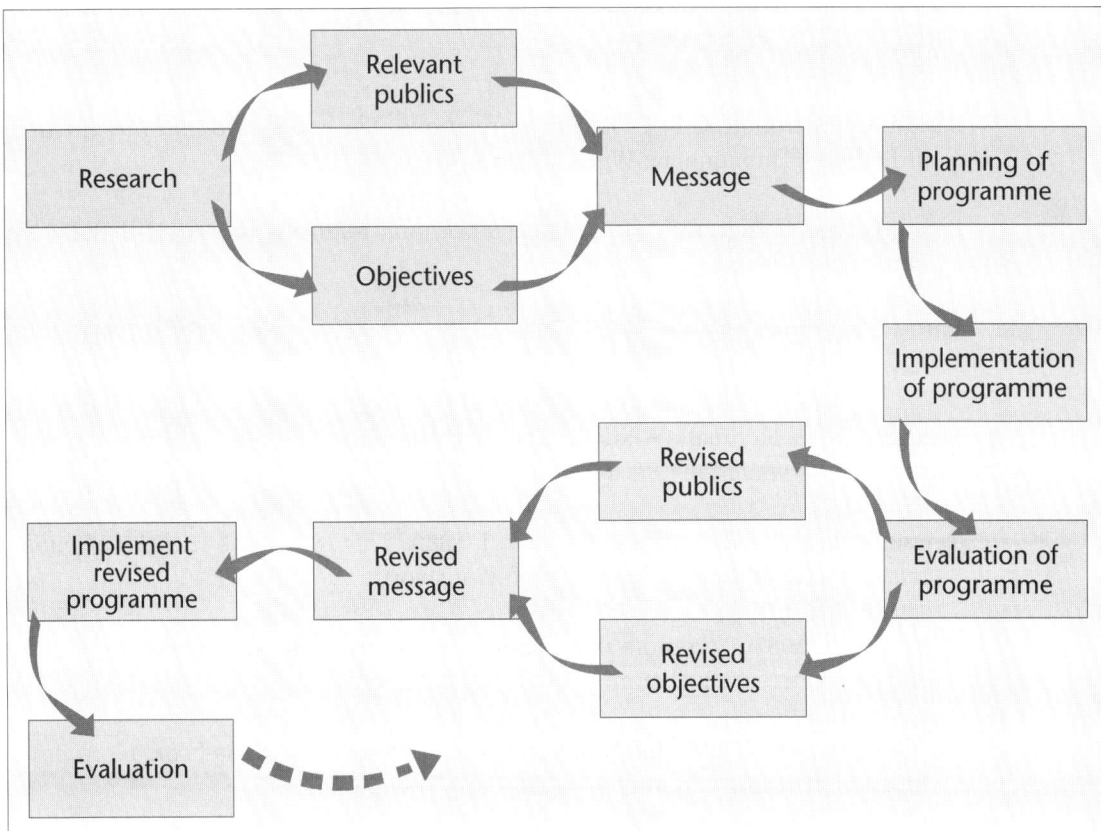

Figure 2.7 **Development of a public relations programme**

ACTIVITY

You have been appointed as public relations practitioner for New Nation Bank (Pty) Ltd and need to plan a public relations programme for the organisation to maintain and develop goodwill, to maintain and increase deposits and loans, to maintain and develop branch banking, and to build up the image of the organisation.

Write out a public relations programme for the management of New Nation Bank (Pty) Ltd in which you try to convince management that you need an "unlimited" budget to implement such a programme.

Summary

In this unit we discussed the meaning of public relations and described its historical origins. We also discussed various theoretical approaches to public relations and distinguished between various publics within the public relations context. We illustrated the significance of planning in public relations and highlighted the important steps to be followed in the planning of a public relations campaign and the phases of a public relations programme.

SUGGESTED READING

Baskin, O. & Aronoff, C.E. 1992. *Public relations. The profession and the practice.* 3rd edition. Dubuque, Ia: Wm. C. Brown.

Botan, C.H. & Hazelton, V. Jr. (eds) 1989. *Public relations theory.* Hillsdale, NJ: Lawrence Erlbaum.

Cutlip, S.M. 1994. *The unseen power: public relations. A history.* Hillsdale, NJ: Lawrence Erlbaum.

Moscardi, M. & Honiball, A-M. 1993. Public relations in Southern Africa. *International Public Relations Review* 16(1):2–6.

Newsom, D., Scott, A. & VanSlyke Turk, J. 1989. *This is PR. The realities of public relations.* 4th edition. Belmont, Calif: Wadsworth.

Olasky, M.N. 1987. *Corporate public relations. A new historical perspective.* Hillsdale, NJ: Lawrence Erlbaum.

Rensburg, R.S. (ed.) 1996. *Introduction to communication: course book 4 – communication planning and management.* Cape Town: Juta.

Rensburg, R.S., Mersham, G.M. & Skinner, J.C. 1995. *Public relations, development and social investment. A southern African perspective.* Pretoria: J.L. van Schaik.

Skinner, C. & Von Essen, L. 1995. *The handbook of public relations.* 4th edition. Halfway House: Southern.

Functions and Issues of Public Relations

Berendien Lubbe

Overview

Since public relations has grown from serving mainly a publicity function to a discipline which focuses on building and maintaining relationships within society, we can distinguish between three separate but related functions within public relations: an *interpretative function*, a *management function* and a *communication function*. These functions interact to achieve certain communication effects which we describe in the context of certain established *communication effects theories*. In the practice of public relations, certain techniques and processes are used to achieve its objectives and it is sometimes easy to confuse public relations with these processes. For this reason we examine how public relations uses *advertising, publicity, information, persuasion* and *propaganda*. A number of issues, regarded as critical for the development of public relations, are currently being discussed and researched. Some of these issues, such as *public opinion, image building, social responsibility, ethics* and the so-called *paradigm* struggle, are briefly examined in this unit.

Key terms to understand and remember

communication effects
corporate culture
corporate image
ethics
functionary public relations
information
management function
persuasion
publicity
public relations advertising

communication function
corporate identity
corporate personality
functional public relations
image
interpretative function
paradigm
propaganda
public opinion
social responsibility

Objectives

At the end of this unit you should be able to:

1   Describe the three functions of public relations and explain how they interrelate and support one another.

2   Describe public relations in the context of the communication effects theories.

3   Differentiate between *public relations advertising* and *publicity*.

4   Explain the relationship between public relations, information, persuasion and propaganda.

5   Identify some of the critical issues facing public relations and describe the nature of the debates on these issues.

INTRODUCTION

Organisations practise public relations at different levels of **activities** that provide an indication of the importance with which public relations is regarded by the management of many organisations. Public relations varies from the so-called *technical* level to *management* level. Public relations **technicians** are involved in communication tasks which include activities such as writing news releases, arranging functions, organising meetings and visits, where information is mainly supplied to publics about organisations. Public relations **managers** go beyond communication activities – they take part in the decision-making processes which guide organisations to meet their goals. The communication tasks represent the implementation of the activities planned in an overall public relations strategy. Some organisations appoint only public relations technicians to fulfil the public relations function, while others have fully fledged public relations departments with managers and technicians. The way public relations is **positioned** in an organisation also reflects management's view of its importance and value. Some organisations structure public relations as a major department. This is depicted in Figure 3.1.

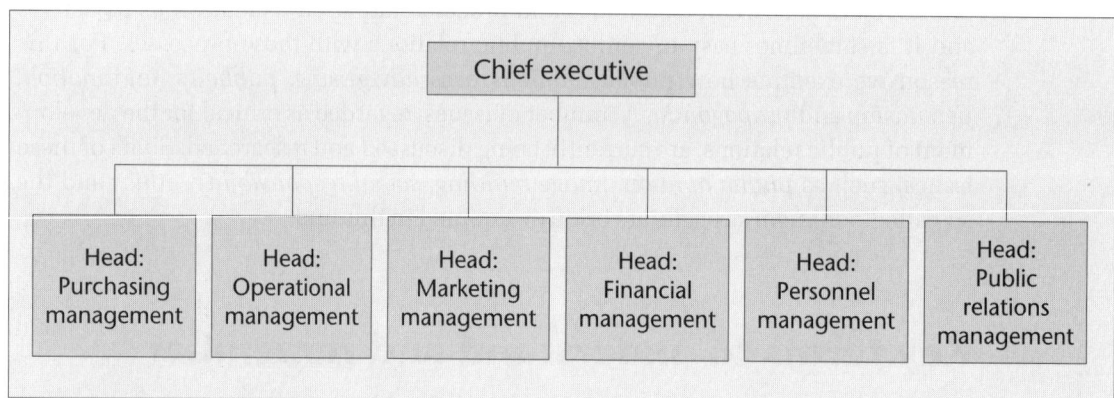

Figure 3.1 **The public relations department as a major department in an organisation**

Other organisations position public relations as a subdepartment of another department, as depicted in Figure 3.2.

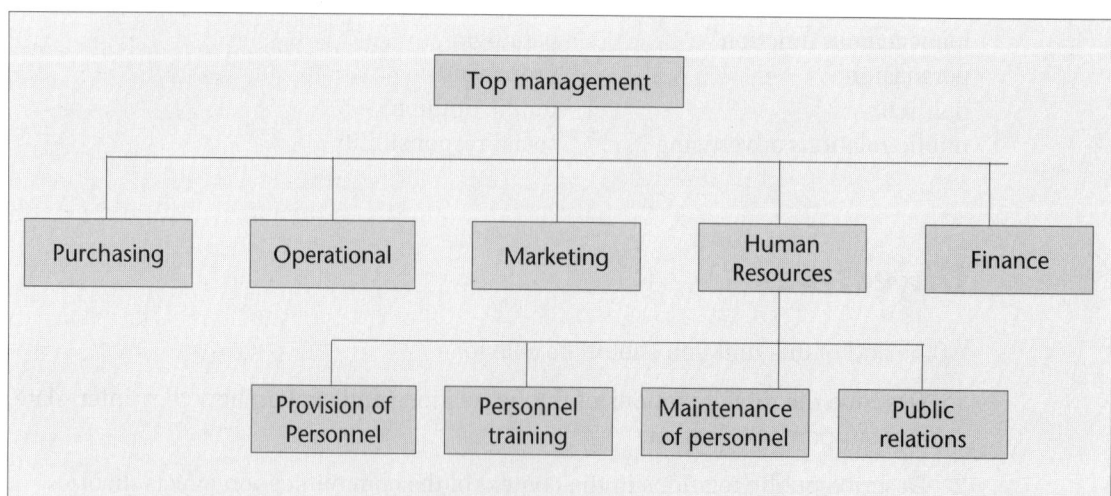

Figure 3.2 **The public relations department as a subdepartment of a major department in an organisation**

Still other organisations appoint only one or two individuals to perform the public relations function without having a separate department. This may suffice in a small organisation, depending on the nature of its activities. For example, a small retail store may not need a separate public relations department and can adequately address its public relations needs through one individual. However, this may be quite inadequate for larger, more complex organisations, particularly if the public relations appointees do not take part in management decision-making processes.

Some managers of organisations are also of the opinion that public relations can be performed by individuals who do not have any specific **qualifications** or **experience** in the fields of communication or public relations. Under these circumstances public relations cannot make an optimal contribution to the success of an organisation.

There is a broad spectrum of seemingly unrelated areas in which public relations practitioners can become involved and even specialise. These areas range from *personal image building* dealing with advice on personal appearance and public speaking, to *financial public relations* dealing with corporate mergers and financial publications. In each of these areas public relations should incorporate three functions, namely an *interpretative* function, a *management* function and a *communication* function.

3.2   THE FUNCTIONS OF PUBLIC RELATIONS

In *Course book 1* (Steinberg 1994) the term *function* was defined as the way in which a phenomenon acts to fulfil its purpose. The purpose of public relations, as found in its numerous definitions, can broadly be described as the management of communication to achieve mutual understanding between people, groups and organisations. Although public relations practitioners are involved in areas of specialisation as varied as *personal image building* and *financial public relations,* they must all ultimately work towards this goal. In **personal image building** this means that practitioners who assist individuals to present themselves, both verbally and nonverbally, in a way which is most acceptable to society, are creating mutual understanding between the individual and the audience. The **financial public relations** practitioner strives to create an understanding of, and generate support for an organisation by providing an insight into the way the organisation operates. Such a practitioner focuses on how the organisation meets the needs of its various publics such as customers, shareholders and financial institutions. In this way mutually beneficial relationships, based on mutual understanding, are established between the organisation and its publics.

In order to achieve the broad purpose of mutual understanding between people, groups and organisations, public relations must fulfil three functions. Firstly, public relations deals with the *interpretation* of the needs, attitudes and opinions of people, groups or organisations. Secondly, these needs, attitudes and opinions must be *communicated* between people, groups and organisations in such a way that an understanding of them is achieved. Finally, public relations must *manage* this process of communication in order to change or maintain needs, attitudes or opinions. Let us examine each of these functions separately.

Public relations as an interpretative function

The essence of public relations as an *interpretative* function lies in how organisations (groups or people) understand and meet the needs of various publics and those of society as a whole. For example, based on the way in which the interests of the *Shell* petroleum company have been projected in the media as a result of their involvement in Nigeria, it is evident that the company did not adequately interpret the attitudes of their publics. Public outcry against *Shell*'s involvement in Nigeria has resulted in the creation of numerous activist groups, which has led to boycotts of their products in various countries, as is illustrated in Figure 3.3.

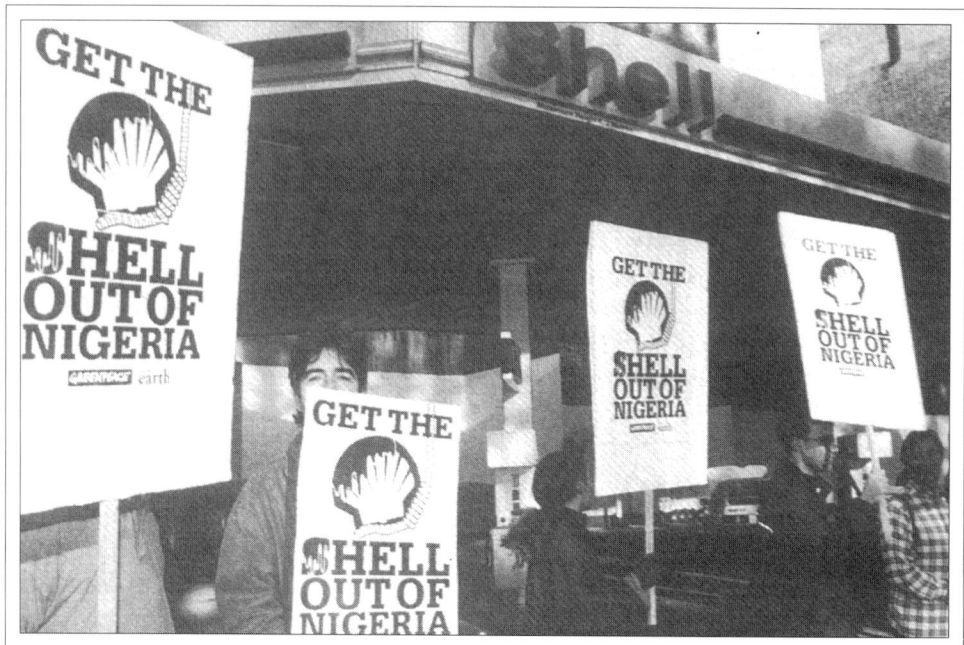

Figure 3.3 **International pressure against** *Shell*

(Photograph courtesy of *Greenpeace,* London and *African Business*)

On the other hand, other organisations give priority to the needs and attitudes of their publics in order to achieve continued support. In South Africa institutions such as universities, government and semi-government departments, as well as private organisations, are constantly monitoring and interpreting the attitudes of their publics and making adjustments to their policies and operations. High-profile public organisations such as the South African Broadcasting Corporation, the South African Police Service, Transnet, ISCOR and several mining companies are constantly under pressure from various activist groups and for them to achieve continued support they must be fully aware of the needs and attitudes of their various publics. In this respect the role of public relations cannot be underestimated.

Public relations did not always have an interpretative function. Historically it was regarded as a mass-communication discipline where the objective was to **inform** the public or publics of what the organisation was doing. Publicity and press agentry were the primary techniques of public relations, and **how** the messages were sent its primary measure of success. Even today, public relations is often practised in this way. Some organisations still believe that publicity (measured in column centimetres) determines the success of the public relations function. Bell and Bell (1976:51) describe this type of public relations as *functionary*. Public relations *functionaries* are mainly concerned with supplying information about the organisation to the environment, often as "a steady stream of press releases", and not with supplying information to the organisation about the environment. The functionary mode **limits** the public relations practitioner's role to that of a **technician** whose responsibilities are mainly to prepare and produce communications. Although public relations technicians fulfil an essential role, it is only when the *interpretative* function is present that public relations becomes a powerful asset in the hands of organisations. Organisations that practise public relations as an *interpretative* function are able to act proactively, anticipating changes within the environment, adjusting their policies and procedures, and also actively influencing the environment. Bell and Bell (1976:52) describe this type of public relations as *functional*. The functional approach places public relations practitioners in the role of managers, concerned with bringing the organisation and its publics together in a mutually responsive relationship. Organisational goals are set and achieved by interpreting the needs and attitudes of those publics that are essential to the organisation's survival and continued success. If we look at the example of the public service of South Africa (at all three levels of government, namely national, provincial and local), the most important goals set for successful transformation and acceptance of the new authorities are **public relations goals**. These goals include knowing and understanding target groups within specific publics better and interpreting the changing environment in order to formulate appropriate **communication strategies**.

In short, it can therefore be said that interpretative public relations is concerned with translating the organisation (its policies, aims and actions) to its publics and the publics (their needs, motives and expectations) to the organisation. The most important differences between public relations practised as an interpretative function (the functional approach) and public relations practised without an interpretative function (the functionary approach) are presented in Table 3.1.

Functional	Functionary
• Open systems approach	• Closed systems approach
• Proactive public relations	• Reactive public relations
• Managerial role	• Technical role
• Anticipates environmental changes	• Reacts to environmental changes
• Involved in: policy formulation; decision making; problem solving	• Not part of top management
• Accountable for results	• Activities regarded as objectives
• Concerned with "what" is said	• Concerned with "how" things are said

Table 3.1 **Functional and functionary public relations**

Public relations as a management function

Interpreting and translating an organisation and its publics to each other provides the foundation for an organisation to communicate effectively with its publics. However, **effective public relations** is more than a technique where communication media are used between an organisation and its publics. The dimension of *managed* communication is added. Grunig (1992:4) gives a simplistic definition of public relations as the "management of communication between an organisation and its publics". According to Grunig, public relations as **communication management** is not only broader than a communication technique but also broader than specialised public relations programmes such as media relations or publicity programmes. Public relations as a management function is the overall planning (based on research), execution and evaluation of an organisation's communication with all those publics, both internal and external, that affect its ability to achieve its goals.

By way of a summary we can say that public relations management in an organisation:

▶ Activates **research** in order to gain an understanding of how the various publics (for example consumers, employees, suppliers, regulating bodies, the community) perceive the organisation; what their expectations are, and also of the way in which the organisation is fulfilling these needs and expectations.

▶ **Plans** communication programmes which can change or shape the attitudes and perceptions of the constituent publics **and** the organisation, where necessary. The overall goal is to establish the organisation's credibility and to provide a positive environment in which it can conduct its activities.

▶ Uses the organisation's resources (staff, finances, technology, et cetera) optimally to **implement** communication programmes effectively.

▶ **Evaluates** the communication programmes to determine whether they have achieved the desired effects amongst target publics or the organisation in terms of attitude or behavioural changes.

By describing public relations in this way, we can differentiate three important implications: firstly, that it fulfils a *strategic* function where long-term planning must be done; secondly, that it should be performed by *communication specialists* at top management level who are capable of translating the needs of both the organisation and the publics into effective communication programmes; thirdly, that it is a *deliberate process* for accomplishing definite objectives, anticipating events through planning and continually adjusting its efforts to a changing environment on a sustained basis. The former South African Police (SAP) is a good example of how public relations was practised traditionally as a communication technique without the management dimension (i.e. *functionary* public relations). Around 1979 the SAP was mainly involved in media liaison and visitor programmes. Subsequently they expanded their activities to include community relations, the SA Police Band, a protocol section, an art section and the SA Police Museum, with the main emphasis being to "improve the image of the SAP". Despite these expansions and activities, public relations was not regarded as an integral part of the overall management process, but as an optional or peripheral function. Public relations was therefore not taken into consideration during decision making at the various management levels. Consequently, there was a lack of shared vision and common objectives and this resulted in reactive rather than proactive public relations. This **functionary** approach to public relations meant that public relations activities, such as organising sports events and environmental cleaning operations in townships, became goals in themselves and not supporting mechanisms within a broader public relations programme.

In more recent years, however, public relations has changed towards a **functional** approach. The overall goal of the South African Police Service (which replaced the SAP in 1995) is to make it more transparent, accessible and accountable to both its members and the public. To achieve this goal public relations was established as a management function which began with the formulation of a national communication policy and strategy involving all role-players (unions, media representatives, et cetera). This national strategy was devised to ensure that a shared vision and approach to internal and external liaison is followed from top management level down to station level. According to Van Deventer (1995:17–18), the key elements of this strategy are: perception management; opportunity identification; innovation (to proactively initiate an agenda-setting function) and contextualisation (to reactively put issues that could negatively reflect on the corporate image of the SAPS in context or to provide differing perspectives on the issue). An explanation of the term *corporate image* is provided in Section 3.6. Through its national strategy the SAPS has extended public relations to include both the **interpretative** and **management** functions.

Public relations as a communication function

According to Budd (1995:178), communication "is the last act in the process of public relations – a process that should appropriately begin with policy and decision-making". This does **not** mean that communication is less important than policy and decision making, but rather that communication is the effective implementation of policy.

Based on contemporary communication theory, to which you were introduced in *Course book 1* (Steinberg 1994), communication is not only regarded as the dynamic process of exchanging meaningful messages, but as a **transaction** between the participants during which a relationship develops between them. This means that the people communicating are **mutually** responsible for the outcome of the communication encounter as they transmit information, create meaning, and elicit responses. Effective communication means that mutual agreement about the meaning of the message is reached. The quality of the relationship which develops between the participants depends on how effective the communication is. From this perspective public relations fulfils its communication function when **transactional communication** occurs between an organisation and its various publics. Practitioners often confuse **dissemination** with **communication** (cf. Cutlip, Center & Broom 1994:228). For example, practitioners who view placements (publicity) in the mass media as successful communication, are guilty of such misconceptions. The problem is that the success of the communication does not lie in sending the message, but rather in the **effect** that the message has on the publics and on the communicator. This is the difference between **sending** messages and **communicating** messages. In the first instance (i.e. dissemination) the recipients of the message are regarded as passive and in the second (i.e. communication) the recipients are regarded as active in so far as their response to the message can have an impact on the communicator.

Public relations is therefore concerned with the **effects** of communication between an organisation and its publics. For example, the Iron and Steel Corporation (ISCOR) had to withdraw from the Saldanha Steel project because mutual agreement could not be reached on the location of the project. While some publics within the local community supported the project, others, such as environmentalists, were opposed to it. The effects of the opposing messages sent via the media, correspondence, meetings, protests and other forms of communication eventually led to ISCOR's withdrawing from the project. ISCOR's withdrawal subsequently led to a new debate on its participation in Saldanha Bay. This example shows the importance of establishing a relationship between participants which is based on mutual agreement.

The effectiveness of public relations practitioners depends on their own ability to communicate effectively and to advise others on how to communicate effectively. Seitel (1995:100) argues that just as the auditor is expected to be adept at accounting and the legal counsel is expected to be an accomplished lawyer, so the public relations practitioner is expected to be an expert communicator. Public relations practitioners must demonstrate their expertise in many communication skills, such as writing, speaking, listening, promoting and counselling.

You are a public relations consultant who has been requested by an organisation to assist it in its decision on whether or not to establish a public relations department. Write a report to management speech explaining why you believe that public relations is essential to an organisation and why the public relations manager should be appointed as part of the top management team.

3.3 PUBLIC RELATIONS COMMUNICATION EFFECTS

Public relations practitioners constantly grapple with the question of how programmes and campaigns should be designed to achieve various communication and behavioural effects. Various theories can be applied to guide the formulation of public relations programmes to achieve the desired effects (cf. Baskin & Aronoff 1992:61). Five of these theories and models, where various communication forms are used, from interpersonal to mass communication, are briefly discussed below. These are the *learning effects hierarchy*, the *social learning model*, the *low-involvement theory*, the *agenda-setting theory* and the *spiral of silence theory*. You may recall some of these theories from previous studies; however, here we describe them specifically in the context of **public relations**.

Learning effects hierarchy

This theory basically holds that once new ideas are known and understood by people they can be **persuaded to accept new attitudes and change their behaviour** if they are positively reinforced to do so. Communication is used to effect changes from the cognitive (knowledge aspects) to the attitudinal and finally the behavioural aspects. One application of this theory which is widely referred to in the marketing, development communication and public relations fields is the *diffusion of innovations* approach. Two processes can be identified within this approach. First is the *diffusion process* which emphasises the **communication** of new ideas from communicators to target publics (i.e. the **positive reinforcement** referred to above), the acceptance or rejection of the new ideas and the further **distribution** of these ideas by members within the target publics. The diffusion process therefore takes place within the target public. Secondly, there is the *adoption process* which takes place within the mind of the individual and which has five stages – awareness, interest, evaluation, trial and adoption.

▶ **Awareness** – People are aware of the idea or practice, although their knowledge is limited.

▶ **Interest** – People begin to develop an interest in the idea and seek more information about it.

▶ **Evaluation** – People begin to mentally apply the idea to their individual situations. Simultaneously, they obtain more information and make a decision to try the new idea.

▶ **Trials** – At this point, actual application begins, usually on a small scale. Potential adopters are primarily interested in the practice, techniques, and conditions necessary for application.

▶ **Adoption** – Once the idea has proved worthwhile, it is adopted.

The diffusion and adoption processes function together when, at each of the five stages, media of communication are used to influence target publics to adopt new ideas. These media vary from mass media to interpersonal communication. According to Baskin and Aronoff (1992:162), mass media are most effective at creating awareness and interest, while specialised media such as brochures are effective at creating knowledge. At the later stages of evaluation and trial, interpersonal communication media are best for influencing attitude change. Personal experience is most important at the point of adoption.

From a public relations point of view, a public can begin as a latent public where an issue (idea, problem or organisation) is still unrecognised, and move through the various stages of awareness, interest and evaluation, to become a so-called aware public. Once the public has moved through the stages of trial and adoption, becoming actively involved with the issue (idea, problem or organisation), it can be called an active public.

Public relations campaigns which are well suited to applying this approach are

► those aimed at publics adopting new ideas or behaviour (e.g. a campaign to promote changes in existing behaviour, such as one which promotes a change from manual banking to new developments such as electronic banking);

► where publics are already involved in the topic (e.g. people who are already actively involved in a cause such as protection of the environment will adopt new issues relating to the environment more easily);

► where the position advocated in the campaign is different from other campaigns (e.g. a campaign advocating a "yes" vote as opposed to a "no" vote on any particular issue).

Social learning model

This theory focuses on **sustained behavioural change**. Communication media such as the mass media and interpersonal communication are used together (not sequentially as in the diffusion of innovations approach) to educate and train target publics (not only to persuade). This theory holds that there is a continuous interaction between a person's behaviour and the consequences of that behaviour within his or her environment. The more positive consequences a person experiences as a result of a certain behaviour, the more that behaviour is likely to continue. According to this theory, social learning and behavioural change can occur at the awareness stage where the mass media are used not only to create awareness but also to inform and persuade publics to change their behaviour. Reinforcement is provided on an interpersonal level to support the changed behaviour. Campaigns promoting well-being and health are well suited to this model. For example, the Heart Foundation does not only inform people of the risks involved in smoking, obesity, unhealthy eating, and so on, but also provides guidelines through the mass media for healthier living.

Low-involvement theory

According to Baskin and Aronoff (1992:63), this theory, which was developed from the advertising and marketing literature, holds that **changes in behaviour can occur without cognitive or attitudinal change**. This is because certain behaviours are not dependent on large amounts of knowledge or reconciliation with existing attitudes. Awareness campaigns with short, simple messages are launched to achieve behavioural change but without necessarily affecting attitudes or knowledge. The public moves from the awareness stage immediately to behavioural change, and then perhaps, to attitudinal change. Each year, before the Christmas and New Year season, the South African Breweries launches an awareness campaign to prevent people from driving when they have been drinking. The aim is to immediately prevent accidents from the outset in a period when the most accidents can potentially occur. People react to these messages by changing their behaviour in response to the campaign (e.g. drinking less or asking someone else to drive if they feel that they have had too much to drink), but these changes may not be of a permanent nature.

Agenda-setting theory

Agenda setting is described in *Course book 1* (Steinberg 1994) as the way **the mass media create public awareness and concern about important issues**, thereby contributing to the shaping of public opinion. The mass media focus attention on certain issues, with the result that people begin to consider those issues as important. Public relations practitioners attempt to get certain issues onto the mass media agenda which in turn become the issues which people talk about. Public relations practitioners involved in government or in the private sector will focus on issues that may have an impact on their organisations, and through the mass media try to influence the relevant publics. One of the major problems encountered in South Africa at the time of writing is labour unrest and continuous demands for higher wages, particularly in the mining industry. The public relations practitioners in the latter industry are constantly providing the mass media with information on the long-term effects of labour unrest, thereby aiming to influence the broader "labour" public. They do not focus on their own organisations, but rather keep the broader issue alive, thereby attempting to create a healthier climate in which they can operate.

Spiral of silence theory

This theory proposes that individuals who think that their opinions regarding an issue conflict with the majority of other opinions, will be inclined to remain silent on that issue. The spiral begins when a person decides either **to express his/her opinion or to remain silent**. It continues when others realise that their views are either supported or contradicted. As more opinions are expressed in support of an issue, the issue appears to become legitimate. However, because of the fact that people have remained silent on the issue, the **majority** opinion is **not** necessarily the **expressed** opinion. Media coverage can reflect, enforce, or challenge the spiral of silence effect on public opinion (cf. Cutlip et al. 1994:241). Public relations, through the use of public information campaigns, can break the spiral of silence on issues such as child abuse, smoking, sexually transmitted diseases, white collar fraud and homosexuality. The recent emergence of the previously unvoiced issue of sexual harassment in the workplace is an example of a spiral of silence which has been broken.

ACTIVITY

We have provided you with examples of public relations campaigns in each of the five communication effects theories. In addition to the examples provided, try to think of at least one more example in each of the five theories and explain, in one paragraph each, why these examples relate to each theory.

3.4   PUBLIC RELATIONS MEDIA: ADVERTISING AND PUBLICITY

Organisations practising public relations as a strategic management function will set overall communication strategies to achieve certain communication effects.

These strategies must be translated into specific programmes, projects and campaigns where identification of the publics, specific communication objectives, media selection and message content is done, and decisions are taken regarding the timing and frequency of messages. The communication function is put into operation by allocating and scheduling tasks and budgeting in the public relations department. These programmes, campaigns and projects must support the broader public relations goals, which, in turn, support the overall goals of the organisation.

Public relations uses two types of communication media, *controlled* and *uncontrolled media*. **Controlled media** refers to communication over which the public relations practitioner has control in terms of the timing of the message, frequency, content, format and placement. The communication can take the form of brochures, advertisements, newsletters, annual reports, audiovisual material, meetings, interviews and even special events. Controlled media are used to communicate both internally and externally. **Internal** organisational media include letters, notice boards, magazines, newsletters, interviews, meetings and even staff functions. **External** organisational media include pamphlets, brochures, information guides, letters, posters, publications, advertising, meetings (e.g. shareholder meetings), functions and audiovisual material such as videos and documentary films.

Uncontrolled media, as the name indicates, refers to media over which the practitioner does not have the final say regarding placement, content, and so on. These media include publicity releases, media conferences, photo captions and feature stories. You may recall the documentary films which were broadcast by SABC-TV on Sol Kerzner and the Palace of the Lost City at its launch. Uncontrolled media used by public relations practitioners are mainly publicity releases. Although prepared by the public relations practitioner for the mass media such as newspapers, magazines, radio and television, the ultimate decision on the content, timing and placement lies with the editors of the respective mass media.

ACTIVITY

Identify the internal and external communication media used by any organisation of your choice and make a list of each under the categories internal and external media.

Since *advertising* and *publicity* are major public relations techniques, they are discussed in more depth in the section below.

Public relations advertising

Advertising is a **controlled** method of communication and is defined by Cutlip et al. (1994) as the placing of information in the media by an identified sponsor that pays for the time and space (see Unit 4 for a detailed discussion of advertising). Advertising in newspapers, magazines, radio, television, cinema and outdoors (e.g. billboards, bus stations, et cetera) is used for both marketing and public relations purposes. Marketing uses mainly *product advertising*, while public relations advertising takes two forms. The first is *public service advertising*, which covers social issues such as antismoking campaigns, traffic safety, race relations and conservation (cf. Moore & Kalupa 1985). A well-known example of the use of public service advertising is the annual Red Nose Day campaign in support of child welfare. The second is *institutional* or *corporate advertising*, which concentrates on projecting the organisation to establish a favourable public image. Both institutional and public service advertising are used by private and public sector organisations. An example of an organisation in the public sector which uses **public service** advertising is the Department of Health with its antismoking advertising campaigns. An example of a business organisation using public service advertising is the South African Breweries' campaign against drunken driving.

Institutional or corporate advertising is done for a variety of reasons, of which the following six can be distinguished:

► correcting misconceptions;

► improving labour relations;

► informing the community;

► arousing the interest of potential shareholders;

► developing a favourable image;

► creating awareness.

Some well-known South African examples of **institutional** or **corporate** advertising include South African Airways' 1996 campaign to launch their change in corporate identity, Telkom's 1995 image promotion campaign, Denel's 1992 campaign to establish itself as an entity independent of Armscor, the campaign launched by the Iron and Steel Corporation (ISCOR) prior to its listing on the Johannesburg Stock Exchange in 1991, and the campaign run by First National Bank when it changed its name from Barclays Bank in 1988. All of these campaigns were run to achieve certain public relations objectives. Figure 3.4 is an illustration of an advertisement which focuses more on the image of the organisation ("91 international awards"), while Figure 3.5 shows an airline advertisement which focuses more specifically on its services ("Fly direct"). An example of institutional advertising used by a public sector organisation is the television advertising campaign run by the Free State Province in 1995, aimed at creating awareness of aspects such as the low crime rate and the business infrastructure to draw potential investors and residents to the province.

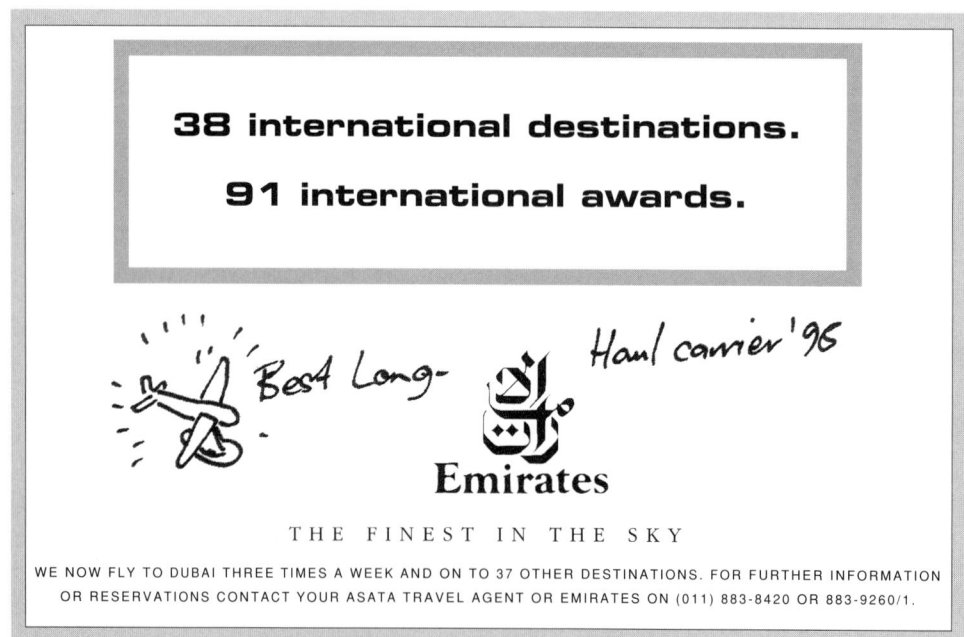

Figure 3.4 **An example of an advertisement which focuses on the image elements of an organisation: "91 International Awards"**
(Reproduced with the kind permission of *Emirates Air*)

Figure 3.5 **An example of an advertisement which focuses on the product/service elements of an organisation**

(Reproduced with the kind permission of *Air Austral*)

The **publics** of an organisation can also use advertising to influence the organisation's policies or actions. For example, activist groups such as environmental groups use advertising to create awareness among the general public if an organisation is deemed to be acting in an unacceptable way. The demise of practically the entire fur industry is an excellent example of the important role played by, among others, advertising campaigns launched by animal anticruelty activists. Individuals are also known to use public relations advertising to influence organisations and their decisions. In the case of the proposed 1995 merger between Lonrho's platinum division and Gencor's platinum arm, Implats, the former chief executive of Lonrho used a full-page advertisement in the *Financial Times* to prevent the merger, albeit unsuccessfully.

Another form of public relations advertising which is increasingly being used is that of *advocacy* or *issues* advertising. Organisations position themselves on certain issues and through advertising inform their publics of their positions, which are particularly important if the organisation's existence depends on the support and goodwill of different publics. Issues relating to sexual orientation, smoking, nuclear testing, affirmative action, women's rights and the environment are all issues on which organisations may be called to take a stand. An example of advocacy advertising is the combined stand that a number of organisations took during the 1992 South African referendum for a "yes" vote.

Public relations advertising is an effective medium of communication for a number of reasons:

▶ A large number of people can be reached at a relatively low cost per person.

▶ A variety of media are available in which messages can be placed.

▶ Timing, placement, frequency and space can be controlled by the communicator.

▶ Particular publics can be targeted.

▶ The intensity of the campaign can be controlled through the use of more than one medium.

▶ Communication is quick.

ACTIVITY

1   When next you read a newspaper or magazine, select at least one example of product advertising, public service advertising and corporate advertising, and explain why each example falls into that particular category.

2   Take the example that you selected in the category of corporate advertising and try to define what the purpose of the advertisement is.

Publicity

Publicity can be defined as information from an outside communicator that is used by the media because it has news value. The communicator does not pay the media for placement of the information and therefore loses control of placement, content and timing.

Public relations is most often confused with publicity. There are a number of reasons for this confusion. The most important reason is that **historically** public relations developed from a publicity function where practitioners were mainly concerned with informing publics of the organisation's policies and practices, while basically ignoring their attitudes. Another reason is that, even today, publicity remains a **major technique** of public relations, resulting in the misconception that public relations *is* publicity. Finally, many public relations practitioners are drawn from the mass-media industry, particularly **journalists** who often practise publicity as public relations.

Publicity is still a major technique in public relations, but today publicity is part of the communication plan where certain objectives are set. Publicity is no longer an aim in itself, but a supporting technique applied to achieve the aims of a public relations campaign or programme, and as such can be a powerful tool. An organisation or institution can use five different types of publicity to communicate its activities, policies and plans (cf. Moore & Kalupa 1985). These are dealt with below.

News

The most common type of publicity is news of a local, regional or national nature, prepared and disseminated by publicity agents or public relations departments. There are two categories of news publicity: spontaneous and planned news. **Spontaneous news** is brought about by an unplanned event such as a strike or a serious accident. News media are informed and reporters, photographers and camera teams sent to the scene. In the event of a major crisis, such as the "Helderberg" disaster suffered by South African Airways in 1987, the proper handling of so-called **emergency publicity** by public relations practitioners is remembered by the media long after the emergency or crisis. Public relations management should plan a well-formulated emergency publicity programme in advance. Aspects such as how members of staff should liaise with the media in a crisis are important. **Planned news**, on the other hand, has to do with daily developments and events inside an organisation which may interest the public and therefore be newsworthy. Such news can include mergers, management changes, financial results and new directions or expansions. The public relations department of an organisation prepares and distributes news releases publicising these activities.

Special news articles

These articles can be written by public relations practitioners in conjunction with journalists, to give newspaper and magazine readers information, advice and suggestions on home improvements, road safety, fashion, food, travel, beauty and numerous other subjects.

Pictorial publicity

Imaginative and unusual photographs are becoming more sought after by newspapers, magazines and television. Many organisations employ their own photographers in an effort to optimise this source. Photographs of special events, new offices or facilities, interviews and local news events are sent to newspapers for publication. Video tapes produced by organisations about themselves and which are suitable for use on television for news, documentary or talk-show programmes, although not widely used, are also a form of pictorial publicity.

Background and editorial material

Editors of news media such as newspapers, radio and television are supplied with background information not included in news releases. This deals with subjects such as financial projections of companies, special events, management changes, disasters or any other newsworthy events. Statistical and reference data such as biographical details on executives and historical data on organisations can clarify issues and sometimes earn favourable publicity. An example of the use of background information is one of the longest-standing environmental controversies in South Africa. It lasted from 1989 to 1996 and it concerned the mining of the St Lucia dunes. Much of the publicity that was generated was based on background material supplied to the news media by both the environmentalists and Richards Bay Minerals (RBM). In 1989 RBM announced that it intended to mine a section of the dunes north of St Lucia. This resulted in a public outcry and a great deal of publicity opposing this intention was generated. The issue became highly controversial because both sides had a strong case. RBM had the potential economic advantages on its side, while the environmentalists had the conservation "lobby" on their side. In response to the negative publicity, part of RBM's public relations strategy was to provide the news media with as much material on RBM itself, its social responsibility programmes and scientific data on dune rehabilitation. This kind of background material was essential for presenting RBM's case to the broader public. On the other side the environmental groups also provided the news media with scientific data from environmental impact studies which served to further their case in the media. The final result of the controversy was that the government banned mining operations in the St Lucia wetlands area.

Because publicity constitutes such a large part of the daily task of public relations practitioners, and because these practitioners are the link between organisations and the media, their relations with the media are extremely important. Knowing how to liaise with the media, produce news releases, meet deadlines, and so on, are essential for successful publicity.

Practitioners play a mediating role between organisations and the media and must gain the confidence of both. In other words, practitioners have a responsibility towards their organisations and towards the media. This relationship should be fostered by applying the principles of professional conduct, openness and honesty. Problems occur when practitioners flood the media with news releases which have little relevance to the particular medium or which have little news value. Good publicity can only be achieved if there is trust on both sides. It is mainly the responsibility of the practitioner to foster this trust.

ACTIVITY

When next you read your newspaper, look at some of the articles or reports that deal with organisations or issues. Evaluate the article, and write a short paragraph on the type of publicity that each represents.

3.5 PUBLIC RELATIONS AND INFORMATION, PERSUASION AND PROPAGANDA

The theories of communication effects described in Section 3.3 provide the theoretical foundation for the way in which public relations campaigns are planned and executed. As we explained in this section, the goal of some public relations campaigns is to provide publics with *information,* while the goal of others is *persuasion,* that is, to persuade publics to change their attitudes or their behaviour. In the ensuing section we discuss **information** and **persuasion** as integral **parts** of public relations and highlight that these concepts do not constitute public relations per se. Another concept which has been confused with public relations because of certain historical associations is that of *propaganda*, and we therefore discuss propaganda in relation to public relations.

Public relations and information

Information has been defined as "the number of signals required to reduce completely the uncertainty in the situation" (Littlejohn 1996:52). In other words, the greater the uncertainty in a situation, the more information required. People accumulate and organise information about some person, object, situation or idea in order to form an attitude towards that particular concept. Where new attitudes need to be formed or existing attitudes maintained, it is necessary for public relations programmes to **inform** publics, that is, to share sufficient information to reduce the uncertainty about the particular issue. Information is therefore fundamental to any public relations programme. Cutlip et al. (1994:230) say that the **process** of *informing* involves drawing attention to what is being communicated, achieving acceptance of the message, having it interpreted as it is intended and storing the message for later use.

At the turn of the century **information transmission** was the primary method used by public relations practitioners for enlisting the support of publics for the organisation. This phase came into being as a result of public resistance to the manipulative tactics used by press agents in the eighteenth century to conduct political campaigns. Organisations attempted, mainly through **publicity**, to spread information about themselves and public relations practitioners were generally known as **publicity agents**. Organisations were more concerned about informing the publics about themselves than they were about gaining inputs from the publics on their attitudes towards organisations. At this stage public relations was practised mainly in the *functionary* mode.

Although public relations has developed into a function which **manages** the relationship between an organisation and its publics through planned two-way communication, information provision must, by definition, still form an essential part of any public relations campaign. Public relations as a management function now includes the exchange of messages, not only to inform but also to instruct or persuade through shared meanings. According to Cutlip et al. (1994:230), **instruction** goes one step further than informing because active learning and practice are stimulated. **Persuasion** goes even further because the aim is to gain acceptance of the communicator's point of view and to effect behavioural change.

Public relations and persuasion

Although often referred to as a technique, persuasion is actually a process whereby a deliberate attempt is made to change a person's or a group's attitude, beliefs or behaviour (cf. Kaye 1994). Persuasive communication can take the form of emotional appeals or reasonable arguments and can be conveyed through interpersonal, small group, and mass-communication means. Public relations practitioners most often use persuasion to influence public opinion. **Effective** persuasion means that the persuasive properties inherent in each of the four elements of the communication process – the communicator, the message, the medium, and the recipient – have been successfully applied; that is, each of the four elements has been successfully applied within the context of relationships and the social environment. Let us discuss each of the elements separately.

Verwey (1994:67) describes the most significant source (**communicator**) in public relations as the practitioner, who is not only responsible for selecting the message that is to be communicated but also for selecting the media of communication. However, a distinction must be made between two roles that a public relations practitioner can play. The first role is where practitioners research, plan and formulate communication programmes on behalf of their organisations or clients. In this instance practitioners are **not perceived** by the public to be the **communicators** of the message since their role is mostly to advise others in an organisation on what and how to communicate. The second role is where practitioners act as spokespersons on behalf of organisations or clients and **are perceived** by the public to be the **communicators** of the message, although an organisation is the actual communicator. The implication is that, although an organisation may be the actual communicator of the message, the practitioner, as the spokesperson, is perceived as such and it is the **credibility** which is attached to the **perceived communicator** which often determines the effectiveness of the message. Kaye (1994:35) is of the opinion that credibility lies in the attitude of a recipient towards a message source (the perceived communicator) and is made up of factors such as expertise, trustworthiness and dynamism. If the communicator has high credibility in the eyes of the recipient, the message is more likely to be accepted.

Even though the same **messages** can be interpreted differently by different people, message characteristics can influence the effectiveness of persuasion. Cutlip et al. (1994:231) suggest taking the position of recipients into account when formulating messages. For example, if recipients of a message are opposed to a particular issue, messages should contain both sides of an argument. If recipients are in agreement, messages should be consistent with the recipients' views. If recipients are well educated, messages should contain both sides of an argument and, if both sides of an argument are presented, relevant arguments on the opposing side should not be left out, as this will create suspicion. Finally, if recipients may be exposed to future persuasive messages opposing the argument, two-sided messages should be used to build resistance to later messages.

Persuasive messages can contain emotional appeals such as humour or fear which are used to elicit responses from individuals. However, different people respond differently to such appeals. Nothing illustrates this point better than the "fear" appeals used in antismoking campaigns because many people persist in smoking even though they have been made aware of its dangers.

The role of the **media** in persuasive communication can be explained with reference to media effects. Print media are regarded as *high-involvement* media which, according to Cutlip et al. (1994:234), tend to follow a "see-learn-feel-do" sequence, while television is seen as a *low-involvement* medium which produces gradual shifts in perceptions, often through repetition.

The role of the **recipients** in persuasive communication is particularly important in public relations as the essence of public relations is the management of relationships based on two-way communication. Understanding the needs and attitudes of the publics provides the foundation for effective communication whereby both the organisation and the publics adjust to one another (cf. Unit 2 for a discussion of the phases in the public relations process whereby research is conducted into the needs and attitudes of the publics).

Persuasive communication is affected by the nature of the **relationships** that exist, as well as the **social setting** within which the communication occurs. In a public relations context, relationships refer to those that exist between an organisation and its publics. A different relationship exists between an organisation and its workers and an organisation and its customers. This means that different messages and media will be selected to reach each audience. In public relations the social setting within which an organisation and its publics communicate may generate more group communication than interpersonal communication, since the environment is such that group action may produce the best results.

Public relations and propaganda

The word *propaganda* originated in the seventeenth century when the Catholic Church set up a congregation for propagating the faith (cf. Seitel 1995:28). Propaganda was aimed at facilitating communication between the church and its congregation. From these early beginnings it grew as a technique used mainly to manipulate public opinion. Some individuals, such as P T Barnum, Matthew St Clair and Ivy Lee, to whom the early development of public relations is ascribed (cf. Unit 2 for an in-depth discussion of the development of public relations), used manipulative techniques to a greater or lesser degree to influence public opinion. The manipulation of public opinion, or propaganda, came to be distrusted by the public who regarded it as being manipulative and dishonest.

Moore and Kalupa (1985:65) describe the extreme form of propaganda as *subversive propaganda* which is fundamentally the evasion of the truth. Deliberate falsehoods are fabricated with the intention of deceiving the public. Propagandists use different forms of falsehoods, including evasion of the truth, omitting significant facts, gross exaggerations and presentation of only those arguments that support the viewpoint of the propagandist. Although these practices still exist, the ethical principles on which public relations is based, as well as the professionalism with which it strives to attain its objectives, are **contrary** to such practices. The legacy of *bad* propaganda continues today where we see some people in developing countries being critical of foreign broadcasts because they regard such broadcasts as propaganda for foreign cultures.

The difference between propaganda and public relations is that propaganda presents an issue by focusing only on the good, and its success depends on a biased view of the issue. Public relations, on the other hand, strives to present an unbiased view and, in so doing, seeks to achieve **mutual understanding** between an institution or organisation and its publics. The greatest difference between propaganda and public relations in the political arena is that, whereas propaganda is issued to seek votes, public relations explains policy to make a party better understood. Propaganda presents one side of a case; public relations presents all sides.

Public relations has increasingly divorced itself from the concept *propaganda* to the extent that most textbooks and literature on public relations do not refer to propaganda at all. It is generally no longer recognised as a communication technique to be used in public relations.

ACTIVITY

1   Write your own definitions of information, persuasion and propaganda.

2   You have been requested by Government to draw up a public relations campaign to tell the general public about the new constitution and what it will mean to them. Do you think that this campaign should incorporate informative messages, persuasive messages, propaganda or a combination of any of these? Write a short summary explaining the basis for your decision.

3.6   CRITICAL ISSUES IN PUBLIC RELATIONS

Public opinion

The concept *public opinion* is fundamental to public relations as it is often seen as a means of influencing public opinion through information, instruction or persuasion.

Public opinion is traditionally defined as the sum total of individual opinions concerning a matter of common interest. This approach holds that individuals make up the publics of an organisation or of any particular issue (e.g. abortion, AIDS, the environment), and that these individuals have certain opinions regarding that organisation or issue. These opinions can reflect goodwill or ill will towards the organisation or issue. From this viewpoint the collective opinion of the majority of these individuals is described as public opinion. However, this agreement-of-individuals approach to defining public opinion misses the point that it is **public** and that public opinion represents more than the collected views held by a particular category of individuals at any one point in time.

Public opinion is not simply a **state** of individual agreement, but rather a dynamic **process** in which ideas are expressed and adjusted in order to reach a collective decision on a course of action. The concern is that researchers and practitioners following this approach view public opinion only at one point in time. They therefore measure only the *direction* (for-or-against predisposition) and *intensity* (strength of the feelings) of the opinion. Other important dimensions are left out. Firstly, the *stability* of the collective opinion is not measured – in other words, how long people have held or will hold the same direction. Secondly, the amount of knowledge that people have about the object of the opinion, the *informational support*, is not measured. Finally, the extent to which people think their opinions are shared by others or the so-called *social support* is not measured (cf. Cutlip et al. 1994:243–245).

According to Baskin and Aronoff (1992:120), public relations practitioners who rely on so-called *public opinion polls* to provide insight into the characteristics of their potential audience may be operating with erroneous data. Most polls of this nature actually measure *mass* opinion rather than public opinion. **Mass opinion** represents an average calculated from a group with many different opinions. However, the average of these opinions can be substantially different from the original opinions stated.

Traditional public opinion polls typically break down their results into demographic categories that seldom identify groups of people with common interests. Cutlip et al. (1994:245) therefore contend that to understand public opinion fully the traditional approach of viewing the collective opinion of a number of individuals at any one point in time does not suffice, and greater sensitivity in terms of measuring public opinion as a process which leads to certain actions is required. Thus the concept **general public** should be discarded and **target publics** be identified and defined, and the nature of their relationship with the organisation or issue be established. In this respect Baskin and Aronoff (1992) provide three categories of publics that indicate their level of involvement in any particular issue, namely *latent* publics, *aware* publics and *active* publics (cf. Unit 2 for a discussion on publics). If a public does not recognise a problem or issue it is called a **latent** public; if and when a public recognises the problem or issue as relevant to its interests it becomes an **aware** public; and if it begins to seek information or take other actions related to the issue it is called an **active** public.

In this way public relations decisions can be made which are "actionable" because, as Broom, Lauzen and Tucker (1991:222) state "… we don't care any more about public opinion, we care about actionable public opinion because there isn't enough money to deal with everybody …".

ACTIVITY

Do you agree with the statement that practitioners may be working with erroneous data if they rely on public opinion polls to provide insight into the characteristics of their potential audience? Write a paragraph stating your opinion and explain the reasoning behind your viewpoint.

Public relations as "image building"

A number of questions have been raised on the issue of public relations and image building or image management, of which we consider three of the most important. The first relates to the **illusionary** nature of the concept *image*, the second to the problem of **accountability** and the third to the way in which **images** are **formed** by publics.

The concept *image* is disliked by some public relations practitioners and academics because it has the connotation of an **illusion**. When public relations is involved in so-called image building, its negative connotation suggests that public relations is a manipulative technique. The problem of image "manipulation" has its roots in the dual role that public relations practitioners must fulfil. On the one hand, public relations practitioners serve an organisation and further its interests. In this role they have certain loyalties towards the organisation. On the other hand, because an organisation's *raison d'être* in society stems from its ability to meet the needs of its publics, the public relations practitioner must also serve the interests of the publics. As far back as 1965 Sullivan, in his work on public relations and images, described this as the central dilemma of public relations, calling it a tension between partisan and mutual values. Partisanship assumes without question that the organisation is right and that its interpretation of its image is complete and correct, whilst mutual values, on the other hand, take into account the viewpoints, interests and rights of others which must balance partisan values (cf. Sullivan 1965).

Pearson (1989) raises the question whether a balance between partisan and mutual values is attainable, since practitioners are ultimately employed by organisations and institutions. If not, they can be accused of the manipulation of an image. Manipulation of an image can mean two things. On the one hand, it can mean the unethical use of techniques producing inaccurate images which are not based on reality and which are ultimately not in the interests of the relevant publics. The debacle surrounding Masterbond in the early 1990s, where members of the public lost vast sums of money, was due to the inaccurate images created in the media by the Masterbond Group regarding its stability and growth prospects. Two of the managing partners were subsequently jailed for twelve years for their role in the deception of investors. On the other hand, manipulation of an image can also be because people do not fully see reality and images then become incomplete interpretations of reality. Messages are sent by a public relations practitioner based on images that the practitioner has about the reality of his or her organisation. In the case of the demise of the domestic airline, Flitestar, in 1994, the general public, and particularly airline ticketholders, were constantly reassured of the airline's continuation almost to the day that it ceased operating. This was ascribed to the incomplete information given to the staff of the airline regarding the seriousness of the problems confronting Flitestar.

Some public relations specialists (cf. Broom et al. 1991) have questioned the wisdom of assigning image building to public relations on the basis that **accountability** is difficult because the concept *image* is murky and cannot be operationalised. Practitioners are therefore discouraged to act in a scientifically accountable way. The open-systems approach to public relations (cf. Unit 2 for a discussion of the systems approach) is specifically based on two-way communication and mutual understanding which means that a desired image should not be a product of how an organisation wishes to be seen, but rather a reflection of the reality of how an organisation can meet the needs and expectations of its publics. This raises the question of how image can be translated into action and behaviour that is measurable. Public relations must have goals that are attainable, measurable and economically worthwhile. Image making must therefore fulfil these requirements.

The final question relates to the way in which publics **form images**. According to traditional public relations theory, the terms **public** and **image** are different but related. From a public relations perspective, a **public** is generally viewed as a group of individuals who share similar attitudes and behaviours towards an organisation and because of this generally have a similar image of the organisation. Organisations have traditionally been seen as determining their own images. This traditional theory has now been questioned by a number of researchers, among them Moffit (1994:159–170). He suggests that **image** is ultimately determined by the publics who process it and not by the organisation, and that multiple factors, such as organisational, cultural, historical and personal factors, affect image. This means that each individual can have unique and different images of an organisation based on a unique combination of factors at any point in time. In other words, an individual can view an organisation in a negative and in a positive way, for example the organisation can be seen as providing a good service but at the same time lacking in social responsibility towards society as a whole. This effectively means that one individual can associate with a broad number of publics at any given time. This has two implications for public relations. Firstly, a **public** can be identified as relating to an organisation based on a **shared** image. Secondly, **individuals** within that public can be researched, analysed and communicated to in terms of all the potential publics that may exist within the individual. Moffit (1994:167) suggests that the concept **public** and the concept **image** be collapsed into a single concept and that the notions of public and individuality be reconciled.

As a result of the complex nature of image and the various criticisms levelled at public relations as an image-building technique, the concept **corporate image** has, in many instances, been used interchangeably with (or substituted for) concepts such as **corporate identity** or **corporate personality**. However, distinct differences do exist between these concepts and we shall discuss the meaning of each in the next section.

ACTIVITY

Write at least one paragraph in response to each of the following questions.

1   What does "manipulation of image" mean?

2   Think of at least two organisations about which you have "mixed feelings". What are the aspects that you feel positive about and what are the aspects that you feel negative about? Try to think of one word to sum up your feelings about each organisation.

3   Why, do you think, should the public relations practitioner of an organisation be held accountable for the image he/she creates of the organisation?

Corporate image, corporate identity, corporate personality and corporate culture

Corporate image can be defined as the beliefs or feelings which the publics of an organisation hold towards that organisation. These impressions will vary because they are based on everyone's knowledge and experience of the organisation, its products and/or services. Van Riel (1995:28) simply states that "image is the picture of an organisation as perceived by target groups". If we asked different people what their general feelings were towards an organisation, we would get a variety of answers ranging from positive to negative (e.g. good–bad, pleasant–unpleasant), depending on their knowledge of, and experience with the organisation. Images are formed as a result of the way in which individuals **perceive** objects. The way in which an individual perceives determines the way in which the perceived object is represented in his or her cognitive system (the image). Examining the perceptual process is therefore necessary to provide an understanding of how individuals perceive organisations. In *Course book* 1 (Steinberg 1994) perception was defined as the process whereby we acquire information about our environment through our five senses: hearing, sight, touch, taste and smell. People perceive the same objects, situations or organisations differently because each person attends to, organises and interprets this sensory data in a different way (cf. *Course book 1*, Unit 3 for a discussion of the perception process). A number of factors are important in the formation of corporate image by both internal publics (e.g. employees) and external publics (e.g. clients, media, government and the community):

▶ The **internal behaviour of the organisation** – This is reflected in its formal policies and corporate culture (corporate culture is defined further on in this section). The policy of an organisation is depicted in materials such as its annual reports and other information available to outsiders, such as details of products and prices. Corporate culture is reflected in the behaviour of management, its reward structures, its values and organisational rituals.

▶ **Communication** transmitted via the media to the outside world – This includes publicity and marketing media communications. The media are particularly important in creating awareness and knowledge about an organisation.

▶ **Interpersonal communication** – This relates mainly to personal contact with the employees of an organisation. Since employees play an important role in determining the external image of an organisation, the information they transmit must be compatible with the way management wishes the organisation to be perceived. The attitude of employees towards an organisation will determine the way outsiders perceive that organisation when they come into contact with employees. Desirable policies and a healthy culture within an organisation are therefore of the utmost importance in the formation of corporate image.

▶ **Personal experiences** – These include previous personal experiences with the product or service of an organisation.

▶ **External factors** – These are factors which are generally outside the control of an organisation. Rumour formation, the negative influence of the conduct of certain members of an organisation and the rational or irrational ways in which members of publics selectively retain information on an organisation, all fall within this category.

Van Riel (1995:98–99) suggests a multistage plan of five steps to be followed by any organisation which wants to adjust its corporate image. In the first step, the image dimensions which are important to an organisation's publics must be identified. For example, these dimensions may include the financial soundness of an organisation, the quality of its services and products, the quality of its management, its innovativeness and its social responsibility. Images of competitors in terms of these dimensions should also be taken into account so that an organisation's relative position can be determined. The second step entails a comparison of the picture that an organisation wishes to create among its publics with the needs of those publics and with reality. For example, if an organisation serves a conservative public, it should not present itself as a fast-moving risk taker. Policies should reflect the needs of the publics. These policies can include changes in a variety of areas such as products, prices, corporate investment, visual symbols (e.g. logos), marketing or employee conditions. In the third step, the chosen policy should be explained to employees by way of internal communication media such as brochures or seminars, so that they may convey it to the public. The fourth step entails the implementation of the policy through a corporate image campaign which can include advertising and public relations. The choice of media and the nature of the campaign are determined by the specific objectives of the corporate image campaign. The final step is the evaluation of the campaign, which can include research into changes in attitudes or behaviour by relevant publics.

The concept **corporate image** is closely related to the concept **corporate identity**. Simplistically stated, corporate image is what people feel about an organisation, while corporate identity is what organisations do to create that feeling. **Corporate identity** can be defined as the visually perceptible and unique ways which an organisation selects to identify itself to its publics, for example, by means of letterheads, office furniture, colour schemes, uniforms, logotype. According to Van Riel (1995:27), corporate image "can be described as the picture that people have of a company, whereas 'corporate identity' denotes the sum total of all the forms of expression that a company uses to offer insight into its nature". Corporate image can therefore be seen as reflecting the identity of an organisation. The good or bad images that people have of an organisation are determined to a considerable degree by the messages it transmits about itself.

Van Riel (1995:28) suggests that corporate identity is associated with the way in which an organisation presents itself to its target groups through **three** specific areas.

▶ Through its **behaviour**. This is the most important and effective medium through which corporate identity is created. An organisation's actions constitute its behaviour and certain actions can also be emphasised through communication and symbols to create corporate identity. The organisation's actions must, however, support these messages. For example, an organisation which wants to establish itself as "innovative" can do so by telling target groups by means of verbal or visual messages, but if the organisation's actions do not confirm these messages, the communication is pointless.

▶ Through its **communication**. Communication can be seen as the most flexible instrument in establishing corporate identity since verbal or visual messages about the organisation can be sent directly to target publics. This includes communication campaigns which inform publics about an organisation. For example, First National Bank had to launch new corporate image campaigns to reassure investors that the future was secure when divested from Barclays Bank. Nedbank continuously conveys information to investors through communication campaigns, which highlight the seriousness with which it regards their investments.

▶ Through its use of **symbols**. Symbols are the implicit indication of what the organisation stands for. Symbols include slogans, logos, interiors and all equipment (such as transport vehicles) which carry the organisation's symbols. Figure 3.6 presents an example of a specific logo which was changed.

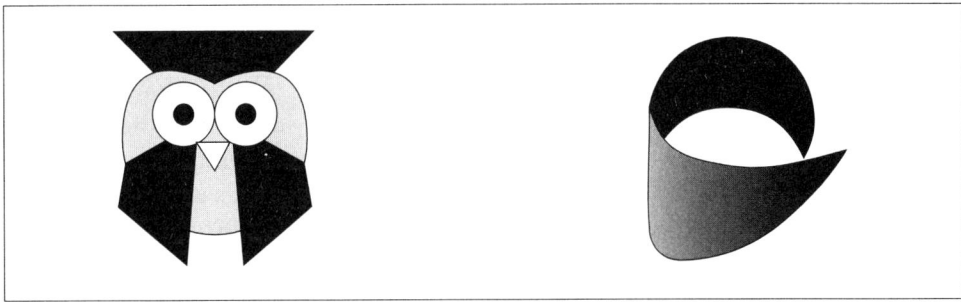

Figure 3.6 **Previous and current logo of the Bureau for University Teaching (UNISA)**
(Reproduced with the kind permission of the Bureau for University Teaching, UNISA)

Motivation behind the selection of a specific logo

In January 1996 the **Bureau for University Teaching** at the University of South Africa changed its logo from the owl to the "curl". After numerous remarks about the cultural relevance of the owl and in accordance with the policy of change and the mission of the Bureau, it was decided to change its logo to prevent any conflict or misunderstanding in the future. The symbol of the owl not only creates problems within an African context, but research has also shown that there are negative connotations in its association with Western culture. The brief to the graphic artist was to design a logo which eliminates any cultural or other bias (such as animals, plants or other recognisable objects); that it should be simple and yet reflect the dynamic nature of the Bureau's activities.

After a number of designs had been presented, the "curl" was finally selected. It has no specific symbolism, is in line with modern corporate designs and, typographically, is easily applied. The "curl" supports the Bureau's aspiration towards a neutral, objective process.

An organisation attempts to present a unified visual presentation which creates a coherent picture and a sense of belonging together. For example, Avis uses the colour red in its advertising, logo, slogans, airport kiosks and in its uniforms. Part of the symbolism of an organisation may also be reflected in less concrete ways such as an organisation's willingness to involve itself in social responsibility programmes or even its commitment to service (e.g. its delivery period).

Another concept which must be clarified is **corporate personality.** Corporate personality is viewed by Van Riel (1995:33) as a "manifestation of the organisation's self-perception". The corporate identity, behaviour, communication and symbols can be regarded as the outer forms of expression, while the corporate personality represents the deeper element which lies behind them. This is the **unique character** of an organisation which is found in its **characteristics** and **behaviour.** These characteristics are attributed to an organisation on the basis of its behaviour. Much the same as with any individual, an organisation's personality is unique due to its characteristics and distinguishing features which are presented through its behaviour. An organisation sends out visual and verbal signals and cues, just like a person, which provide the basis for determining its identity. Van Riel (1995:33) states: "The communication, behaviour and symbolism of a company are in fact the concrete forms into which the company's personality crystallizes."

The way in which public relations is managed in an organisation, including the presentation of an organisation's identity to its target publics, is influenced by the organisation's culture. **Corporate culture** is defined by Grunig (1992:591) as "the sum total of shared values, symbols, meanings, beliefs, assumptions, and expectations that organise and integrate a group of people who work together". It is an abstract concept which is difficult to observe and manage, but it is an integral part of an organisation's daily life. It describes the way things are done in an organisation and represents the shared values of a group of individuals within an organisation. A number of variables determine an organisation's culture. These include:

▶ The structure of an organisation such as its size, policies, rules, degree of centralisation of decision making, complexity and co-ordination between departments.

▶ The type of technology used in an organisation in its production and operational processes which determine service levels.

▶ The prescribed ways of doing things reflected in the various systems of control, feedback, remuneration, et cetera.

▶ The people who form the culture, the most important being the top management of an organisation. The leader's management style and personality strongly influence the culture in an organisation.

▶ The way in which public relations is practised in an organisation is strongly linked to the organisation's culture. Put simply, the view that top management holds of the role of public relations in an organisation will determine the way in which public relations is practised. Whether it is practised as a management function or simply as a communication function is largely dependent on the culture of the organisation.

ACTIVITY

1 Describe the relationship between corporate image, corporate identity and corporate personality and draw a diagram to illustrate this relationship.

2 When next you watch television, try to recognise corporate image advertisements and write down what you think the organisation or institution is trying to convey about its personality.

3 Do you think that corporate culture can determine whether public relations is practised as an interpretative, management and/or communication function in an organisation? Explain your reasoning.

Social responsibility and corporate investment

South Africa is at the time of writing heavily involved in social upliftment and empowerment. These issues are of major importance in public relations, particularly in government and business. Specialisation in the field of social responsibility is one of the major trends in public relations practice and is particularly relevant to the transformation process taking place in South Africa. Where many South Africans are still suspicious of the motives of business and have experienced no personal benefits from social responsibility programmes, the issue of corporate social responsibility is highly sensitive and practitioners are required, more than ever, to practise public relations as an interpretative function.

Organisations become involved in social responsibility programmes because this can eventually determine the climate in which businesses function. This argument is based on the following assumptions:

▶ Business improves when the welfare of society improves.

▶ The improvement in public attitudes towards business creates a favourable climate in which business can be conducted.

▶ Social responsibility programmes have an effect on land development, particularly where environmental protection is concerned. Land development and environmental protection affect the location of businesses.

▶ Businesses that appear not to be socially conscious are more prone to strikes and product boycotts, which affect long-term investment.

Overton-De Klerk (1994:179) defines corporate social responsibility as a generic term that refers to "the business organisation's concern and active two-way involvement with social, economic and political forces which influence the environment within which it exists".

Organisations are involved in social responsibility programmes in two ways. The first can be seen as a narrow involvement within the organisation itself and is reflected in, for example, fair labour practices, support for minimum household subsistence levels, provision for employee housing, maintenance of quality standards and the upholding of certain management practices. The second is the broader involvement outside the organisation, reflected in the organisation's policies towards, for example, nature conservation, housing, education, culture and health care. It is generally within the broader sphere of corporate investment and social responsibility that public relations is involved.

An organisation generally develops a policy concerning social responsibility. This policy is based on internal, external and comparative research. Internal research is done within an organisation and covers its current philosophy, past practices, beneficiaries, amounts donated and decision-makers' views on contributions. External research evaluates the merits of causes such as health, education, welfare and the environment in which an organisation can become involved. Comparative studies are done on what other organisations are doing so that an organisation's contributions do not duplicate those of another organisation. Large organisations usually have foundations which decide on and control contributions. For example, Anglo American has its Chairman's Fund which runs the social responsibility programmes of the organisation. Examples of corporate social responsibility are Standard Bank's sponsorship of the Grahamstown Arts Festival, Sasol's support of wildlife and Liberty Life's support of education and community upliftment.

Public relations plays a fundamental role in the field of social responsibility in terms of initiating programmes based on an understanding of the issues and applying the steps in social investment.

ACTIVITY

Write short notes on the following:

1 Do you agree with the assumptions stated above on why organisations become involved in social responsibility programmes? Explain the reasoning behind your standpoint.

2 Explain what is meant by a "narrow" and a "broader" involvement in social responsibility and provide some practical examples of each.

3 If you were appointed to launch an organisation's social responsibility programmes, how would you decide what areas the organisation should support?

Ethics in public relations

Ethics in the practice of public relations (as in most other professions) is becoming an increasingly important concern. Leading public relations practitioners, academics and associations such as the Public Relations Institute of South Africa believe that the success of public relations depends on the degree of ethical conduct in the field. A number of studies have already questioned the ethics of public relations practitioners and have shown that the standards of honesty and ethics assigned to practitioners are generally low, and also lower than those assigned to, for example, business executives, clergymen and journalists (cf. Pratt 1991). This has led to much debate and theorising on the question of ethics in public relations.

The basic dilemma of public relations is that a practitioner must serve the **interests** of his or her organisation, as well as the interests of society. Added to this dilemma are the **number of publics** towards which a practitioner has an ethical responsibility. Newsom, Scott and VanSlyke Turk (1989) identify the following ten publics: clients, media, government agencies, educational institutions, information consumers, financial stakeholders such as stockholders and analysts, the community, the organisation's competition and critics, and other public relations practitioners. Furthermore, the **role of the practitioner** also has an effect on ethical decision making, with the *technician* having to act on decisions made by the employer/client, whilst the so-called *manager* is able to act more autonomously. Finally, **where** practitioners work, either as in-house employees or outside consultants acting under contract, can also influence their ethical obligations in a decision-making situation (cf. Bivins 1992).

A number of theories have been proposed as framework, for ethical decision making and conduct in public relations. We briefly review two theories which focus on the loyalties of the practitioner and on the environment in which he/she operates.

Loyalties and potential conflict situations in ethical decision making

Parsons (1993) is of the opinion that the modern public relations practitioner has four loyalties – to **self**, to an **organisation** (or to a client), to the **profession** and to **society**. Practitioners must first consider loyalties to themselves. Practitioners can be faced with situations where their beliefs and values differ from those of the organisation and they must decide how far they will go to uphold their values. Secondly, practitioners must consider their loyalty to the organisation which provides employment. Accepting a position in an organisation implies acceptance of its philosophy, and a practitioner's commitment, trust and loyalty may affect objective reasoning. This also applies when accepting a contract with a client. The third loyalty is towards the profession to uphold certain standards. Practitioners must decide whether to place recognition from their peers above recognition from organisational superiors who determine promotions and salaries. Finally, loyalty to society suggests that practitioners are accountable to society for any misdeeds. Practitioners need to determine when and to what extent these loyalties conflict.

A framework is suggested that might be used as a tool in situations where a practitioner's loyalties may be unclear and potential conflicts that may arise unknown. By analysing these conflicting loyalties practitioners are able to make defensible ethical decisions about how to meet their obligations. This framework is depicted in Figure 3.7.

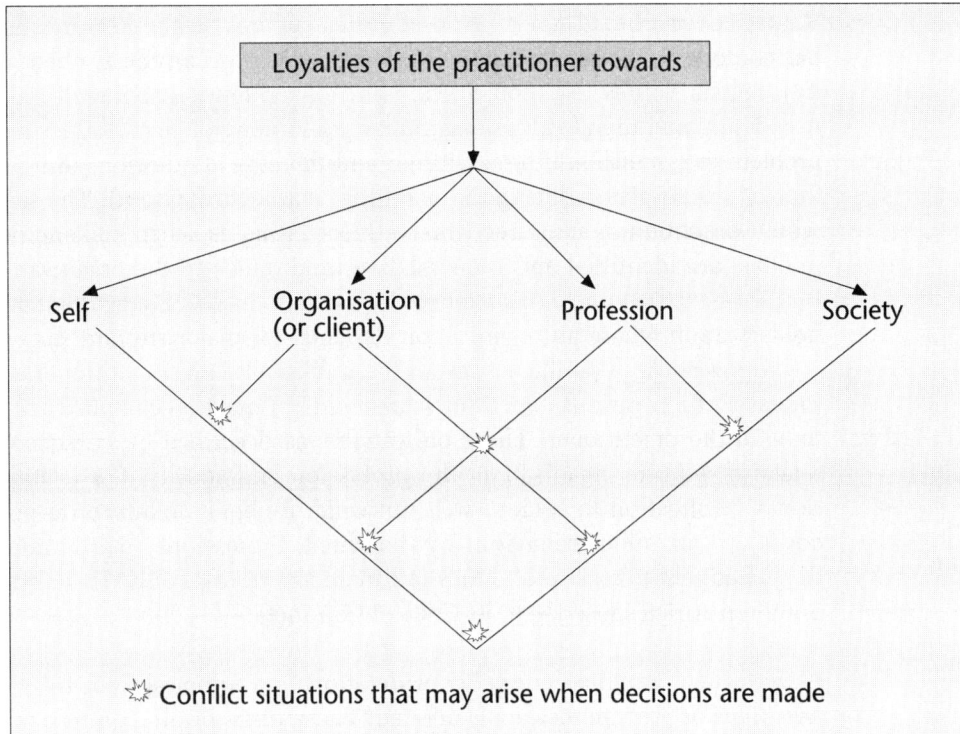

Figure 3.7 **Loyalties and potential conflict situations in ethical decision making**
(Adapted from Parsons 1993:54)

A systems model for ethical decision making in public relations

The systems model can be adapted to ethical decision making in public relations by identifying the relevant inputs and the proper decision making levels at which decisions are made (cf. Bivins 1992).

Simplistically stated, systems theory basically means a process whereby resources are received from the environment (input), processed (throughput) and products and services are produced and then returned to the environment (output). Feedback is then sought to determine the effects of the output (cf. *Course book 4* [Rensburg 1996], Unit 3 for a discussion of the systems approach to organisations). For public relations, input is information which indicates any opportunities or threats to the system's stability, and throughput is organising the information and formulating responses. Output is released into the environment as public relations campaigns in order to restore stability or make use of opportunities. Feedback provides the effects of the communication on the recipients and allows for further adjustment in the system. These processes in the system (input, throughput, output and feedback) can be equated with the four stages of the public relations process, namely problem definition and situation analysis, planning, implementation and evaluation (cf. Unit 2 for a discussion on the process approach to public relations). The entire four-step process is one of decision making. Decisions are made at every stage as to the importance of information for a complete understanding of the issue (threat or opportunity).

The process begins with the recognition of a problem or issue (**input**). This is the first level at which the practitioner needs to recognise his own values and principles. For example, a practitioner who is opposed to abortion would have strong conflicting values if he/she were to become involved in a proabortion campaign. Values cover a broad range of possibilities such as aesthetic values (something is harmonious or pleasing), professional values (e.g. promptness, client confidentiality), logical values (e.g. consistency and competency), sociocultural values (e.g. hard work) and moral values (e.g. honesty and nonviolence). Values relevant to the problem or issue should be identified and the ethical questions and potential conflict situations stated during the planning phase (**throughput**). The second level at which practitioners must recognise ethical issues is when stakeholders (relevant publics) are identified and their relative importance to the organisation analysed. Bivins (1992:376) refers to stakeholders as *claimants* and suggests that those stakeholders upon whom an organisation depends for major support (e.g. clients) have the strongest claim on the actions of the public relations practitioner. However, the interests of the various claimants (stakeholders) must be balanced with the obligations of the practitioner. These obligations, as described by Parsons (1993:52–53) relate to self, the organisation, the profession and society. For example, a practitioner's obligation to society will outweigh a client's claim on a practitioner to cover up fraudulent behaviour by the client. Professional public relations practitioners adhere to a code of ethics (all members of the Public Relations Institute of Southern Africa subscribe to its Code of Conduct).

A third level at which ethical considerations are important occurs where alternative plans or programmes are generated. These plans or programmes must be evaluated by taking all the possible consequences of each one into account. This is done by asking who will be affected by the decision, how they will be affected, and how the answers to these first two questions affect a practitioner's decisions in terms of objectives, alternative strategies and implementation. When an alternative action is chosen, a fourth level of ethical decision making arises. Bivins (1992:374) suggests applying certain analytical frameworks to the final choice of a plan of action, namely:

▶ **Consequential** – considering the consequences of the action to all **claimants,** as well as the potential outcomes.

▶ **Rule-based** – determining whether the proposed action complies with set rules or codes.

Once the final decision has been made regarding the choice of an alternative, and communication and action are implemented in the environment (**output**), the reactions of all stakeholders are carefully monitored and evaluated so that the practitioner can defend his/her decision (**feedback**). If a strong ethical component is present throughout the process, defence of decisions should not be difficult for the practitioner.

By applying the above process, Bivins (1992:365–383) combines the systems model with the process approach to public relations to produce a model for ethical decision making in public relations.

ACTIVITY

Review Case 2.1 in Unit 2. If you were the public relations practitioner involved in this case:

1 How would you describe your loyalties in terms of Parsons's (1993) theory?

2 Identify and describe potential conflict situations that may arise as a result of your loyalties.

3 Describe the ethical decisions that may arise during each phase of the campaign.

The paradigmatic struggle in public relations

One of the problems facing public relations today is the lack of a common framework. This should already have become apparent to you when you were introduced to various definitions of public relations and the concomitant difficulty in finding a universally acceptable definition (cf. Unit 2 for a discussion of the definitions of public relations). The problem in achieving a universally accepted definition of public relations is due to the so-called paradigmatic struggle in public relations which is rooted in the lack of consensus as to what public relations really is and does. A **paradigm** can be defined as a model or pattern of thinking about a problem. Paradigms are important because they delineate a field and control what and how phenomena are studied in that field. A number of different views, based on various assumptions and different goals, exist in public relations. Nevertheless, one generally accepted view is that public relations entails **persuasion** and **communication** and operates according to a **four-step process**. Beyond this view, the practice of public relations and related research constantly shifts from one model or *paradigm* to the next. Various authors categorise these models in different ways and a brief mention of some of the approaches and models will serve as an introduction to this particular debate.

Botan (1993:107–110) suggests that there are two branches of public relations, namely the **applied** branch and the **theoretical** branch, and that each of these describes public relations from a different perspective. The *applied* branch describes public relations from a traditionally business-oriented perspective, that is, its role in organisation–publics relationships. Some public relations theories and models that fall within this category are the process theory, the systems model, the rhetorical model and the symmetrical and asymmetrical models (cf. Unit 2 for a discussion of these models). The *theoretical* branch first describes the role of public relations in society as a whole and then its role in supporting business. Questions on how public relations is used to contribute to society as a whole are relevant to the theoretical branch. Theories that can be distinguished under this category are the social-scientific theories such as the persuasion and learning effects theory, the social learning theory and the low-involvement theory (cf. Section 3.3 for a discussion of these theories).

The major problem in public relations is determining how effective it is and according to which model or theory public relations work should be evaluated. Hallahan (1993:197–205) identifies at least seven paradigms for assessing public relations efforts. Each paradigm focuses on a different focal question according to which public relations can be evaluated.

- In the *process paradigm* public relations is examined as a series of routine or accepted procedures, often as a continuous cycle. Public relations is assessed by determining if all four steps in the process, namely problem definition, planning, implementation and evaluation, were followed. If all four steps were followed, public relations should be successful; in other words, the **activities** conducted by the practitioner are analysed.

- The *plan or programme paradigm* examines public relations within the context of a work plan or campaign and public relations effectiveness is determined by whether the campaign was well executed in terms of strategies, objectives, tactics and within the budget. Although the activities in terms of a process are not analysed, the basis for analysis is still the **efforts** of the practitioner rather than the results of the campaign.

- According to the *communication/practice style paradigm* public relations is assessed on the basis of the methods or techniques of communication used. Evaluation occurs by asking if the principles of effective communication were incorporated and, as was the case with the previous paradigm, the focus is on analysing the practitioner's **efforts**, rather than the results of the campaign.

- The *organisational/managerial effectiveness paradigm,* suggests that public relations is effective when management is satisfied with the effort; in other words, public relations is deemed successful if the expectations of management are met. This includes how effective the working relationship between management and the public relations practitioner is. Since **organisational expectations** are the basis of analysis of public relations in an organisation, its success will differ in different organisations.

- In the *systems paradigm* public relations is regarded as an effort to strike a balance between an organisation and its environment and the effectiveness of public relations is determined by whether the equilibrium is maintained. In other words, the success of public relations depends on how well an organisation and its publics build consensus and reduce conflicts. **Organisational** and **environmental expectations** form the basis for analysing public relations.

The above five paradigms fall within the so-called **applied branch** of public relations suggested by Botan (1993:107–110).

- In the *behavioural paradigm* public relations is examined in terms of changes in the knowledge, attitudes or behaviour of individuals or groups. Public relations effectiveness depends on whether a desired change took place in predispositions or actual patterns of behaviour. Public relations is analysed in terms of the **impact** of public relations efforts on individuals and publics.

- The *social problems paradigm* examines public relations as a response to sociological or political problems or opportunities. The focus of public relations is on the group rather than on the individual, and public opinion in terms of issues. The effectiveness of public relations is evaluated according to whether the social problem was satisfactorily **resolved**.

The above two paradigms fall within the so-called **theoretical branch** of public relations suggested by Botan (1993:107–110).

It is evident from the above that a redefinition of the public relations domain is necessary in order to adequately separate public relations from other fields. A more coherent body of knowledge according to which public relations effectiveness can be assessed is also required.

Review the seven paradigms suggested by Hallahan (1993). Identify the focal point of each paradigm and the basis used for analysing the effectiveness of public relations.

Case 3.1

"GOOD LUCK BOKKE" South African Airways/ Rugby World Cup 1995 Campaign

Introduction

It is widely recognised that the inception of the Rugby World Cup (RWC) as an independent entity within the game has since 1987 placed the rugby union on a course of universal acceptance and dynamic expansion. The Rugby World Cup takes place (as is the case with most other major events) on a four-yearly basis. It is one of the few sports other than the Olympics, the Soccer World Cup and World Track and Field events which draws such vast numbers of spectators both on the field as well as in the media, particularly television. For example, the Rugby World Cup drew more than 2,5 billion viewers in 1995.

South African Airways (SAA) decided to become a major sponsor of the Rugby World Cup for three very important reasons, quite apart from the fact that the event was taking place in South Africa.

The first reason related to the obvious commercial benefit to be derived from carrying passengers to South Africa for the event. These passengers came from countries where enthusiasm for rugby is very high, such as Australia, the United Kingdom, New Zealand, France and Argentina. The second reason related to SAA's status as an international airline and included the potential for exposure in markets not traditionally reached, for example in countries such as America, Japan and African and Eastern European countries. The third reason related to the airline's finding a new audience in South Africa amongst people who had previously not regarded SAA as part of their national culture.

Planning

SAA realised right from the start that there were two key issues which had to be taken into account in planning the campaign. The first issue was SAA's practical ability, from a logistics point of view, to handle the increase in passenger traffic over the two-month period during which most of the rugby enthusiasts would arrive in South Africa. SAA could also not ignore the fact that a person visiting South Africa would not only travel to and from the country but would also use many other services such as accommodation, taxis, buses, restaurants and airports. Visitors would also make use of the opportunity to see South Africa as a tourist destination. SAA saw itself as a link in this chain. The aim was to move all passengers successfully through the

➡

various stages of their journey and included support of passengers before and after flights.

The second issue related to the enormous potential for publicity on both an international and local scale. The investment SAA was making in the Rugby World Cup would have a return in terms of SAA's positioning as an international airline. However, greater than this was SAA's desire to find a new audience within South Africa after all the dynamic changes of recent years. SAA saw this as potentially the greatest long-term benefit that could be derived from involvement in the RWC. The aim was therefore twofold: firstly, to position SAA as an international airline and, secondly, to create awareness of SAA amongst an audience that was previously largely unaware of, neutral or negative towards the airline.

Since SAA, and indeed South Africa as well, had never before been involved in an event of such magnitude, planning had to start early. Two years prior to the actual event, SAA had already identified specific key areas where action had to be taken:

▶ the movement of spectators, media, teams and officials, which is the core business of the airline;

▶ airport logistics;

▶ marketing and promotions; and

▶ internal communication.

Campaign implementation

The movement of spectators, media, teams and officials

SAA first addressed the issue of physically finding the ways and means of moving all the potential visitors into and around the country. This proved operationally possible and was, indeed, successful. This included the movement of international media, teams and officials. To SAA this was a key area because it was the first experience many of these people would have of South Africa. Certain actions were taken, for example in-flight staff were briefed on the handling of passengers for this specific event, which meant that they had to familiarise themselves not only with general information on South Africa but also with the rugby events themselves in order to be able to answer the variety of queries expected. However, since SAA had positioned itself as a link in the travel chain, it could not divorce itself from the passengers once they had arrived in the country. A system was therefore put in place whereby the airline could liaise with the relevant people in each of the cities where the events would take place. This system, described in the next section, encompassed all the peripheral activities such as overland transport, accommodation, tourist and rugby activities.

Airport logistics

Besides an overall steering committee – called the RWC Operations Co-ordination Centre – which was allocated the task of co-ordinating logistics and promotions in each city where an event was to take place, SAA also had local committees and public relations staff in each city. They would deal with issues such as guiding visitors on the next step of their journey once they had arrived in a particular city. SAA did not leave passengers when they left the aircraft. This personal contact with passengers and the service provided proved to be one of the most powerful public relations exercises in the campaign. This exercise was also exceptionally cost-effective.

Internal communication

Preparing SAA staff through internal communication covered two main areas. The first area concerned briefings to check-in staff, in-flight cabin crew and ground staff at points of arrival. Specific procedures for handling and relating to RWC supporters had to be performed, for example special ticketholders with a picture of Chester Williams were distributed. Staff were also prepared for the handling of the more "exuberant" supporters who might create problems aboard. In this way all predictable eventualities were taken into consideration and staff prepared in the use of public relations, with the emphasis on dealing with the individual rather than the crowd.

The second area covered was to prepare SAA staff to make concessions in passenger handling. SAA could not work within the normal boundaries of reservations, airport or flight procedures and staff had to be prepared to use initiative to handle problems.

Marketing and promotions

The first public relations initiative that SAA took at the start of the campaign was to involve both local and international media in rugby events that took place prior to the Rugby World Cup. This began in New Zealand and Scotland where media representatives were invited to attend matches and promotional functions together with SAA staff to meet the **new** Springboks. The reason for doing this was to proactively position SAA as a major sponsor early on and to create awareness of its involvement in the Rugby World Cup before the international media came to South Africa. This also provided an opportunity for SAA to become a "familiar face" when the media representatives arrived in South Africa.

With the advertising and merchandising campaign SAA took a "nontraditional" approach. Since the contract allowing SAA to use all RWC logos, slogans, et cetera, had been signed two years prior to the event, the traditional approach would have been to make use of all media, together with other sponsors, over a long period (approximately one year) prior to the event. SAA decided to launch its advertising campaign initially with pure "teasers", only in poster form, of which an example is depicted in Figure 3.8. These posters were distributed in each city, through service providers, municipalities, corporations, clients, et cetera.

SAA's main thrust was to concentrate most of its advertising in the two months prior to the start of the event in print media, and one month prior to the event on television. The aim of this approach was to capture and build on the enthusiasm of the nation for the event. Other sponsors took the traditional route of advertising over longer periods, such as two years prior to the event.

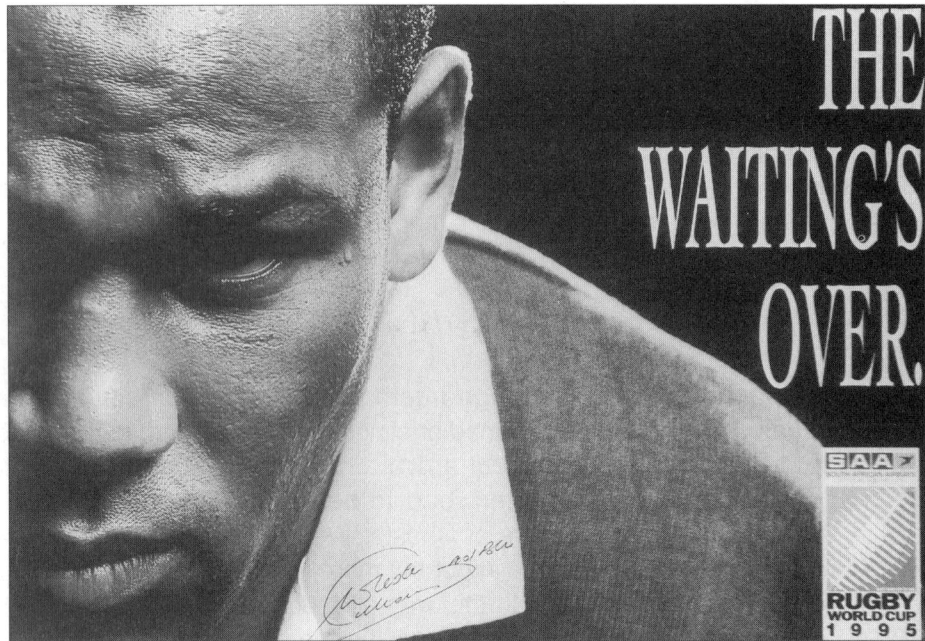

Figure 3.8 **SAA poster advertisement**

Like all the other sponsors SAA was afforded the opportunity of creating mer-chandising material (e.g. T-shirts, caps, badges, bags, et cetera, with the RWC and SAA logos). SAA used the merchandising material in two ways. The first was as a promotional tool to reach SAA's existing client base, by giving items such as caps and bags to SAA clients, including corporations, Voyager members and influential political and business people. The second required a special dispensation from the RWC and allowed SAA to provide the informal sector with these items. Vendors in the informal sector could sell the items at the major games and all SAA required was that the costs of the items be covered; the profits then accrued to the vendors in the informal sector. This succeeded in reaching people who had previously never regarded SAA as part of their own culture or who did not associate with rugby, which was regarded until that time as an elitist Afrikaner sport.

The advertising campaign was aimed at a broader audience than the tradi-tional rugby enthusiasts. Advertising covered print media and television, as well as outdoor media such as billboards, particularly at airports. SAA also joined forces with local organisations such as the Durban Municipality, pro-viding them with material which was initially used to advertise the event in Durban. This material then became strategically important since the munici-pality decided to use it to assist people in getting to the various matches and functions, for example SAA/RWC posters were placed at strategic points, publicised through the media, and directed people to their destinations.

The approach taken in developing the advertising message was to encom-pass not only SAA's involvement in the event but to embody the broader vision of a new South Africa. This was captured in the slogan "The waiting is over!". Once the campaign began the general public adopted this slogan with enormous enthusiasm. This was particularly true for the "new" audiences who viewed this slogan as an announcement of the arrival of the **new** South Africa. According to a survey conducted on television audiences who watched the various matches and the profiles of viewers, the responses indi-cated a high level of interest from most groups. For example, with Xhosa speakers as many as 77 per cent of respondents gave a positive response.

On-field advertising of the various events through television coverage and print media showed SAA as the official carrier for the RWC and reached local and international audiences. An example is provided in Figure 3.9.

Figure 3.9 **An example of on-field advertising**

Public relations used during the event itself included inviting valuable clients to watch games and be entertained prior to and after matches in all the cities.

Promotional items were given to all invited clients as mementos. In all cases the media were invited to the games as guests of SAA. As enthusiasm increased with each victory that the South African team achieved, SAA was able to enhance and increase its role in the whole event – it was drawn into the momentum where it almost became part of this winning team.

The most spectacular public relations event was undoubtedly the fly-over. Approximately three months before the RWC event started SAA decided that a fly-past of its Boeing 747-200 would add to the lustre of the final ceremony. When SAA realised that the Springboks were taking part in the final match, three issues became very important. The first was that SAA was suddenly part of a **winning** team as sponsor. The second was that it created an inordinate interest from SAA's client base to attend matches. The third was that SAA, although having had decided on a fly-past irrespective of who played, realised that it now promised to be a far more spectacular opportunity (and a first in aviation in the world at any sporting event). Subsequently SAA decided to use the aircraft as a symbol of all the hopes and dreams of South Africa becoming the world champions. This was a public relations opportunity which presented itself in the final stages of the campaign and SAA used it to talk to the South African public, the Springbok team and international audiences by emblazoning a message ("Good Luck Bokke") painted in bold letters under the aircraft, as shown in Figure 3.10. This can be regarded as a public relations coup, since this fly-over is still shown on many television stations internationally.

Figure 3.10 **Photograph of "Good luck Bokke" fly-over**

Problems experienced

Some problems did occur but these were mainly logistical, such as reservations problems and tour costings. Problems that occurred in the public relations campaign related mainly to a period where the media were negative towards SAA as a result of the logistical problems. Constant communication with the media became vital.

Since SAA had taken on the responsibility of being a link in the travel chain, problems which occurred outside the airline's core sphere of activities also had to be addressed by the airline public relations staff.

Evaluation of campaign

The campaign proved enormously successful. RWC and SAA's association with the event achieved two things. The first was that it positioned SAA as a mainstream international carrier which brought subsequent financial benefits.

The media exposure and the relationships built with representatives of the international (and local) media proved to be successful in terms of SAA's positioning as an international player.

The most important consequence of all the elements of this campaign was that it positioned SAA as the airline of the people and it made it possible to cast off the cloak of being perceived as a pre-apartheid airline serving only a small portion of the population. SAA had become recognisably a national asset. This made it possible for SAA to sponsor, with great confidence, support and enthusiasm, the "BAFANA BAFANA" African Cup of Nations event. The infrastructure was in place to handle such an event, the expertise was available and the recognition that SAA could handle such an event as sponsor was no longer in doubt.

Concluding note

SAA became involved in the Rugby World Cup without the benefit of any prior experience in terms of such major events. The success of the campaign and its positive long-term implications for the airline can be ascribed to the way the people involved in the campaign were totally committed to ensuring its ultimate success. SAA and all its partners in this event were dedicated and enthusiastic throughout and their commitment to making it a success for South Africa was the driving force behind the success.

SAA used the opportunity provided by the Rugby World Cup to present itself to audiences throughout the world and to re-establish itself as South Africa's national carrier.

The Corporate Relations Department of South African Airways ensured a high profile presence in the media throughout the event by means of communicating on a daily basis.

SAA's corporate relations spokespeople addressed the media at a number of SAA media conferences and were available to attend to media queries on a 24-hour basis. This assisted in creating the positive image that South African Airways was prepared to handle the big event and to deal with any eventualities.

ACTIVITY

Read Case 3.1 "Good luck Bokke" South African Airways/Rugby World Cup Campaign and identify the public relations and promotional activities which were used.

Summary

From a theoretical perspective three distinct but related functions of public relations were identified: an *interpretative function*, a *management function* and a *communication function*. The relationship between public relations and *persuasion*, *propaganda* and *information* was discussed. The communication function of public relations was also described from a practical perspective by explaining how two of its most important tools are used, namely *advertising* and *publicity*.

Certain critical issues in public relations were discussed. The issues and dilemmas of *public opinion* and *image building* as part of public relations were described. A distinction was made between *corporate image*, *corporate identity*, *corporate personality* and *corporate culture*. The importance of social responsibility was highlighted, as were the issues of *ethics* and *ethical decision making* in public relations. Finally, the so-called *paradigmatic* struggle in public relations was described in terms of some of the models identified by various authors.

A case on the campaign launched by South African Airways for the Rugby World Cup was included to provide an example of the use of media and aspects related to corporate image.

SUGGESTED READING

Baskin, O. & Aronoff, C.E. 1992. *Public relations. The profession and the practice.* 3rd edition. Dubuque, Ia: Wm. C. Brown.

Cutlip, S.M., Center, A.H. & Broom, G.M. 1994. *Effective public relations.* 7th edition. Englewood Cliffs, NJ: Prentice-Hall.

Kaye, M. 1994. *Communication management.* Englewood Cliffs, NJ: Prentice-Hall.

Lubbe, B.A. & Puth, G. (eds) 1994. *Public relations in South Africa. A management reader.* Durban: Butterworths.

Newsom, D., Scott, A. & VanSlyke Turk, J. 1989. *This is PR. The realities of public relations.* Belmont, Calif: Wadsworth.

Seitel, F.P. 1995. *The practice of public relations.* 6th edition. Englewood Cliffs, NJ: Prentice-Hall.

Introduction to Advertising

George Angelopulo

Danie du Plessis

UNIT

4

Overview

In this unit we look at advertising. We pay particular attention to the position of advertising within the marketing process, and note its historical development. Some of the more pertinent theories of advertising are discussed, and we consider one model for the implementation of an advertising campaign. We give an overview of the functions and powers that are ascribed to advertising.

Objectives

At the end of this unit you should be able to:

1   Give an overview of the history of advertising and its international and South African development.

2   Define marketing both narrowly and widely.

3   Define the position of advertising within the marketing mix.

4   Describe the categories of advertising and provide examples of each.

5   Describe the traditional theories of advertising.

6   Describe and apply Baker's Relevance Accessibility Model of Advertising Effectiveness.

7   Describe the advertising campaign process.

8   Identify the primary areas of advertising research.

9   Describe the functions and powers that are most commonly ascribed to advertising.

4.1   INTRODUCTION

Advertising has become such a part of our lives that we barely notice its presence around us. The mass media to which we are exposed are permeated with paid-for messages, and the very concept of these media has extended beyond the traditional – today advertising is evident on our buildings, in our art and sport, and even on the tickets that we receive to attend sports and arts events!

Advertising can be viewed from many perspectives. We look at advertising from the point of view of the communicator, but we do not ignore the audience. The position of the audience is considered in the analysis of the advertising message and in our discussion of the functions and power of advertising.

Moving from a historical analysis of the advertising phenomenon, we shift to an analysis of the role of advertising in the existence of organisations, and the processes of advertising implementation. In this unit we further consider advertising as an academic pursuit, and in terms of the effects, powers and functions that are ascribed to it.

4.2   A BRIEF OVERVIEW OF THE HISTORY AND DEVELOPMENT OF ADVERTISING

Key terms to understand and remember

advertising agents	barkers
branded products	broadsides
column	crier
handbills	periodicals
signboards	space salesmen
type size	

Advertising before the modern era

Although contemporary advertising as we know it is less than a hundred years old, its roots can be traced far back in history. The underlying concept of advertising – the transfer of information – can be traced back to ancient history. Babylonian merchants employed *barkers*. A barker would advertise his employer's business orally by shouting his wares to passers-by. Over the door of the merchant was hung the symbol of his trade. The first written advertisements also appeared in the Babylonian era. These first advertisements were announcements of rewards for the return of runaway slaves with a description of the runaways – these were probably posted in the temples (cf. Presbrey 1968:3–4).

The only form of commercial advertising known to the people of early Egypt was the *crier*. The crier would announce the arrival of ships and the offering of items from their cargoes. It was also a custom of early Greeks to affix advertisements to the statues of their infernal deities and demons calling down the vengeance of the gods on those who had found lost articles and had not returned them. The later Greeks also made use of public criers who were selected for their pleasing voices and elocutionary ability. They were used mainly to advertise auctions of slaves and animals. *Signboards* outside shop doors are known to have been a form of advertising in ancient Athens. In ancient times signs and symbols were used to mark the location of houses of commerce. For example, in ancient Greece an inn was indicated by a pine cone, a practice that stemmed from the habit of sealing wine jugs with pine resin (cf. Presbrey 1968:4–5).

It is in records of Rome, Herculaneum and Pompeii that we find advertising in the modern sense of the word. This advertising consisted of persuasive announcements painted on walls in black or red. Examples of these kinds of advertisements uncovered by excavators in the ruins of Pompeii indicate that written advertising came soon after the spread of literacy in ancient Rome (from 200 BC onwards). In Pompeii there were walls that may have been controlled by an advertising contractor, for they carried a variety of painted announcements of theatrical performances, sports, baths and gladiatorial exhibitions. The walls selected were at places where crowds gathered or where people passed in great numbers (cf. Presbrey 1968:6–7).

ACTIVITY

When next you find yourself in a business area, observe the way in which shops make use of signs and symbols (other than their names) on signboards to identify their trade.

Written advertising disappeared with the decline in literacy that followed the fall of the Roman Empire in the fourth century, and it lasted through ten centuries of the Middle Ages (more or less from the fourth to the fourteenth centuries). During the Middle Ages advertising was limited mainly to signs. By the fourteenth century these were painted on wood, but they were mostly symbols. Barkers were used mainly for official purposes but gradually were again used for commercial purposes. In 1141 in France, twelve criers organised a company and obtained a charter from Louis VII giving them the exclusive privilege of town crying in their province. Five of them were assigned to crying wines on behalf of the taverns. They went about extolling the wines, each man crying for a particular tavern and giving samples of the wine. For each blowing of the horn and sampling to the gathered group, this advertising man would receive a small fee from the tavern. Also in Paris there were numerous wine criers. In the thirteenth century, town criers were in general use and were paid by the merchants whose wares they touted. They sometimes even used songs and rhymes – very much like the music used in today's advertising jingles (cf. Presbrey 1968:10–11).

After the Renaissance of the fourteenth, fifteenth and later centuries, the invention of the printing press and subsequent improvement of literacy, the media began to play an important role in society. This enabled the advertising message to be relayed much faster and to reach more people than ever before.

The international advertising industry

The British roots

The use of the word *advertisement* in the modern sense first appears in 1655 when book publishers began to head their announcements, *An advertisement of books newly published*. By 1660 the word became generally used as a heading for commercial announcements. A seventeenth century man who saw the possibilities of advertising was John Houghton. He was a merchant, publicist and book reviewer who started a circular called *Collection for improvement of husbandry and trade* (cf. Presbrey 1968:56). At first the advertisements in Houghton's price bulletin dealt only with books, but he had general advertising in mind from the beginning. He suggested advertising for other products. The advertising in Houghton's paper at first was all of the registry office type with the advertiser remaining anonymous until application for his name was made to the editor, who wrote the advertisements in the first person. Later on the names of advertisers were included and the next improvement was the inclusion of addresses (cf. Presbrey 1968:56–60).

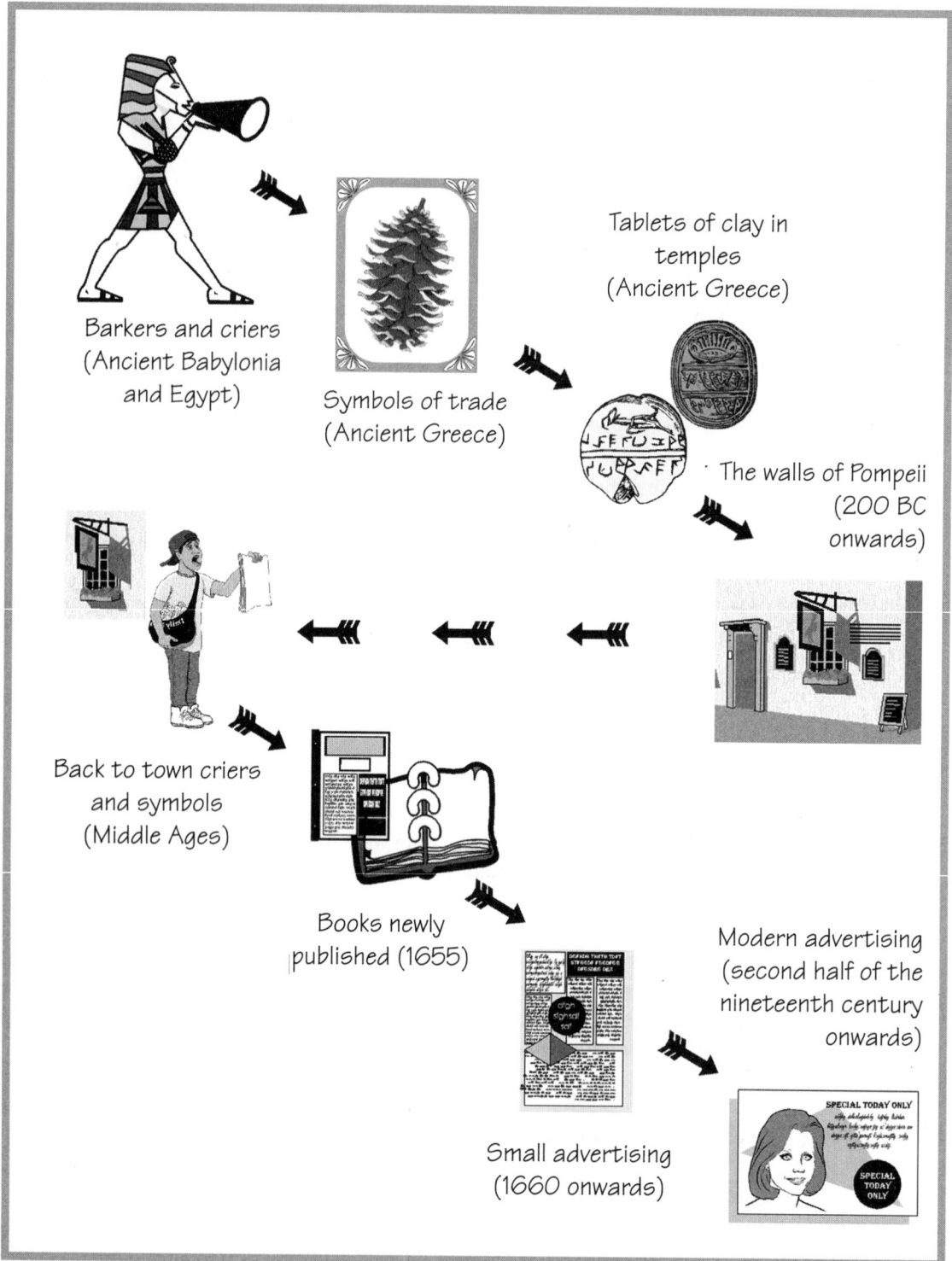

Figure 4.1 **Historical development of advertising**

The customary charge in London was a shilling for an advertisement, whatever the number of lines (usually eight to ten lines). The first paper to establish a line rate was the *London Country Gentleman's Courant* at the rate of twopence a line. On 1 December 1702 the first English daily newspaper appeared on the scene – the *London Daily Courant* (cf. Presbrey 1968:62).

In 1712, during the reign of Queen Anne, a tax on newspapers and advertisements was introduced. With illiteracy in England as high as elsewhere in Europe and the New World during the eighteenth century, the British government, instead of encouraging the spread of the press and a growth in literacy, put a tax on every copy of a newspaper. Every advertisement was also taxed three shillings and a sixpence, regardless of size, with the result that newspapers could not survive profitably. This tax was meant to control seditious libel and the funds collected were used to maintain a licence bureau. In later years the tax was continued as a source of revenue for general purposes. This tax was levied for nearly 150 years with devastating effects for the news and advertising industries in England. The effects of the newspaper tax in Britain can be judged by comparing the situation to that in the United States of America (USA) in 1850. The USA, with no tax on newspapers or advertising and with about 23 million inhabitants against 27 million people in Britain, had more than four times as many newspapers and more than four times the circulation. The annual subscription rate of a London daily in 1853 ranged from 30 to 45 dollars, but in the USA the price of a popular daily was 5 dollars a year (cf. Presbrey 1968:74–76).

After the introduction of restrictions on the press and the advertising industry in England, other countries would take the lead in the advertising business. Our focus now shifts to the USA. In that country the media and the art of advertising flourished because the media were free to fulfil their function in society. England laid a firm foundation for modern advertising and the later development of successful advertising ideas and commercial publicity.

ACTIVITY

Contact any local or regional newspaper close to you and enquire about their advertising tariffs. Ask them to explain the units (col/cm) that are used to sell advertising space.

United States of America (USA)

The printing press was a prerequisite for printed advertising. The first printing press in the USA arrived in 1638 and was imported by Harvard University at Cambridge – the beginning of what is now known as the Harvard University Press. It was fifty-two years after the arrival of the first press before the first attempt was made to print a newspaper in America (cf. Presbrey 1968:118–119).

By the end of the American Revolution (1775–1783) there were forty-three weekly newspapers in existence and in 1784 the first daily newspaper was established in Philadelphia. The topics of advertisements of the time consisted mostly of land, runaway slaves and transportation. Only about 20 per cent of the advertisements were lists of goods offered for sale by local merchants and descriptions of books newly published. These were simple announcements. The first daily newspaper had 10 *columns* of advertising in a paper of 16 columns. The first New York daily in 1785 consisted mostly of advertising, interspersed with a thin sprinkling of news. This ratio of advertisements to news continued without change right into the 1800s. By the end of the 1780s paper was so scarce that the *type size* went from standard 12 point to 6 point – a standard that would last for almost seventy years. This had two effects on advertising. Firstly, it limited newspaper advertising to abbreviated statements of product lists. Secondly, it moved creative advertising to *handbills*, trade cards and *broadsides*, which are one-shot advertisements similar to the magazine advertisements of today (cf. Goodrum & Dalrymple 1990:13–16).

Cut out a page of classified advertising in any newspaper. Hold the classified advertisements against the first editorial page of the newspaper. Compare the type size and typography of classified advertising in a newspaper to that of the main body of the newspaper and describe the differences.

By 1850 the American nation was booming and industrial production was expanding. The need to advertise new products grew with the increase in production. Newspaper advertisements were more off-putting than ever. Most major newspapers required that no advertisement could be longer than two or three lines and all advertisements had to be in small type and in the same type style throughout the paper. No advertisement could be wider than one column. The reason for this was the belief that to do otherwise would be unfair to the small advertiser (cf. Goodrum & Dalrymple 1990:19–20).

One of the great early American advertisers was P T Barnum. Although Barnum was responsible for a heavy increase in newspaper advertising in the last half of the nineteenth century, his main contribution was to outdoor advertising. He was much more original and creative in his printed advertising in the form of pamphlets, posters and other media. In his newspaper advertising Barnum did not show the originality he displayed in other printed advertising. Barnum's service to advertising was in awakening commercial America to the possibilities of publicity and his success sold the idea of advertising. Barnum grouped all his efforts – news-column publicity, posters, handbills, newspaper advertising, parades and street stunts – under the word *advertising* (cf. Presbrey 1968:224–226).

In the final years before the Civil War (1861–1865), newspapers proliferated and their readership increased throughout the community. Improved technology, adequate paper supply and increasingly prosperous merchants led to the growth of the advertising industry. It was not easy to advertise because the location and number of newspapers were unknown. None of the newspapers knew how many readers they had and there were no set rates for commercial accounts – these were bargained over during each submission. The extent of these unknown factors produced the first *advertising agents*, the first of whom were merely newspaper *space salesmen*. The two that are usually credited with creating the idea were VB Palmer who started in Boston in 1841 and soon opened offices in New York and Philadelphia, and John L Hooper who had an office in New York (cf. Goodrum & Dalrymple 1990:21). The advertising agencies started as independent brokers between the newspapers and advertisers. By the last part of the nineteenth century the agencies began to offer their services to advertisers, promising help with the writing of the advertisements, seeing that they were placed in the best possible positions, and presenting themselves as allies of the advertisers by trying to get the best possible deals from the newspapers (cf. Goodrum & Dalrymple 1990:20–22).

One of the most famous of the advertising agents in the USA was Albert Davis Lasker. He realised that there was more to advertising than just the repetition of the brand name. He believed that advertising was salesmanship in print and his technique was to find the news in the product and then tell readers why they should buy the product. He was assisted by a brilliant writer, Claude Hopkins, who believed that products and markets had to be researched before producing an advertisement. It was, however, George Batten who conceived the idea of providing a media and creative service in one agency at no additional cost to his clients – he would be paid through the standard commission that he would negotiate with the publications in whose pages he placed the advertising (cf. Barenblatt & Sinclair 1989:17; Lears 1994:199).

After the Civil War a new era opened for the advertising profession. Wartime shortages led to the invention of wood pulp newsprint, and paper became cheaper and more abundant than ever before. The war also caused women to enter the labour market. It became possible for them to buy basic commodities (bread, soap, ready-made clothes) from the shops without the shame of being branded inadequate housewives. The manufacturers of soap and typewriters were the first to put pictures in their advertisements others followed quickly. The single-column-no-display-type rule was broken and the techniques that had been developed for handbills and broadsides moved to the newspaper pages (cf. Goodrum & Dalrymple 1990:22–23).

Trademarking and *packaging* was a new development which had an effect on advertising. Before this development, basic commodities were bought in bulk and sold generically to consumers by the grocer. After the Civil War, trademarked products flooded the market. Although the *branded products* were more expensive than the traditional ones, the products were cleaner, better kept, and of consistent quality. Nationwide advertising introduced the trademarks to the readers and the copy told them why the products were better. The customer knew which brand to buy before entering the store. Advertising also played the role of introducing new products and explaining what they were and how they were to be used (cf. Goodrum & Dalrymple 1990:23–24).

The publication of magazines was also an important development with consequences for the advertising business. Magazines began as house organs for book-publishing houses. The first was *Harper's Magazine*, which was founded in 1850 (cf. Russel & Lane 1990:9). The *periodicals* did not immediately contribute directly to advertising advancement, but they very soon became essential in the intellectual life of the nation, thus creating a medium for the advertising that would follow. Some of the most famous writers in American literary history were closely connected to particular magazines. Mark Twain began writing for *Harper's Magazine* in 1866. For fourteen years after its establishment *Harper's Magazine* refused advertising (other than its own book announcements). *The Atlantic* was the first magazine to accept advertising and others followed slowly. *Scribner's Century* eventually broke away from the disinclination of the high-class literary periodical to canvass actively for advertisements. Full-page space in periodicals first appeared in the *Century* and then in *Harper's*. They were the first to demonstrate that large space was good business and not an extravagance (cf. Presbrey 1968:464–478; Russel & Lane 1990:9).

Various developments influenced the American advertising scene around the time of World War I. The invention of aspirin coupled with the passage of the Pure Food and Drug Act reduced the role of patent medicine advertisements, the most prominent advertisers up to that time. The advertising of patent medicines almost disappeared. The invention of the motorcar resulted in a sudden advertising war between competing companies which manufactured different car parts and accessories. During the war, two other changes appeared on the advertising scene. Firstly, the federal government made use for the first time of paid advertising to sell war bonds, recruit soldiers, generate female volunteers and underwrite relief programmes. These advertisements were so innovative and the quality of their artwork so high that they became the standard of advertising after the war. Secondly, during the war it became clear to advertisers that women played an important role in purchasing decisions. By the end of the war the advertising industry assumed that most advertisements were read by women and that most products were purchased by women. Emancipated women became the prime targets of advertising (cf. Goodrum & Dalrymple 1990:35–37).

The prosperity of the 1920s collapsed during the Great Depression (1929–1933). High unemployment rates and little money to spend resulted in fewer goods being sold. Many advertising agencies were wiped out and advertisers did not have much money to spend on advertising. They began asking questions about the effectiveness of advertising because they could not afford to advertise without being sure that every advertisement would be worth the money spent on it. This development introduced the *age of research*. George Gallup began polling and selling his results and Nielson began selling indexes of food and drug sales (cf. Goodrum & Dalrymple 1990:39). The agencies developed research methodologies to be able to explain, predict and quantify advertising effectiveness. At the same time advertising went for the "hard sell". This resulted in a backlash from two sides. The government introduced stringent regulatory measures and, from the consumer side, organisations developed that began to test and monitor (and publicise) products and product claims. Radio began to dominate the media scene with soap operas (so named for the soap companies that sponsored them), and national magazines with their large audiences were plentiful (cf. Goodrum & Dalrymple 1990:39–42).

The period after World War II was similar to the period after World War I. The major changes would come in the 1960s and 1970s. The design revolution led to the complete advertisement becoming a visual statement and not just a literary one. A new tradition developed where the copywriter and graphic artistic teams were assigned as equals to each new advertising project. In the 1960s the circulation of the major magazines became so large that they simply could not charge enough for their advertising space to print and distribute that many copies. Many of them simply went bankrupt and disappeared. The introduction of television advertising affected print advertising severely. The new generation of both copywriters and graphic designers were challenged to design the perfect television advertisement. The majority of goods had, however, become *parity products*, with five or more major companies that produced essentially the same thing (cf. Goodrum & Dalrymple 1990:43–45).

ACTIVITY

In a modern market you will find a variety of brands of a specific product (e.g. a personal computer with certain specifications and performance requirements). The various brands will be more or less equal with few differences between them. When you are next visiting the supermarket, compare the information on the packaging of your favourite washing powder with the information on the competition's labels. Can you substantiate your own preference on the strength of the information provided on the label?

The fact that products became more and more similar led to the segmentation of the audience (see the discussion on segmentation later in this unit). The need to refine the message and focus its audience put more emphasis on the important role of research. This costly activity exceeded the resources of the smaller agencies and gave rise to the development of large agencies when agencies combined, bought others and formed huge corporations that were able to survive in the highly competitive world of advertising (cf. Goodrum & Dalrymple 1990:42–47)

Figure 4.2 **Five Roses – then and now**

(© E.K. Wilshere-Preston – the original appeared in colour)

Five Roses – there is probably not a single South African who does not know this brand name and what it stands for. South Africans have made Five Roses their first choice in quality tea since its introduction to the country by Mr T W Beckett in 1909.

Since then the growth of Five Roses has been a two-way partnership between the brand and discerning tea drinkers who have continued to demand strength, aroma, flavour and the best of Ceylon from their favourite brand of tea. Five Roses has never compromised in its promise to deliver the very best. In fact, so important is the distinction of quality to the brand that, during World War II when tea was scarce, Becketts temporarily withdrew the brand.

Great brands are not just those that turn huge volumes and enjoy massive awareness, although Five Roses achieves in both these areas. A great brand is not defined by one with a large adspend, timeous updates and impressive promotional spends. Five Roses, however, enjoys all of these benefits too.

To define what makes Five Roses a great brand would be to look back on a near century of a rich and proud heritage – a period where Five Roses has been consistent in keeping its promise of quality. It has a continuing philosophy of innovation, be it in its advertising promotion, packaging, or in the variety of quality teas it now offers the South African tea drinker – at home or in the countless restaurants and hotels who have made it their choice. Now Five Roses has also become the choice abroad, being found as far afield as Saudi Arabia where tea is the main social drink.

All these things have made the Five Roses brand a truly great one. Since the inception of its proposition more than 50 years ago of "Nobody makes better tea than you and Five Roses" the company has felt no need to change this promise. The partnership between the brand and the consumer grows each year to a level of involvement that only a truly great brand can enjoy.

To Five Roses, brand building is a never-ending journey. Its path is to continually offer its loyal supporters, new and old, the very best in quality teas, year after year, cup after quality cup.

The South African advertising scene

Newspapers – On 16 August 1800 the Cape Colony's first newspaper appeared. The bilingual *Cape Town Gazette and African Advertiser/Kaapsche Stads Courant en Afrikaansche Berigter* was owned by slave dealers and privateers Alexander Walker and John Robertson (cf. Nelson 1990:8). The newspaper announced that the cost for advertisements would be in proportion to their length and position in the paper. The newspaper lasted only thirteen months because, among other reasons, it was seen as too expensive and charged too much for its advertising space. Thereafter it became the official government newspaper *The Cape of Good Hope Government Gazette*. In January 1824 George Greig established the weekly *South African Commercial Advertiser*. Of the eight pages of the first issue, more than four were filled with advertisements. In May of that year Lord Charles Somerset prohibited the *Commercial Advertiser*, but Greig was willing to produce the next issue only with advertisements. Somerset nonetheless sealed his presses (cf. Nelson 1990:8).

A year after the *Eastern Province Herald* appeared in Port Elizabeth, David Buchanan began the *Natal Witness* in Pietermaritzburg in 1846. One of the reasons for the success of this newspaper was the additional revenue generated through advertising. The first Dutch-Afrikaans weekly newspaper was *De Verzamelaar* which appeared in 1826. It was followed by *De Zuid-Afrikaan* in 1830. In January 1849 *De Kerkbode*, official mouthpiece of the Dutch Reformed Church, appeared and from the start indicated that it would accept advertising. *The Friend* was established in Bloemfontein 1850 and the *Natal Mercury* in 1852. The *Cape Argus* followed in 1857 with an announcement that it would offer the best medium for communicating with the general public. The *Cape Times and Daily Advertiser* appeared on the scene twenty years later. With the discovery of gold in the Transvaal in 1886, the *Eastern Star* moved to Johannesburg where it became *The Star* (cf. Sinclair & Barenblatt 1993:238–239; Nelson 1990:8–9).

The first newspaper aimed at black readers, *Imvo Zabantsundu*, was published in King Williams Town in 1884. The editor was John Tengo Jabavu, who had been the first journalist in South Africa to write in a black language. This newspaper was also the first newspaper to be written and owned by black people, and is still in existence today.

The press industry in South Africa today is dominated by four major press groups, but there are also smaller companies and individuals that produce smaller publications.

By 1910, products were generally illustrated by means of cartoons, and testimonials, both real and fabricated, were used to sell products. By the 1920s black and white photographs displaced the line drawings and in turn were displaced by colour after World War II. Only in the late 1950s was a library of local models established by advertising agencies to enable them to make use of local models instead of overseas photographs (cf. Nelson 1990:16).

Electronic media – The South African broadcasting history dates back to 1924, but it was not until 1951 that advertisers were able to make use of radio as a powerful advertising medium. The early radio broadcasting was privately owned, called JB, and served Johannesburg, Durban and eventually also Cape Town. In January 1927 the station was closed down. The station was rescued by I W Schlesinger, a wealthy businessman, but on 1 August 1936, by Act of Parliament, the company was sold to the South African Broadcasting Corporation (SABC). E H Cameron McClure, who became the head of the newly established commercial service in 1949, was the initiator of commercial radio for the SABC. The commercial station, Springbok Radio, came onto the airwaves on 1 May 1951. It quickly became a favourite with both the public and the advertisers (cf. Barenblatt & Sinclair 1989:24).

There was such a huge demand for advertising time on Springbok Radio that commercial time was booked long in advance. The supply of commercial time could not cope with the huge demand for radio advertising. In the mid-sixties the SABC introduced three new radio stations not only to provide more advertising time but also to satisfy an entertainment need. The three stations, Radio Highveld, Radio Good Hope and Radio Port Natal were the initial users of the new FM broadcast network. In 1955 the Association of Advertisers pressed the SABC for another channel and asked the Minister in 1956 for a separate commercial station that would broadcast to the black population. The result was the introduction of Radio Bantu in 1960 (cf. Barenblatt & Sinclair 1989:25). Since then, eight of the public radio stations have been commercialised, and advertising money spent in the field of radio increased immensely.

The introduction of a television service was a long-awaited occasion for advertisers, and since the first broadcast of a television commercial in 1978, advertisers have recognised the size of the audience and the potency of the medium from an advertising point of view (cf. Sinclair & Barenblatt 1993:247). The SABC enjoyed a monopoly for a few years until M-Net was established in 1986. M-Net was the first private subscription television network in South Africa and the first that could challenge the SABC's monopoly. It belongs to a consortium of newspaper groups and was established because the English and Afrikaans newspaper groups objected to the loss of revenue as a result of the commercialisation of the SABC's television service. The government permitted the newspaper groups to start a commercial television channel to share in the advertising income from broadcasting.

The first major changes occurred only after political changes took place at the beginning of 1990. In 1990 the government appointed a task group under the leadership of Christo Viljoen (at the time chairman of the board of the SABC). One of the task group's main proposals was that an impartial Independent Broadcasting Authority (IBA) should be established to manage and control the spectrum of broadcasting and monitor the technical quality of broadcasts. The IBA was established in 1993.

The result of the establishment of the IBA was that various private community radio stations applied for broadcasting licences at the IBA. The IBA granted most of the licences for community radio stations under certain conditions. Some commercial broadcasters were (at the time of writing) still awaiting licences.

The introduction of satellite television in 1995 has had a further impact on the broadcasting scene in South Africa. In a few years many things have changed on the electronic media scene because of political, economic, social and technological developments – a process that is not yet finalised. At the time of writing most of the issues have not yet been resolved.

Other media – The cinema industry in South Africa survived the challenge of television and did well in the long term. Cinema advertising takes a substantial part of total advertising spending and is seen as a medium capable of reaching well-defined audiences in defined regional areas. Another advantage is that it may carry advertisements for products that are not allowed to be screened on television, such as cigarettes.

Outdoor advertising represents almost the same amount of advertising spending as cinema advertising and therefore comprises a substantial part of the advertising industry of South Africa (cf. Nelson 1990:17–18; Barenblatt & Sinclair 1989:24–25).

For the advertising industry, a new world has opened up with new challenges that relate to the targeting of audiences and the selection of media. The new electronic media, a dramatic increase in the number of radio stations, new publications aimed at specific markets and sociopolitical changes have impacted on the advertising industry in South Africa. Audiences are smaller and more dispersed at a given time because they can choose between tens of television and radio channels. The greater variety and competition, on the other hand, provide the opportunity for advertisers to target their audiences with more accuracy and more cost-effectively (cf. Gorton 1996:S16).

Advertising professionalism – The first advertising agents in South Africa opened their doors in the 1880s. It appears as if the first South African advertising agents were playing the role of space brokers, as the agent has traditionally done in Britain and the USA. Agents would simply serve as salespeople to sell the space to advertisers on behalf of one or more publications without offering any additional services. The flourishing newspaper industry in the last few decades of the nineteenth century also gave rise to a prosperous advertising industry. The Newspaper Press Union (founded in 1882) was very soon confronted with space salespeople who demanded discounted tariffs and still received commissions. The NPU congress of 1890 resolved the problem by deciding that all newspaper proprietors should be invited to adopt a minimum tariff of nine pence per single column inch with a discount of up to 25 per cent at the discretion of the individual proprietor (cf. Nelson 1990:10; Barenblatt & Sinclair 1989:18–19).

The NPU was keen to canvass more advertising from the advertisers, but it was also taking precautions to ensure that the agencies' revenues, credit and methods of operation were controlled. In 1912 the NPU decided to recognise certain agencies that would receive commission. Only four agencies were recognised, and it was agreed that the newspapers would register their tariffs with the NPU. The commissions to agencies would be restricted to 15 per cent. The number of recognised agencies had grown to fourteen by 1924. In that year rules regulating the accreditation of advertising agents were adopted by the NPU and these formed the basis of the rules that applied until the Joint Accreditation Committee (JAC) took over the task of accreditation in January 1983. Some of those original agencies still exist today. Only after World War II could the agencies convince the NPU to increase the commission to 16,5 per cent. The proposition was accepted on condition that the additional 1,5 per cent was only payable if accounts were received by the newspapers by the fifteenth of the month following the appearance of the advertisement (cf. Sinclair & Barenblatt 1993:241).

Key terms to understand and remember

advertising	distribution
marketing communication	marketing
market orientation	marketing mix
personal selling	place
price	product
promotion	promotional mix
publicity	sales promotion

Advertising as a phenomenon of marketing

Advertising and the communication objectives it seeks to achieve do not exist or operate independently. Advertising is an extension of an organisation's other activities, and most commonly an extension of its marketing operations. Before looking at the applications of advertising, it is important to consider the position of advertising within the broader perspective of the organisation and the role that it plays in marketing. *Marketing* is viewed in two ways: in the wide sense, and in the traditional sense as a business activity.

A wide definition of marketing

Kotler (1981:65–67) gives a wide definition of marketing. His definition includes programmes and activities that go beyond the business parameters traditionally associated with marketing. Kotler (1981:65–67) proposes four axioms of marketing:

▶ marketing involves two or more social units, each consisting of two or more human actors;

▶ at least one of the social units is seeking a specific response from one or more other units concerning some social object;

▶ the market's response probability is not fixed;

▶ marketing is the attempt to produce the desired response by creating and offering values to the market.

When viewed so widely, every purpose to which advertising is applied can be described as marketing. Advertising is therefore a means of reaching consumers (the people who buy or use products), but also other important publics such as shareholders, employees, government, trade unions, suppliers or agents. It promotes goods and services, but also organisations, people, places and ideas. Advertisers include business organisations, but also political, social, religious, cultural, and knowledge organisations. We may therefore define all advertising as a marketing activity, including those applications that deal with activities outside the traditional field of business. Examples therefore include AIDS awareness, political, water saving, or constitution-writing campaigns, and the more conventional advertising that promotes cars, insurance, holiday trips and household goods. There is some correspondence between this form of advertising and the public relations advertising discussed in Unit 3.

A traditional definition of marketing

Bearing Kotler's (1981) broad definition of marketing in mind, let us consider the more traditional concept of marketing. In this sense marketing is the process of identifying some need or demand by an identified market, and satisfying that demand with the creation and supply of a product, service or idea within realistic production, distribution and pricing parameters.

Runyon (1984:6) and Sinclair and Barenblatt (1993:77) see marketing in this sense as the **genesis** of advertising. Marketing in this sense creates, uses, controls, starts and stops advertising. Business-related marketing activity accounts for more than 90 per cent of all advertising. More than any other source, business creates and maintains the advertising industry and the advertising agencies, vendors and media that form part of it. The marketer uses advertising to increase sales, build brands, and launch products. Marketing is the engine of advertising. Without marketing activity (in the traditional sense), no advertising industry would exist.

Businesses that survive in the long term tend to be market oriented. In other words, they:

▶ find out what their market wants and needs;

▶ supply the products that will satisfy those wants and needs;

▶ do so better than the competition;

▶ make sure that their customers are happy with the company and its products;

▶ make a profit.

Such businesses practise the marketing concept, that is "a management philosophy stating that an organisation should strive to satisfy the needs of consumers through a coordinated set of activities that also allows the organization to achieve its objectives" (Skinner 1994:14).

The *market orientation* (or *marketing orientation*) differs from the *selling* and *product orientations*, where the business looks at its own needs and abilities, concentrates on selling or product development, attempts to force its products onto its customers, or expects the market to beat a path to its door because of the superiority of its product.

The market orientation is a reconceptualisation of the way that business should operate. Instead of seeing the product as the starting point, a business begins with the customer and the customer's needs, working backwards to delivery of the product, then the creation of that product, and lastly the procurement of the material that is necessary to produce it. To be useful and effective, advertising must extend from a market orientation.

Advertising and the marketing mix

We have noted that advertising is part of marketing, but how exactly is it related to the broader marketing process? To answer this question it is necessary to think of marketing as a "mix" of components. These components are also known as the *four P's*: *product*; *price*; *place* (or *distribution*); and *promotion* (or *marketing communication*). These elements form the *marketing mix* which, in various combinations and applications, deliver need-satisfying products to consumers and generate the exchange between marketer and consumer that is the objective of all marketing activity.

Aspects relating to the *product* include branding, style, sizes, options, features, quality, packaging, warranty and service. Products are goods, services, or ideas that satisfy needs or wants. A product is a combination of tangible features and a combination of intangible attributes with social, functional and psychological benefits. Much advertising is used to build up a brand from the basic attributes of the product. The product is not initially a brand – a product is manufactured, while a brand is created by the full spectrum of the marketing mix. Skinner (1994:324) defines a brand as "a name, term, design, symbol, or any other feature that identifies one seller's good or service as distinct from those of other sellers".

Pricing is related to the product's basic price, quantity and trade discounts, credit facilities offered, legal constraints, economic conditions and pricing policy. It is the value that is given to products during exchange. Pricing is the only element of the marketing mix that produces revenue and profit; the others represent cost.

Distribution is the process of most effectively making the product available to the end user. Distribution occurs via a marketing channel, which is the route that the product follows from the manufacturer to the end user. The marketing channel is best seen as one part of a whole unit that delivers the product to a final user. Good relations with the distribution network permit good support of the marketing programme.

Marketing communication is the process of presenting the product to the consumer. Marketing communication itself comprises the *promotional mix* or *communication mix*. The communication mix includes four parts: *personal selling*; *sales promotion*; *publicity*; and *advertising*.

Personal selling is the presentation of the product by a salesperson in direct contact with the customer. It allows interpersonal communication, is the best marketing communication tool for closing a sale, but it is expensive.

Publicity can be defined as information from an outside communicator that is used by the media because it has news value. It is the distribution of information through media that are not controlled by the information source. Publicity is generally seen to be less biased than advertising and it is less costly, but there is little control over the media coverage, and the original promoter of the message is not always identified. Publicity is not to be confused with public relations in the sphere of marketing communication. See Unit 3 for the discussion on publicity and public relations to identify the difference.

Sales promotion is an incentive that increases the value of the product. It includes the use of contests, point-of-purchase materials, samples, trade shows, coupons and exhibits. It is an attempt to move products through distribution channels by providing incentives to the sales staff, distributors, and consumers. Sales promotion is more effective as a temporary incentive. It combines the sales-closing advantages of personal selling with the great reach of advertising, gives quick feedback, and is relatively cheap. However, it generally contributes little to branding, cannot build a market, and cannot replace the other elements of the marketing communication mix.

Advertising is the paid, nonpersonal presentation of goods, ideas, products or services, undertaken by an identified communicator.

Advertising generally costs little per person reached, is present where a salesperson cannot be, and creates images that a salesperson cannot. However, in most forms advertising must be supplemented by other elements of the marketing mix as it rarely closes a sale, is perceived as biased, and has effects that are difficult to assess because direct feedback is rare.

Every aspect of the marketing mix plays a role in the delivery of need-satisfying products to the final consumer. Each part affects and is affected by the operation of the whole mix. This is also the case with the marketing communication component of the marketing mix. Every aspect of a company's communication reflects upon the image and message that all other company activities project. Advertising affects and is affected by every other bit of company communication such as publicity, letterheads, logo, customer relations, product presentation, and even pricing and packaging. The elements of the marketing and promotional mixes are highly inter-dependent. Each should reinforce the others, and be co-ordinated to maximise the benefits offered by the individual elements of the mix.

It is within this marketing perspective that advertising must be viewed. Advertising exists to attain marketing goals that always fit into the broad framework suggested by Kotler (1981), but which fit mostly into the limited, business framework that is traditionally associated with marketing.

ACTIVITY

1   Identify two advertisements, one of which represents the broad marketing perspective that is described by Kotler (1981). It should describe advertising that is not a part of *traditional* marketing, unlike the second advertisement.

2   Explain why you categorise each advertisement as you do.

3   Identify the *product* of each advertisement.

4   Identify the *tangible* properties of the goods, idea(s), product(s) or service(s) of each advertisement, and the *intangible* properties and values, both positive and negative, that you associate with the advertised *product*.

4.4   THE COMMUNICATIVE NATURE OF ADVERTISING

The classification of advertising

Not all the advertisements to which we are exposed daily are exactly the same or have the same objectives. Advertising can be classified into a number of broad categories. From Russel and Lane (1990:33–42), as well as Sinclair and Barenblatt (1993:13–16), a commonly used classification can be devised. This is outlined below.

National advertising

National advertising refers to advertising of trademarked (branded) products or services that are sold anywhere by different distributors or stores. The product or service is usually (but not necessarily) sold nationwide. The purpose of this type of advertising, which is more widespread than any other, is to establish demand for the specific product or service. The idea is for customers or clients to decide on a specific brand before entering the store or service provider's outlet. (Cf. Russel & Lane 1990:33. See Figures 4.3 and 4.4 for examples of national advertising.)

Retail advertising

Retail advertising emphasises the specific retail outlet as the place to buy a specific range of brands. It can be a local store advertising in the local newspaper or it may be one of the major chain stores encouraging customers to make use of their special sales items for a limited period of time – with the hope that customers will buy other more expensive items once they are in the store. This type of advertising is not merely intended to achieve increased product sales but also to encourage the consumer to buy the product at a particular store (cf. Russel & Lane 1990:34; Sinclair & Barenblatt 1993:15). Good examples of retail advertising are the *Joshua Doore* or *Pick 'n Pay* advertisements.

Nonproduct advertising

Nonproduct advertising is not aimed at selling a product or service. It is used by commercial enterprises and nonprofit organisations or individuals to convey ideas or attitudes, or to promote ideologies, religious doctrines, et cetera. The advertisers may be, for example, political parties, social clubs or professional associations (cf. Russel & Lane 1990:40). Companies may also comment on some environmental issue (e.g. ISCOR in relation to the Saldanha project in 1995) or specific labour practices (the employer may state his position in an advertisement during a much-publicised labour dispute, for example the car manufacturers during the massive strike in the industry in 1994). See Figure 4.5 for an example of nonproduct advertising.

Trade advertising

All the articles that are sold in a shop have first to be purchased by somebody. Trade advertisements are presented to tradespeople in trade journals, giving information about the product, its attributes, price and packaging. The readers of trade journals are, for example, supermarket managers, salespeople, caterers and others who are interested in the announcement of new brands and products. The purpose of trade advertising may be to indicate the profit that can be realised on goods stocked by the retailer. An example would be the advertisements of the wholesalers *Makro* in trade journals or in ordinary newspapers (cf. Russel & Lane 1990:37; Sinclair & Barenblatt 1993:16).

Industrial advertising

In order to manufacture or produce products, the manufacturer or producer has to get raw materials, machines or specific equipment to implement the process of manufacturing or producing. For example, a farmer needs fertiliser to cultivate his lands and the gold mines need steel pipes for the ventilation of their underground operations. A producer of raw materials, equipment or machinery may wish to advertise his products. The main purposes of industrial advertising are to create a quality image for a product, to establish name recognition and to communicate product benefits in support of the sales process. Industrial advertising is directed at a very specialised and relatively small audience and often contains product specifications and details that only those familiar with a specific manufacturing, construction or agricultural enterprise would understand (cf. Russel & Lane 1990:38). See Figures 4.6 and 4.7 for examples of industrial advertising.

Professional advertising

Professional advertising is also directed at people who are not the actual users of a product, but who are instrumental in getting other people to use the product. Professionals such as medical doctors, architects, engineers or pharmacists often make the final purchase decision for their customers or clients by recommending or prescribing the use of certain products. This type of advertising is frequently placed in professional publications or it is directed at the professional target market through direct mail advertising. *Drug companies* may, for example, advertise their products in medical journals (cf. Russel & Lane 1990:38). See Figure 4.8 for an example of professional advertising.

Since 1986 certain professions such as architects, quantity surveyors, chartered accountants, consulting engineers and attorneys have been permitted to advertise their professional services under certain conditions (cf. Sinclair & Barenblatt 1993:13).

Institutional, public relations or corporate advertising

This category of advertising is described by Du Plooy (1991:16) as:

> Advertising designed to sell ideas related to the corporate values of an organisation; as opposed to advertising that supports a specific product/ service. Is used by commercial and noncommercial advertisers for purposes of patronage, public relations and/or public service.

Usually this kind of advertising is used as a basic promotional tool to communicate a company's image of excellence, social responsibility and/or quality (cf. Russel & Lane 1990:40). In Units 2 and 3 (in this book) you also find a discussion of institutional, public relations or corporate advertising. See Figures 4.9 and 4.10 for examples of institutional, public relations or corporate advertising.

Recruitment advertising

Companies or institutions make use of *recruitment advertising* to get the right person to fill a position in that company. Recruitment advertising has two purposes. Firstly, it tries to catch the right person's attention by focusing on the job title and requirements for the position. Secondly, it contributes to the organisation's corporate image. Often specialist advertising agencies are used to assist the organisation with recruitment advertising (cf. Sinclair & Barenblatt 1993:14). See Figure 4.11 for an example of recruitment advertising.

Government advertising

During World War I, the federal government of the USA introduced paid government advertising for selling war bonds, recruiting soldiers, et cetera (cf. Goodrum & Dalrymple 1990:35) Since then, governments have made wide use of advertisements for a number of purposes. For example, invitations to tender for public projects such as roads, bridges, hospitals and schools are advertised in publications read by potential contractors. Paid advertising is also used by governments for other purposes. The Government of National Unity, for example, made use of paid advertisements in 1995 and 1996 to make the public aware of the constitution-writing process, with an invitation to the public and organisations to share in the writing of the new constitution, and also to encourage voters to participate in the November 1995 local elections. As part of the building of the concept **transparency** in government, various committees of national and provincial government invited the public by means of advertisements to participate in the activities of those committees. The Department of Health launched a campaign for primary health care in 1995 – see the advertisement in Figure 4.12.

Financial advertising

In the financial pages of most papers you will find *financial advertising* every day. By law, quoted companies are obliged to announce their trading results in the press, also listing statements, announcements or dividends, rights issues or takeovers of quoted companies. All these must be advertised. This kind of advertising is very dull because of the sombre look of the columns of uninterrupted figures. However, to the interested reader and financial experts such advertisements contain important financial information on which they rely to make investment decisions. Please note that the daily report on stock market prices is not financial advertising because it is not paid for and must be viewed rather as a service delivered by the newspaper (cf. Barenblatt & Sinclair 1989:11).

Pharmaceutical advertising

Although the drug companies and those producing equipment in the medical field rely heavily on personal selling and promotions as a marketing strategy, they need to advertise their products to the medical fraternity. Medical equipment and drugs are subjected to stringent regulation. Legislation ensures that products are fully tested and safe before they are marketed, and severe limitations are placed on advertising claims. Antibiotics, for example, are advertised in medical journals but not in general publications because they must be prescribed by a medical doctor and are not freely available to the public. Some unscheduled pharmaceutical products may be advertised directly to the public, for example *Panado* – for headaches, pain and fever.

Comparative advertising

In South Africa the explicit use of *comparative advertising* is not allowed by law. The law specifically prohibits the identification of competitors' brand names in advertising. In recent years advertising that makes direct reference to competitive products or services has become quite popular abroad. There is, however, increasing discontent over the issue and at the time of writing the issue has not been resolved (cf. Overton-De Klerk 1996:S16). Some examples of subtle comparative advertising appeared recently in South Africa, for example the "Beat the bends" advertisement in which a BMW was subtly compared to a Mercedes (cf. Figure 4.15). Other examples of comparative advertising allowed in South Africa appear in Figures 4.13 and 4.14.

Classified or smalls advertising

A last category of advertising is *classified* or *smalls advertising*. Although this category is not discussed in the books quoted above, it can be included because it is (and has been for a long time) an important part of any newspaper's advertising income. Some announcements such as financial liquidations of companies or individuals are required by law. Classified advertising also provides an opportunity for individuals to have easy and cost-effective access to advertising media. Usually these advertisements, placed by any institution, person or organisation, appear in a specific section of the newspaper reserved for that purpose. The distinctive features of this category are that the advertisements are usually in small print and are very short, that they are not restricted as to type and that they can be classified under identifiable headings such as: *Houses for sale, Death announcements, Personal* and *Social,* et cetera.

ACTIVITY

Find examples of advertisements from the print media for each of the categories of advertising.

Figures 4.3 to 4.15 appear on the following pages.

➡

Figure 4.3 **National advertising**
(Reproduced with the permission of *Saatchi & Saatchi Klerck & Barrett* –
the original appeared in colour)

Figure 4.4 **National advertising**
(Reproduced with the permission of *Saatchi & Saatchi Klerck & Barrett* –
the original appeared in colour)

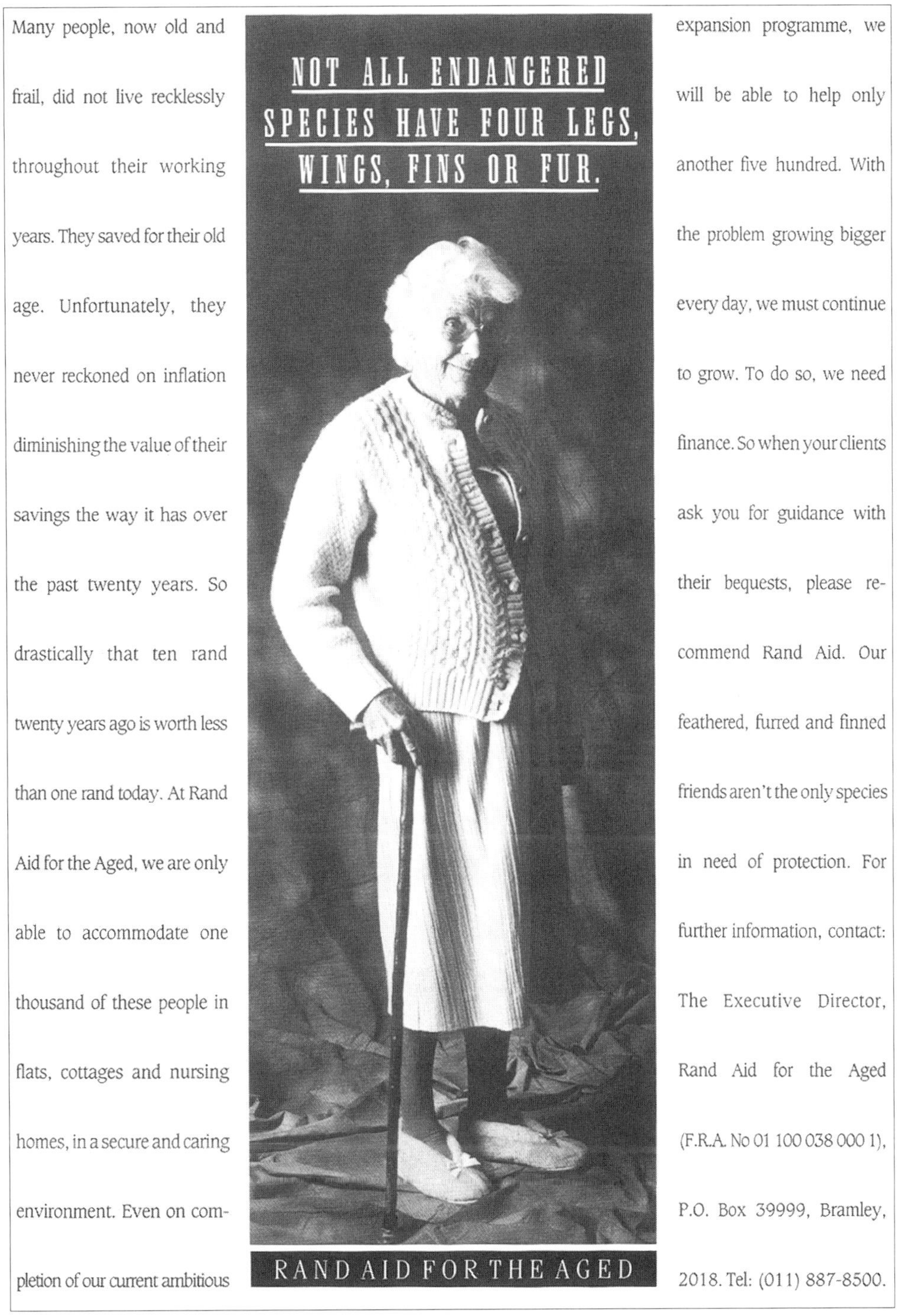

Many people, now old and frail, did not live recklessly throughout their working years. They saved for their old age. Unfortunately, they never reckoned on inflation diminishing the value of their savings the way it has over the past twenty years. So drastically that ten rand twenty years ago is worth less than one rand today. At Rand Aid for the Aged, we are only able to accommodate one thousand of these people in flats, cottages and nursing homes, in a secure and caring environment. Even on completion of our current ambitious expansion programme, we will be able to help only another five hundred. With the problem growing bigger every day, we must continue to grow. To do so, we need finance. So when your clients ask you for guidance with their bequests, please recommend Rand Aid. Our feathered, furred and finned friends aren't the only species in need of protection. For further information, contact: The Executive Director, Rand Aid for the Aged (F.R.A. No 01 100 038 000 1), P.O. Box 39999, Bramley, 2018. Tel: (011) 887-8500.

NOT ALL ENDANGERED SPECIES HAVE FOUR LEGS, WINGS, FINS OR FUR.

RAND AID FOR THE AGED

Figure 4.5 **Nonproduct advertising**

(Reproduced with the permission of *Saatchi & Saatchi Klerck & Barrett* – the original appeared in colour)

Figure 4.6 **Industrial advertising**
(Reproduced with the permission of *Saatchi & Saatchi Klerck & Barrett* –
the original appeared in colour)

Figure 4.7 **Industrial advertising**

(Reproduced with the permission of *Saatchi & Saatchi Klerck & Barrett* –
the original appeared in colour)

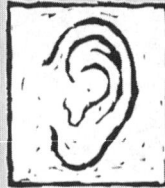

Figure 4.8 **Professional advertising**

(Reproduced with the permission of *Saatchi & Saatchi Klerck & Barrett* –
the original appeared in colour)

Figure 4.9 **Institutional, public relations or corporate advertising**

(Reproduced with the permission of *Saatchi & Saatchi Klerck & Barrett* –
the original appeared in colour)

Figure 4.10 **Institutional, public relations or corporate advertising**
(Reproduced with the permission of *Saatchi & Saatchi Klerck & Barrett* –
the original appeared in colour)

Administrative Posts

UNISA

Applications for the undermentioned vancancies are invited and must reach the Head, Personnel Department, on the prescribed form on or before 31 March 1996. Merit is the sole criterion for appointment to the University irrespective of the candidate's creed, sex, race or political affiliation.

Department of Building Administration
Electrician (Grade 8)

A qualified electrician with a completed apprenticeship is required at our Pretoria campus.

Requirements and qualifications: •Completed N3 certificate (electrical) •Electrician's diploma – Olifantsfontein •Wireman's certificate – Olifantsfontein •A minimum of five years' experience as a qualified electrician.

Salary: The salary is negotiable to R74 955 per annum. Normal fringe benefits are applicable.

Plumber (Grade 9)

The services of a qualified plumber with a broad knowledge of the installation and maintenance of irrigation systems is required on our main campus.

Requirements and qualifications: •Plumber's diploma – Olifantsfontein •Complete N2 certificate (Plumber) •Minimum two years' experience as tradesman •Driver's licence (Code 08)

Salary: The salary is negotiable to R64 095 per annum. Normal fringe benefits are applicable.

Assumption of duty: As soon as possible.

Application forms as well as particulars regarding fringe benefits are obtainable:

BY POST: The Head, Personnel Department, PO Box 392, Pretoria 0001.
IN PRETORIA:
Personally from: Counter 108, Level 10, Administration Building, Muckleneuk Ridge, Pretoria.
By telephone from: (012) 429-2582, 429-2802, 429-2701, 429-2576 or 429-2738.

University of South Africa

✉ 392 PRETORIA 0001 SOUTH AFRICA

☎ (012) 429-3111 • INT +27+12 429-3111 • FAKS/FAX (012) 429-3445

Figure 4.11 **Recruitment advertising**

(Reproduced with the permission of *Unisa*)

HOW TO CATCH TB.

IN TIME.

About 36 people a day die from tuberculosis.

The tragedy of these deaths is that TB is curable, but only if caught in time and therein lies the problem. To catch TB in time, or to avoid catching it in the first place, you have to act promptly and unfortunately the people most at risk of getting TB do not know the signs and symptoms.

You, on the other hand, are at least aware of TB and if you were to pass on the righthand page of this ad to just one other person, you could save an entire family from the tragedy of TB, a highly infectious disease if not treated.

So please think about it. Think of the difference it would make if every reader of this magazine were to do so too.

WHAT IS TB?

TB is a disease that you can get from droplets which tubercular patients expel into the air when they talk, cough or sneeze. While the disease can attack any part of the body, it is usually the lungs that are affected. If left untreated, TB can kill you.

HOW TO TELL IF SOMEONE HAS TB.

Someone with TB of the lungs will have a dry cough that never goes away. Sometimes he will have little desire to eat food. Some people suffering from TB also find it hard to breathe. They may also have pains in the chest and sweat a lot in bed at night.

HOW YOU CAN AVOID GETTING TB.

Immunise your baby at a Clinic within three months of birth.

Eat balanced meals consisting of foods such as meat, fish, chicken, eggs, beans, milk, amasi, brown bread, maize meal, fruit and vegetables.

Alcohol should be avoided because it can lower body resistance.

Smoking causes further damage to the lungs and can also cause heart disease and lung cancer. Get some sunshine, fresh air and live in a clean environment.

HOW TB CAN BE CURED.

To treat tuberculosis, medicines must be started as soon as possible and must be taken regularly according to the instructions given at the Clinic. It takes 6 months or longer for TB to be cured completely, but within 2 weeks of starting treatment, you will no longer spread the disease.

TREATMENT MUST BE COMPLETED.

It is a mistake to stop taking medicines when you feel better. It takes a long time for TB germs to be destroyed. If medicines are stopped too soon and without the instructions of the nurse or doctor, the disease may start all over again.

ALL TREATMENT IS PROVIDED FREE AT CLINICS.

Clinics can make arrangements for you to receive your medicines at your school or work place. Sometimes medicines can cause problems like an upset stomach, ear and eye problems. Should this happen, you must not stop treatment, but go back to the Clinic where a nurse will give you correct advice.

HEALTH BEGINS AT HOME. HEALTH BEGINS WITH YOU.

PRIMARY HEALTH CARE

To learn more about health care, complete the coupon below and return it to PHC Marketing, Private Bag X828, Pretoria 0001. Please send me your free easy-to-use book "Self-help in Health".

Name: _____
Address: _____
Tel: _____ Code: _____

Figure 4.12 **Government advertising**

(Reproduced with the permission of *Saatchi & Saatchi Klerck & Barrett* – the original appeared in colour)

Figure 4.13 **Comparative advertising**
(Reproduced with the permission of *Saatchi & Saatchi Klerck & Barrett* –
the original appeared in colour)

WHAT'S AS CHEAP TO MAINTAIN AS A JAPANESE ECONOMY CAR?

A GERMAN LUXURY SEDAN.

"Toyotas, BMWs and Hyundais are the cheapest cars to maintain." So says Malcolm Kinsey's independent survey on car parts, published in the Sunday Times.

Interesting. But even more interesting are the highlighted price differences between BMW parts and those of other luxury German sedans, identified as M and A.

A price gap? Well, a canyon, if you like. Which, when coupled with our Motorplan* should convince you that there's only one thing more unfortunate than driving other German cars. Buying other German parts.

Unfortunately, comparative advertising restrictions do not permit us to publish the full names of models listed in the table below. However, if you write to P.O. Box 785203, Sandton, 2146, we'll send you the uncensored version.

Independent spare parts survey

1996 Kinsey Report (Prices in Rands)

	JAPANESE 4 X 4	BMW 328i	BMW 318i	JAPANESE SEDAN	KOREAN SEDAN	JAPANESE SEDAN	KOREAN SEDAN	AMERICAN SEDAN	JAPANESE SEDAN	AMERICAN SEDAN	JAPANESE SEDAN	ITALIAN H/BACK	JAPANESE SEDAN	GERMAN ESTATE	GERMAN SEDAN M	GERMAN H/BACK	GERMAN H/BACK	GERMAN SEDAN A	TOTAL	AVERAGE
SELLING PRICE	149500	168300	119700	100947	68950	99750	54650	83150	96221	86485	81179	50180	60710	82392	118298	61200	33950	107519	1623081	90171
PARTS BASKET INCL VAT	45365	57305	42180	44672	31491	48879	28061	43167	50992	49061	48041	30080	37304	54228	79098	55023	30792	104594	880333	48907
% OF SELLING PRICE	30.34	34.05	35.24	44.25	45.67	49	51.35	51.91	52.99	56.73	59.18	59.84	61.45	65.82	66.86	89.91	90.7	97.28	54.85	54.85
PARTS																				
CYLINDER HEAD	4368	9303	3752	4368	1934	3109	1795	3468	3901	4292	4319	3211	2793	4866	9938	6093	5572	14515	91597	5089
SUB-ASSEMBLY	9205	10700	5498	7939	5755	13601	4395	5631	13613	9242	8570	6039	10254	10980	24169	10324	4009	31793	191717	10651
MANUAL GEARBOX	10638	12027	10998	11851	9023	11073	8803	9976	13295	1158	12632	10134	8594	16531	17791	18123	11578	19587	223812	12434
CLUTCH PLATE	427	596	725	425	313	305	268	831	467	371	296	N/A	240	570	542	759	197	1073	8405	467
PRESSURE PLATE	683	497	491	523	225	282	225	384	377	350	226	962	250	478	630	584	224	1033	8424	468
WATER PUMP	596	346	338	596	278	379	226	392	801	492	533	596	319	244	1264	244	343	916	8903	495
REAR SILENCER	1029	3663	1540	846	935	745	693	340	381	962	713	181	571	458	1050	469	286	1723	16585	921
R/R SHOCK ABSORBER	604	123	123	499	383	299	334	333	502	412	327	167	297	268	804	150	154	750	6529	363
R/F SHOCK ABSORBER	604	411	373	507	384	271	362	433	400	404	307	243	269	286	804	286	222	841	7407	412
BRAKE PADS FRONT	258	387	378	169	202	405	200	222	221	645	188	176	164	295	216	205	151	835	5317	295
BRAKE SHOES/REAR PADS	144	352	352	191	201	304	200	340	314	432	202	182	315	156	117	159	222	307	4490	249
FRONT BRAKE DISC	444	196	480	347	256	549	206	225	548	385	368	90	497	174	125	174	118	354	5536	308
REAR BRAKE DRUM/DISC	299	394	142	323	330	435	189	155	592	598	710	95	139	347	161	255	99	1196	6458	359
R/F DRIVE/PROP SHAFT	1114	3795	1679	1846	1222	1655	1127	3290	2094	2018	2014	345	1655	1362	4987	1362	1122	2995	35682	1982
STARTER MOTOR	1177	1006	1006	1344	1112	2299	1002	1171	1448	593	1357	765	524	1161	1151	1161	761	2249	21287	1183
ALTERNATOR	1653	839	1204	1387	1549	2713	1394	2145	1528	1362	1395	513	727	3171	986	4609	923	4253	32351	1797
IGNITION COIL	385	509	743	385	357	434	348	191	465	478	2335	237	669	1135	468	1135	216	1180	11670	648
WINDSCREEN	217	941	941	1444	1283	1268	1258	1883	2655	1187	1431	871	1268	1696	1320	1696	540	1812	25670	1462
FRONT BUMPER	711	1532	1532	766	725	1010	510	1874	409	1949	1184	539	1035	491	1166	491	394	2169	18487	1027
BONNET	1298	1295	1295	1336	803	721	705	1403	1100	1485	1130	790	707	579	2003	689	711	3251	21301	1183
R/F FENDER	628	450	450	674	464	1195	380	616	291	1320	840	279	299	370	1010	370	337	1264	11237	624
R/R TAIL LIGHT ASSEMBLY	378	679	679	695	300	171	261	207	616	481	660	249	171	425	972	457	157	594	8152	453
R/R INDICATOR	254	134	134	178	90	97	107	69	215	153	418	137	97	216	238	216	42	236	3031	168
R/F HEAD LIGHT ASSEMBLY	674	967	967	1188	450	267	500	514	742	1860	777	398	267	609	1705	606	102	997	13590	755
REAR BUMPER	746	2122	2122	829	869	1035	546	1803	509	2050	1317	590	1035	1485	1285	1454	387	2326	22510	1251
R/R FENDER	1754	1471	1471	1215	832	1349	714	1843	1066	1314	1201	472	1349	2000	1333	1621	540	1756	23301	1295
BOOT LID	1965	1062	1062	1437	384	1303	577	2287	915	2015	1039	841	1303	2772	1431	634	1031	2656	24714	1373
OIL FILTER	33	36	32	33	22	67	22	42	33	30	30	29	59	30	54	30	21	57	660	37
AIR FILTER	90	56	162	91	51	43	51	44	76	89	109	29	98	60	113	46	28	179	1415	79
FUEL FILTER	126	159	159	126	64	134	64	67	155	150	142	9	30	130	167	11	7	83	1783	99
SET SPARK PLUGS	33	143	95	33	20	29	18	42	33	40	36	26	29	48	51	48	30	130	884	49
PAIR WIPER BLADES	57	50	50	187	90	46	89	189	57	114	48	43	46	47	79	47	26	186	1451	81
INDICATOR STALK	221	492	492	301	156	787	103	376	201	892	587	912	364	521	224	180	572	8086	449	
CAM BELT	246	304	436	246	270	193	270	205	242	278	223	172	89	91	204	91	49	318	3927	218
AIRCON BELT	157	69	69	157	83	147	81	87	44	82	72	N/A	147	N/A	243	N/A	N/A	112	1550	86
POWER STEERING BELT	137	199	210	137	30	57	N/A	89	100	N/A	N/A	N/A	87	200	N/A	N/A	N/A	62	1308	73
FAN BELT	53	N/A	N/A	53	46	102	38		82	69	N/A	83	N/A	133	N/A	200	13	234	1106	61

The 1996 Kinsey Report compartes the prices of a new vehicle against the cost of a basket of 37 parts, showing the total cost of the parts as a percentage of the car price.

SHEER DRIVING PLEASURE. BMW

*Free maintenance and service for all new FMWs for five years/100 000km, excluding petrol, tyres and top-up oil.

Figure 4.14 **Comparative advertising**

(Reproduced with the permission of *Hunt Lascaris TBWA* and *BMW SA*)

Figure 4.15 **Comparative advertising**
(Reproduced with the permission of *Hunt Lascaris TBWA* and *BMW SA* –
the original appeared in colour)

Theoretical approaches to advertising

4

People differ in their views on the effectiveness of advertising. Some people advocate the restriction of advertising because they believe it to be manipulative. On the other hand, some advertisers question advertising agencies' ability to produce persuasive advertising because their expensive campaigns have not worked the wonders that they believed they would. Despite all the research done and the theories developed, some new products still fail and some advertising campaigns do not deliver the anticipated results. Other advertising campaigns provide spectacular results although they are similar to some that failed. Although there is no final answer to the questions asked on the effectiveness of advertising, several billions of rands are spent every year on advertising all over the world.

Advertising, unlike the associated disciplines of economics and marketing, has not developed a large body of theory. This may be because of a lack of academic tradition or because those most deeply involved in advertising are more interested in short-term results and rely on experience, creativity and experimentation to make advertising work.

Nonetheless, theory does exist in advertising. In this chapter we consider theoretical approaches to advertising that are often referred to as philosophies of advertising. It should be noted that most of these theories are concerned mainly with **how** advertising works and with the **effectiveness** of advertising.

Traditional models of advertising

The main purpose of advertising, amongst others, is to persuade people to buy a product, use a service or consider an idea. Persuasive communication, as described in *Course book 4* (Rensburg 1996), is the basic point of departure for the theory of advertising.

The theoretical approaches to persuasive communication, such as the **theory of attitude change**, the **learning theories**, the **consistency theories**, the **social judgement and involvement theory**, theories about **mass-media effects**, **Rank's model of persuasion**, the **AIDA principle** and **Monroe's motivated sequence,** are all relevant for advertising theory (cf. Rensburg 1996:11–25). All of these theories have been adopted for use in the advertising industry (cf. Sinclair & Barenblatt 1993:17–31).

Involvement theory

A theory specifically relevant to advertising is the **involvement theory** that developed from medical studies on the independence of the two hemispheres of the brain. These studies led to the belief that the left side of the brain is responsible for our logical functions such as reading and writing, with the right hemisphere of the brain being responsible for emotions and the perception of images. Applied to the media, they suggested that television is a low-involvement medium because it is a function of the right hemisphere of the brain to perceive images passively through the focused eye. The print media, on the other hand, was seen as a high-involvement medium because reading employs cognitive processes that are the domain of the left side of the brain (cf. Sinclair & Barenblatt 1993:21).

Later it was discovered that the split between the two hemispheres is not as definitive as had been thought, and that the two hemispheres do not necessarily work independently of one another. The use of the term *involvement* shifted from the media to describing involvement in terms of personal relevance to define the concept. A high-involvement product or service can be described as one that has a high degree of importance to the consumer or client. For example, for an investor, the interest rate offered by a bank or other investment schemes will be a critical factor with high risks involved. On the other hand, the choice between different brands of chewing gum does not comprise risk for most consumers, and it can therefore be considered a low-involvement product (cf. Sinclair & Barenblatt 1993:21).

A further development of the **involvement theory** is the *Relevance Accessibility Model of Advertising Effectiveness* developed by William Baker in the late 1980s (cf. Baker 1993). For the purposes of this course, we concentrate on this model as an example of the way in which advertising theorists try to optimise advertising effectiveness, and to predict the advertising outcomes. Although, in discussing the model, we refer to products and consumers for reasons of convenience, the model also applies to all other categories of advertising.

4.5 THE RELEVANCE ACCESSIBILITY MODEL OF ADVERTISING EFFECTIVENESS (WILLIAM BAKER)

Key terms to understand and remember

accessibility	advertising message involvement
brand choice	brand alternatives
brand quality cues	brand evaluations
brand response involvement	brand response occasion
informational relevance	memory decay
perceived product differentiation	perceived product risk
perceived relevance	pure affect
recognition of relevance	relative brand performance information
satisficing	

Introduction

The *Relevance Accessibility Model of Advertising Effectiveness* (RAM) is directed at maximising advertising message effectiveness. The RAM presumes that the primary purpose of advertising is to present information that will give a brand an advantage over competing *brand alternatives* at the time of *brand choice,* and that this relative advantage will motivate purchase behaviour. Guidelines are provided in the model to make it possible to choose the most effective advertising message strategy from a range of strategic options. Because the choice of a specific brand is the best measure to judge advertising effectiveness, the model aims to predict when a given message strategy is most and least likely to influence brand choice (cf. Baker 1993:50). The following is a summary of Baker's (1993:49–87) theory.

The model consists of two major assumptions and four propositions that transform the assumptions into a theory of advertising effectiveness. From these four propositions evolve the specific rules or principles that the model offers to predict the best message strategy in a given advertising scenario.

Let us begin with the **two main assumptions**.

Assumption 1: Advertising information must be accessible to be effective

According to the RAM, advertising can only be effective when the impressions that it has created in a consumer's memory can be retrieved (accessed) from memory when the consumer evaluates competing brands. *Brand evaluations* therefore depend on visual, verbal or emotional impressions (the mentally transformed advertising message content) created by advertising in the consumer's mind. Various factors can be considered in predicting the accessibility of advertising information.

When a consumer is exposed to advertising, it leaves an impression on his or her memory. The memory impression made by the advertisement may, depending on the level of attention a consumer directs at an advertisement, be weak and difficult to access after a lapse of time, or the impression may be very strong and easy to access. The elements in an advertisement on which a consumer focuses his or her attention will determine which elements of the advertising are most likely to be retrievable. A customer can focus on the executional aspects of an advertisement, such as the scenery or an actor, and that will then be the element that will be the most likely to be remembered. On the other hand, if the consumer focuses on the message, then that is what is most likely to be remembered.

The impressions left in memory may be completely different from the actual content of the advertisement. Consumers could misunderstand the content of the advertisement. They could, for example, believe that a specific insect killer is meant to kill only cockroaches whereas it is to be used against all crawling insects. They may also make a mental summary or mental abstraction of the advertisement, for example to remember the advertisement only as "very funny". These mental summaries and evaluations of advertisements by consumers are more likely to leave a highly accessible impression than the literal elements (meanings) of the advertising.

It must also be borne in mind that consumers are more likely to attend to advertising information that they perceive to be meaningful than information that is not perceived as such. If an advertisement contains situations in which the product is used in such a way that it makes sense and consumers can relate to it, it is more likely to be perceived as meaningful. Meaningful information is attended to and is more likely to be accessible when the consumer must make a decision to buy the product later.

The way in which information is presented may make it more or less accessible. For example, it is much easier to encode pictures and to retrieve them from memory than it is to do so with verbal information. In the same way, unique verbal expressions are easier to remember than ordinary expressions. Information that contains something arousing, erotic, beautiful, mood-evoking, et cetera, is easier to remember than unstimulating information.

Environmental factors also influence the accessibility of information:

▶ Accessibility increases with **repetition** – if information is repeated enough, it is possible that consumers may be able to retrieve some types of information effortlessly when they see a brand or package.

▶ The presence of **memory cues** (such as a brand name, package or scenes and characters from an advertisement) may increase accessibility.

▶ The **delay** between *advertising exposure* and brand evaluation (when consumers actually consider buying the product) may result in decreased accessibility.

- Some **qualitative types of information** (such as specific technical data, e.g. the ingredient *paracetamol* in *Panado*) decay in memory faster than other kinds of information (e.g. *most general practitioners use Panado in their own homes*).

Examine the advertisement in Figure 4.4. Identify the **memory cues** in the advertisement. Distinguish between **qualitative information** and other kinds of information in the advertisement. Which other factors can you identify that will have an influence on the accessibility of the advertisement?

Assumption 2: Advertising information must be relevant to be effective

The RAM assumes that, in order to have a direct effect on brand choice, accessed information must explicitly or implicitly be perceived by the consumer to be relevant at the time of brand choice.

Explicit recognition of relevance. This process take place when consumers consciously and deliberately seek out specific information because they believe it to be a more reliable indicator of quality than other information. If consumers explicitly judge certain information to be irrelevant, it will be discounted in favour of other more relevant information. For example, if a bank advertises high interest rates (the best in the market) on a savings account, the fact that they also offer a free cold drink to each new client will probably be seen as irrelevant. The high interest rate will be seen as the relevant information.

Implicit recognition of relevance. Some advertisements can also contain subtle information that the consumers do not seek out but which can influence behaviour automatically unless it is deliberately discounted. A housewife consumer may, for example, use *Sunlight* dishwashing liquid regularly. Because of influences such as familiarity with the product and classical conditioning (she always uses *Sunlight*), she must make a deliberate decision to consider other brands of dishwashing liquid.

The RAM recognises that there are some factors that may complicate or even make it impossible for consumers to use the type of information that they may prefer to use in a situation. The complicating factors are:

- Environmental factors – such as the unavailability of the preferred information either externally (e.g. inadequate information on the packaging of a product in the store), or internally (the consumer may not remember why he or she thinks a specific product is better).

- Experienced-based factors – such as expertise and the ability to discriminate among different brands.

- Opportunity-based factors – such as time, because it may take too much time to choose a brand using the information a consumer would prefer to use. (For example, the consumer may be dissatisfied with a regularly used product. However, in the supermarket he or she may be in a hurry and therefore unable to compare the ingredients of different brands, with the result that preference is given to the familiar brand.)

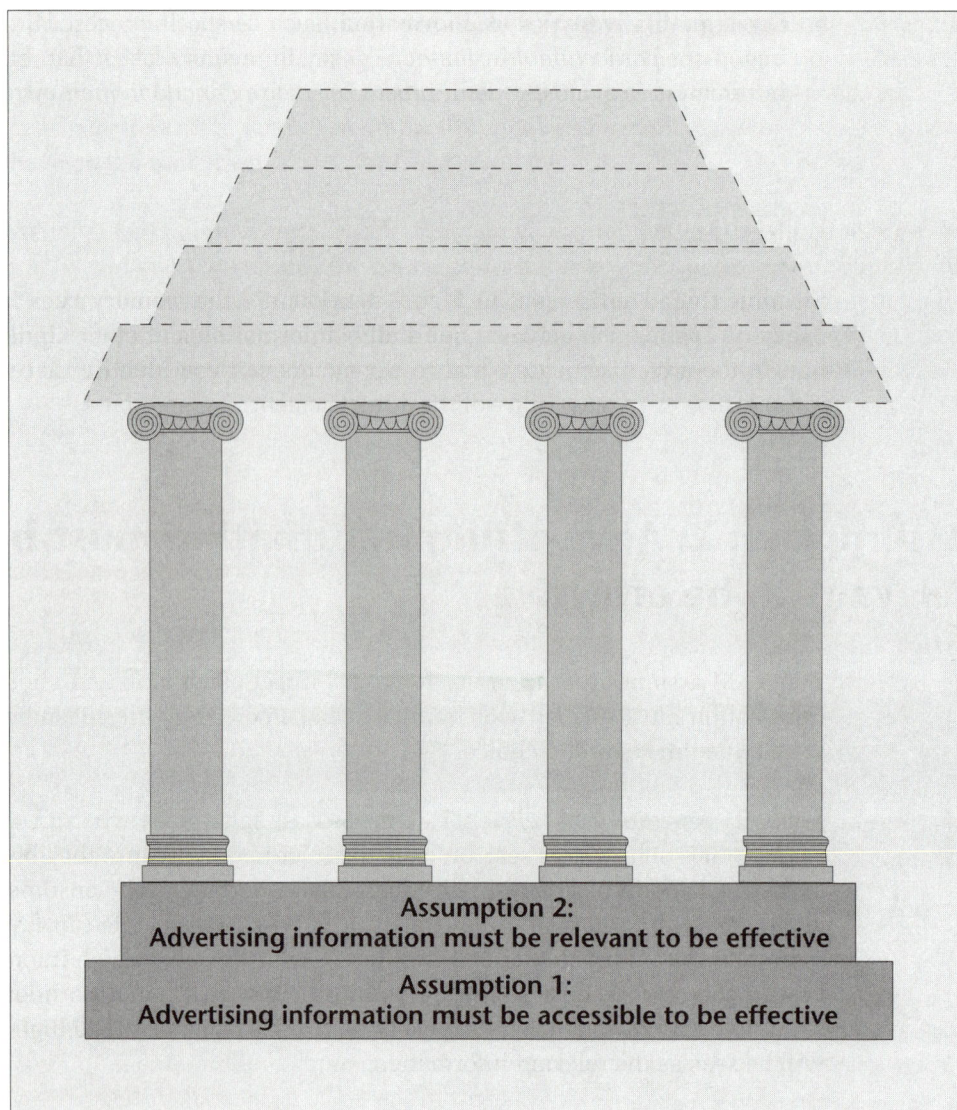

Figure 4.16 **Two assumptions**

The figure shows a temple-like structure with four columns. The base contains two levels:

Assumption 2:
Advertising information must be relevant to be effective

Assumption 1:
Advertising information must be accessible to be effective

ACTIVITY

Study the advertisement in Figure 4.14. Identify the information that you consider as very relevant. Which information will you discard as irrelevant?

The following four propositions are developed on the basis of the two main assumptions discussed above.

Proposition 1: Advertising effectiveness is determined at the point of brand choice

The RAM proposes that the effectiveness of an advertisement must be judged at the *brand response occasion* (i.e. when the brand choice is made) and not the *advertising exposure occasion* (i.e. not when the consumer is exposed to the advertisement). These two occasions are usually separated by time and space with two resultant implications, namely the effect of memory decay and changes in informational relevance (cf. Baker 1993:54–58).

Memory decay

Every day consumers are exposed to hundreds of advertisements and they have a limited ability to remember advertising information over time. Depending on the time lag between listening to, seeing or reading (advertising exposure occasion) an advertisement and the actual decision to buy a specific brand (brand response occasion), the ability to remember advertising information may deteriorate rapidly. The longer the time gap between the two occasions, the bigger the memory decay.

Advertising is also not the only source of information on brands and products. Consumers may base their brand choice decisions on other sources of information, such as *prior* brand usage experiences (the consumer is satisfied with a familiar brand), package information and information displayed at the point of purchase. For example, Cadbury's *Astro* relied solely on package and display information to be a success in a highly competitive market. It may also happen that any persuasive effects of advertising at the advertising exposure occasion may have worn off by the brand response occasion.

Purchase decisions are often quickly made by consumers with little deliberate mental effort. Therefore the easy-to-remember, or *top-of-mind* information, rather than less accessible information that could have been of equal or even greater relevance, is likely to be used to choose a brand in many choice situations.

The longer the time which has elapsed between the advertising exposure occasion and the brand response occasion, the more effort it takes to remember and use advertising information. If more effort is needed to remember advertising information, the danger exists that other, more readily accessible information will be used to make a purchase decision. For example, a customer may be convinced by an advertisement to try a new product with a unique ingredient, but two weeks later he or she may be unable to associate the claims of the advertisement with the specific brand. In this example, the advertisement is unlikely to influence the consumer's choice because other information, such as package information or experience memories, will be used to make a decision.

Changes in informational relevance

The advertising information that is perceived as relevant during the advertising exposure occasion may not be so perceived at the brand response occasion, because other more relevant sources of information may be present or accessible at the time of brand choice. For example, after listening to, reading or seeing an advertisement, the information may be perceived as very relevant and the consumer may be persuaded to buy the product. When the consumer must actually make a decision in the supermarket, he or she may be confronted with other more relevant sources of information that are dominant at that time, such as the prominent display of a competing brand or a special offer. The desired product may also be difficult to find.

During the advertising **exposure** occasions for a given brand (e.g. a customer listening to a radio advertisement while driving), the advertising information for this brand is likely to dominate, because it is heard in an environment where other sources of information are at a disadvantage (you can only listen to one advertisement at a given time). In other words, advertising information for competing brands is less accessible during that advertising exposure occasion because advertisements, packages and point-of-purchase displays are not seen, read or heard. Therefore, the impact of this information is very high in view of the **absence** of competing messages. The consumer may even be convinced of the merits of the product.

However, at the brand **response** occasion (when the consumer must actually decide which brand to buy), the consumer may be introduced to new information and the advertising information may be seen as less relevant and therefore no longer motivational. For example, the brand may be more expensive than competing brands, the consumer may notice other brands that he or she has used before, or he or she may recall another advertisement that was endorsed by a credible personality.

Proposition 2: Consumers use three levels of information to make brand purchase decisions

A central proposition of the RAM is that consumers discriminate between brands by using three types of information, namely *relative performance information, quality cues* and *pure affect* (cf. Baker 1993:58–63).

Relative brand performance information

Relative brand performance information refers to the most detailed and direct information that is available about a brand. Relative brand performance information enables a consumer to make specific and direct comparisons among competing brands.

A consumer may decide to compare a set of brands on the basis of specific features or benefits. The consumer may, for example, be allergic to preservatives in food and therefore he or she will actually study the labels of various brands of cold drink in order to identify those brands that do not contain preservatives.

Brand quality cues

Brand quality cues are those that provide descriptive, but indirect, information that can be used by the consumer to make conclusions about a brand's quality. However, brand quality cues contain no specific evidence of a brand's performance relative to other brands. A consumer may, for example, choose to buy a Mercedes car because it is produced by a manufacturer with a reputation for quality, status or luxury, or simply because it possesses one or more attributes that are symbolic of quality. Another possible example of a quality cue is that of Kenwood's five-year guarantee on certain music systems. Producers' confidence in their products may serve as a quality cue for consumers. Many of these quality cues provide no more than circumstantial evidence of relative quality and performance.

It is assumed that consumers will use brand quality cues when they do not have the motivation, ability, or opportunity to use more specific information with which to compare brands.

Pure affect

Pure affect refers to feelings and emotional responses that have no rational basis relating to any specific brand attributes, benefits, and past promotional or usage experiences at the time of brand choice. Although pure affect provides no evidence of either definitive or relative product quality, consumers may interpret their feeling about a specific brand as such. When individuals make decisions based on pure affect, they are reacting solely to a feeling, and not to the information that triggered that feeling.

If a consumer has a positive feeling about a brand, it will attract him or her to that brand. If a consumer has negative feelings about a brand, the consumer will prefer to avoid the brand. Brand choice will in the end be influenced by the naturally reinforcing properties (attraction or avoidance) of pure affect.

The sources of pure affect (positive or negative) may include:

▶ brand name familiarity – for example, Coca Cola on the one hand, and, on the other, an unknown brand that has recently been introduced to the market;

▶ classical conditioning (cf. learning theories of persuasion in *Course book 4* – Rensburg 1996) – affect-evoking stimuli such as music or visuals associated with the brand through advertising (e.g. some beauty soap advertisements) may lead to positive feelings or, if the consumer dislikes the advertisement, to negative feelings about the product;

▶ affective residue from past experiences – for example, a good or bad experience with a brand;

▶ a combination of these and other affective experiences that have come to be associated with a brand over time.

Implications of the three types of information

Advertisers need to know which type of information their consumer target market is most likely to use when making purchase decisions in a given product category. In any given product category, advertisers need to know if their target is most likely to deliberately compare brand alternatives across performance dimensions, whether consumers are going to use brand quality cues, or whether consumers are going to rely on simple affective reactions on which to base their brand choice decision. The information type that is most likely to be used by targeted consumers for a given brand in a given product category must be emphasised in advertising messages for that product category.

ACTIVITY

Collect product advertisements which exemplify the following types of information needed by consumers in order to discriminate between brands:

- ▶ Relative brand performance information

- ▶ Brand quality cues

- ▶ Pure affect

Proposition 3: Brand response involvement determines a consumer's preferred level of information

Brand response involvement (BRI) refers to the degree to which the consumer makes a mental effort in order to make a brand choice. When brand response involvement is **high** (e.g. when considering whether to buy an expensive car), consumers are motivated to think thoroughly about their brand choice. They are then motivated to search for specific information and compare brand alternatives. When brand response involvement is **low** (e.g. when buying a carton of milk), consumers are not motivated to think about their brand choice and they may not seek information or compare brand alternatives (cf. Baker 1993:63-69).

Two concepts related to brand response involvement are of importance, namely *perceived product differentiation* and *perceived product risk*.

Perceived product differentiation refers to the degree to which consumers believe that performance differences exist between the brand alternatives in a product category. For example, if you have R150 000 available to buy a car, you will make sure that you make the correct choice. You may buy a car with fewer luxury items but a good resale value, or you can choose a car with many luxury features and a lower resale value. As perceived product differentiation increases, the consumer may fear making the wrong choice. Increased differentiation is therefore expected to lead to increased brand response involvement and the consumer will think more about the choice to be made.

Perceived product risk refers to the probability that a nonoptimal brand choice has negative consequences. The consequences may be economic (e.g. loss of money as a result of choosing the wrong car), social (e.g. peer ridicule as a result of buying the wrong style of clothing) or utilitarian (e.g. an appliance with a missing feature that you had not anticipated at the time of purchase).

Perceived **high** product differentiation does not necessarily lead to **high** perceived product risk. The consumer may believe that he/she risks making a nonoptimal choice, but the decision does not necessarily imply serious consequences. For example, if a young couple is interested in buying a vacuum cleaner for the first time, they would like to make an optimal choice. However, if their choice of vacuum cleaner is not ultimately the best choice, it will still perform satisfactorily.

Brand response involvement is important because it is presumed that as brand response involvement changes, different levels of information are sought by consumers at the brand response occasion, and others are avoided or ignored. The RAM proposes that brand response involvement is the primary determinant of the level of information that consumers seek in order to make brand choices.

High brand response involvement leads to "optimisation"

Brand response involvement is most likely to be at its highest level when consumers perceive both high product differentiation and high product risk. At this level consumers believe that major differences exist between brand alternatives and they also believe that the wrong choice will have serious negative consequences. If consumers find themselves in such a situation of high perceived product differentiation coupled with high perceived product risk, they will be motivated to make the best possible decision. Consumers will also be willing to expend the mental effort required to make the best possible choice and will seek the most specific information available to make direct comparisons between brand alternatives (**optimisation**). When consumers are highly involved in the purchase decision, it is presumed that they will seek the highest level of information (*relative performance information*) to make their brand choice.

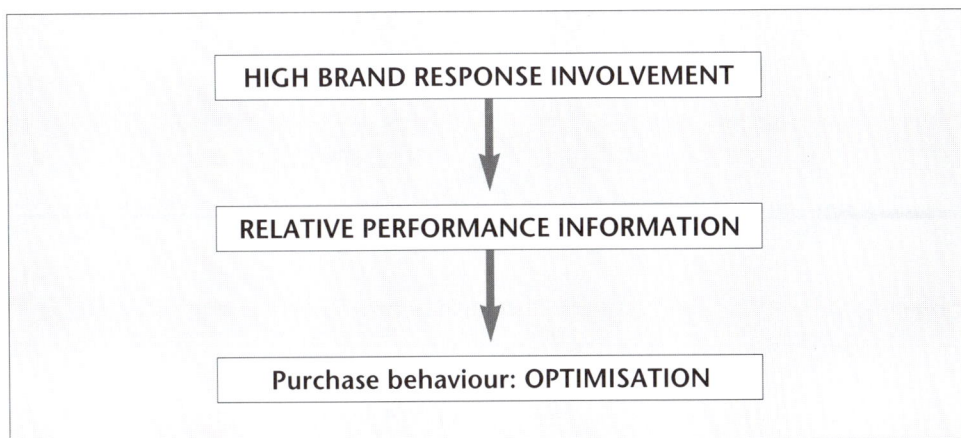

Figure 4.17 **Optimisation**

ACTIVITY

Describe an advertisement for a product of perceived high product differentiation coupled with high product risk. Explain why you decided to choose that specific example.

Moderate brand response involvement leads to "satisficing"

Brand response involvement is likely to be moderate in the following situations:

▶ When consumers perceive **product differentiation** to be significant but product risk as minimal (eg. microwave ovens vary in how quickly they cook food, but all microwaves are fast enough for a specific purpose);

▶ When consumers perceive **product risk** to be significant but little product differentiation exists (eg. buying a television set has serious economic consequences because it is expensive; however, once the decision has been made, the risk involved in choosing between three similar sets is minimal).

Brand response involvement is likely to be **moderate** and optimisation is not likely to occur when consumers believe that there is no benefit to be gained from putting extreme mental energy into their purchase decision (e.g. the example of microwave ovens or television sets discussed above). However, due to the high perceived risk or high perceived differentiation associated with the purchase, consumers need to feel comfortable that they are making a satisfactory brand choice. In this case, consumers are expected to seek information to reassure themselves that they are making a good selection.

The RAM presumes that people will make **satisficing** brand decisions when brand response involvement is moderate. A characteristic of satisficing brand decisions is that consumers may select the first **acceptable** brand, and not necessarily the best of a considered set of brands. The RAM expects that people will typically use **quality cues** to select a brand when they are satisficing.

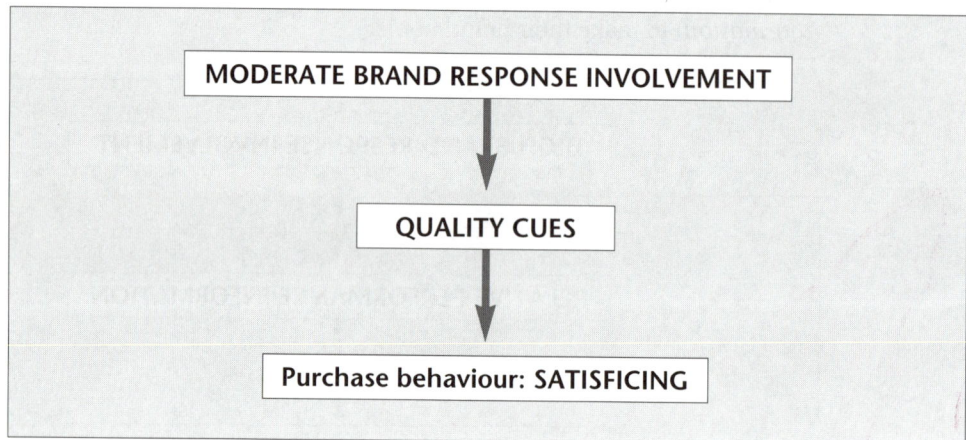

Figure 4.18 **Satisficing**

ACTIVITY

Describe an advertisement for a product where consumers will use quality cues to select a specific brand. Substantiate your choice.

Very low brand response involvement leads to "indifference"

With **low** brand response involvement, consumers perceive little or no product differentiation and little or no product risk. The consumers believe that there is a low probability of making a wrong brand choice and, if a wrong choice is made, the consequences will be trivial (e.g. choosing between different brands of maize meal). There is little reason for a consumer to make any deliberate mental effort when choosing between brands if there are no perceived risks in a product category and no perceived performance differences between brand alternatives in that category. The consumers are expected to be **indifferent** in such a situation.

Indifferent purchase decisions are characterised by consumers selecting the first brand that comes to mind. For example, in a supermarket shopping situation there are multiple salient brand alternatives in a specific product category. Indifferent purchase decisions in the above situation are characterised by consumers selecting the brand in the set with which they feel most comfortable, and decisions are made as quickly as possible. Indifferent decisions are expected to be typically driven by simple **affective** reactions towards brands that come to mind effortlessly at the time of brand choice.

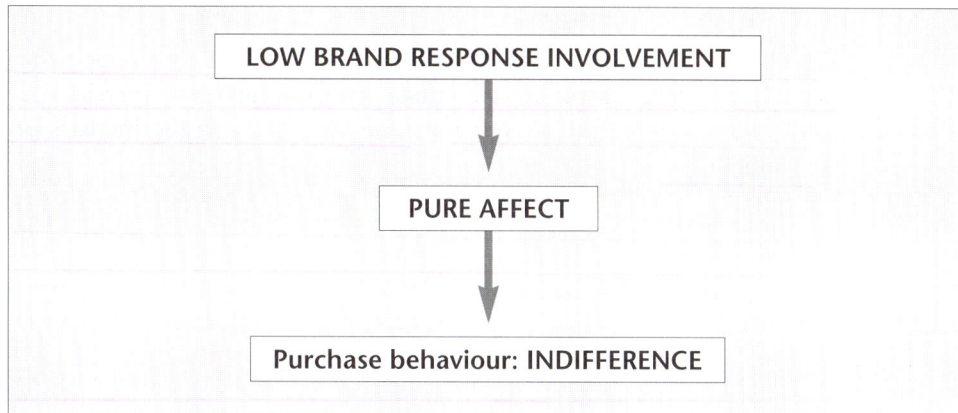

Figure 4.19 **Indifference**

ACTIVITY

Describe an advertisement for a product where consumers will use pure affect to select a specific brand. Substantiate your choice.

Implications of Proposition 3

In the discussion of Proposition 3, three types of purchase behaviour (**optimising**, **satisficing** and **indifference**) have been identified and linked to brand response involvement. Each type of purchase behaviour corresponds to a different decision-making process, and each decision-making process is associated with a different level of information (relative performance information, quality cues and affective reactions).

Advertisers must identify the expected level of brand response involvement of their target market. The advertisers then have to create advertising that corresponds with the required level of information.

Proposition 4: Advertising message involvement (AMI) predicts the level of information learned

In the previous propositions we learned that the identification of the correct level of information is crucial to the success of advertising. However, it is not enough to know the correct level of information that will interest readers. The advertiser also needs to know what kind of information will be relevant for the consumers (cf. Baker 1993:69–76).

Advertising message involvement (AMI)

Advertising messages may communicate the correct level of information (the level of information consumers are expected to use at the brand response occasion), but such advertising messages may not necessarily be effective. For example, an advertisement may contain relative performance information for a brand where brand response involvement is high, but this does not mean that the consumers who are exposed to that advertisement will remember the information or its implications at the time of brand purchase (e.g. an advertisement for an expensive music sound system may contain highly technical information that is difficult to remember).

There are various factors that are likely to influence a consumer's advertising message involvement level, but advertisers can use tactics to increase the consumer's motivation to attend to advertising. One such tactic is the increase of information meaningfulness:

▶ If advertisers include specific **performance information** in their advertising, this information must be about benefits that are most important to consumers (e.g. to emphasise fuel economy in an advertisement for an expensive sports car may be futile).

▶ If the message includes **quality cues**, it must include quality cues that people perceive as reliable predictors of quality (e.g. in an advertisement for a quality Swiss watch, a model driving a cheap car will not be perceived as a quality cue).

▶ If the message intends to make people feel good (**pure affect**), the tactics used to create positive emotions must be such that they will warm the consumers' hearts (e.g. an exotic perfume will be advertised in a very romantic setting with soft lights, beautiful models and warm background).

Advertisers can also employ certain executional tactics (such as unique and appropriate visuals, sounds, dialogue and emotionally intense messages, instead of ordinary unimaginative executions) to increase advertising message involvement.

ACTIVITY

Choose a specific product and identify the level of information consumers will use to distinguish the brand. Describe the way in which you will increase advertising message involvement.

There are, however, four relatively uncontrollable antecedents of advertising message involvement that may influence the interest that consumers will have in the advertising:

▶ anticipated brand response involvement may be wrong because consumers may not perceive any differentiation or risk associated with the product category;

▶ the extent to which the consumer perceives a need for additional information before making purchases in the product category;

▶ consumers may lack interest in the advertised product category;

▶ consumers' attention may be distracted at the time of advertising message exposure.

Advertising message involvement effects

According to the RAM, **advertising message involvement** primarily determines the level of information that consumers most effectively encode in memory at the time of advertising message exposure, and remember at the time when brand purchase decisions are made.

If consumers have a high product class interest, a high expected brand response involvement, as well as a strong perceived need for information, it can be expected that consumers will have a **high** advertising message involvement. In this situation consumers are expected to focus their attention on those aspects that will make it possible to compare the brand to its competitors (**relative brand performance information**).

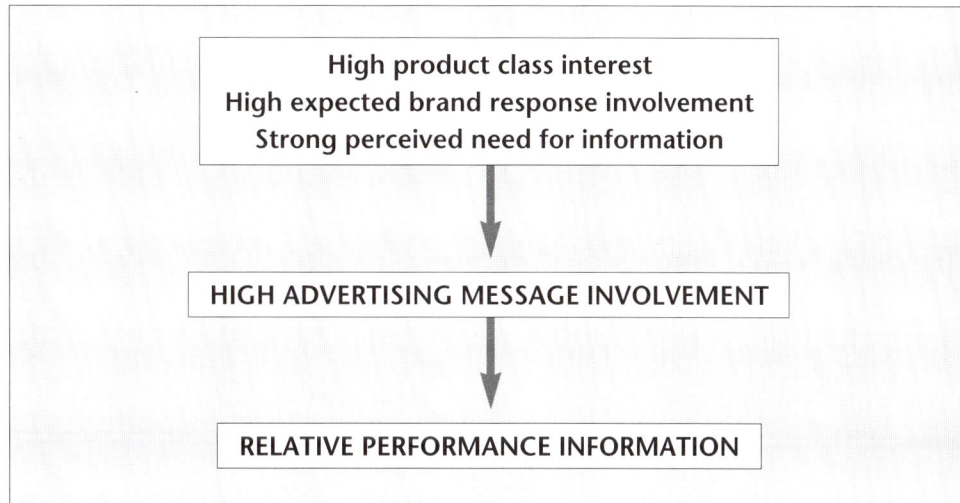

Figure 4.20 **Need for relative performance information**

If consumers have a lower product class interest, a moderate expected brand response involvement, as well as a lower perceived need for information, it can be expected that consumers will have **moderate** advertising message involvement. If the advertising message involvement is low, it can be expected that consumers will comprehend the advertising message, but that they will not analyse and integrate the implications of specific message claims with other brand-related or competitive information in their memory. Consumers will not seek specific information to enable them to make direct comparisons between different brands. When consumers have moderate advertising message involvement, they are more likely to attend to quality-cue type (**brand quality cues**) of information and they will make mental judgements or summaries about the advertisement, the brand and the product in general.

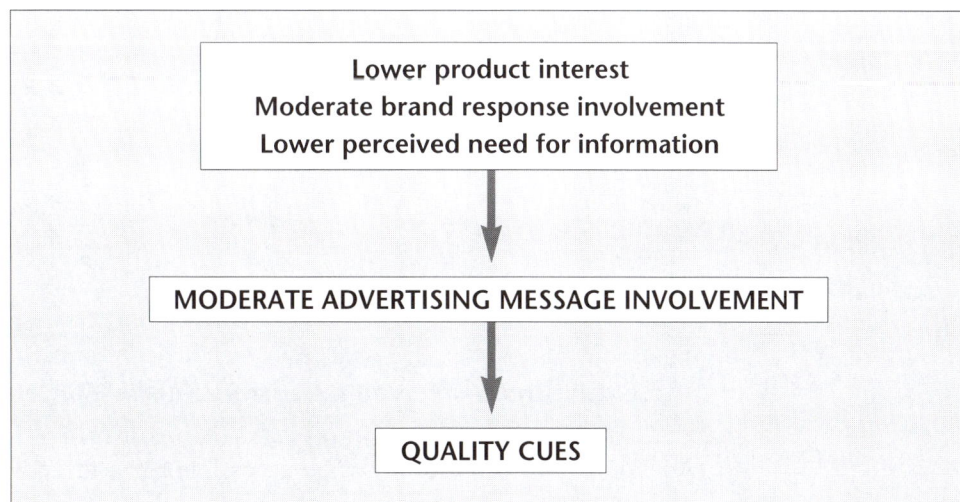

Figure 4.21 **Need for quality cues**

If consumers have very low product class interest, a very low expected brand response involvement, as well as a very low perceived need for information, it can be expected that consumers will have a very **low** advertising message involvement (strong distractions at the time of advertising exposure can also lead to low advertising message involvement). According to the RAM, it is expected that when advertising message involvement is very low, there is no motivation to attend to brand information in the advertising message. Consumers will only attend to the feeling of the advertisement (**pure affect**).

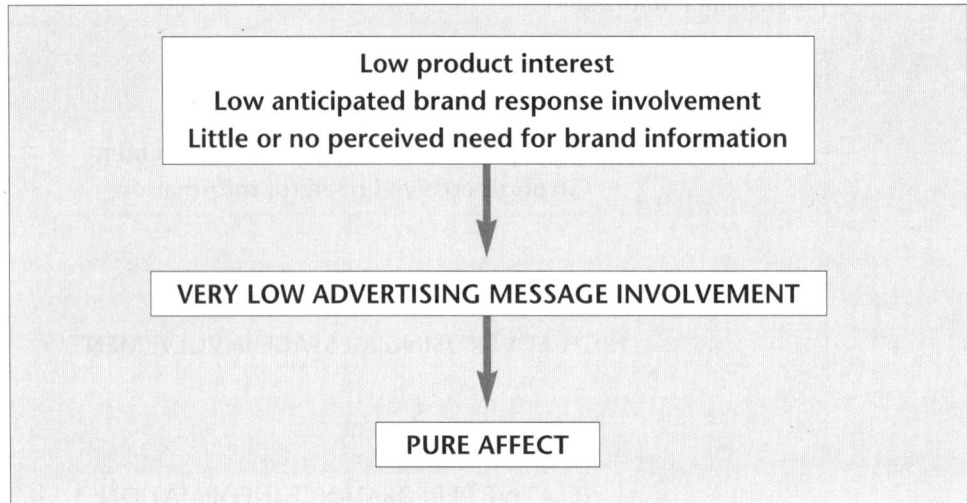

Figure 4.22 **Need for pure affect**

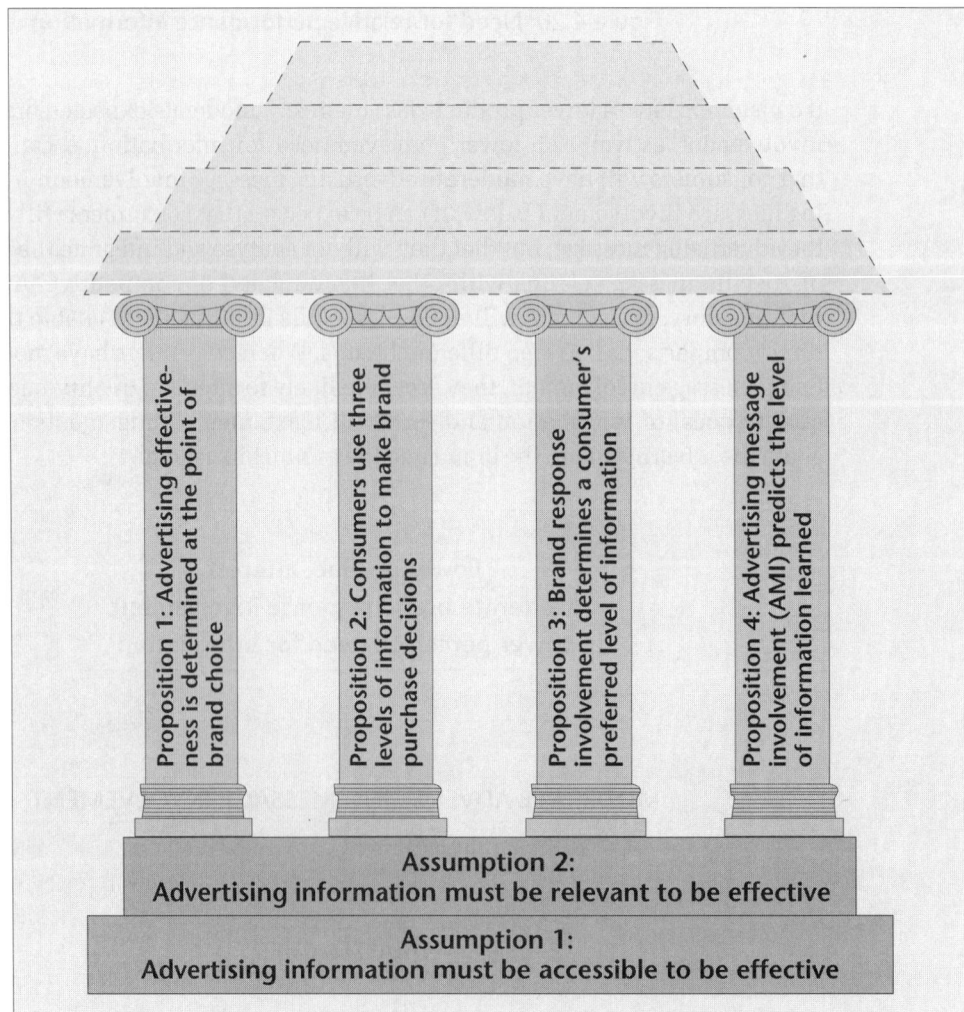

Figure 4.23 **Two assumptions and four propositions**

Application: Advertising effectiveness

Four prerequisites for effective advertising

The RAM identifies four necessary and mutually sufficient conditions that advertising must meet to have the highest probability of directly influencing brand choice (cf. Baker 1993:76–79). Each of these conditions is briefly described below.

Information availability. Advertising cannot influence brand choice unless it has an opportunity to leave an imprint on the consumer's memory. It is also important that an advertisement must affect the consumer's attention in such a way that the message will be attended to, comprehended, and remembered. Advertisements must be presented at times and in places where consumers will be exposed to their content and will be able to attend to and comprehend the message.

Level relevance. Advertising effects are level-relevant if the level of information sought by the consumer to enable him or her to discriminate brand alternatives at the brand purchase occasion correlates with the level of information encoded into memory at the time of advertising exposure. For example, if consumers are seeking quality cues at the point of purchase and quality cues were encoded into memory at the time of advertising exposure, then advertising effects are level-relevant.

Relative accessibility refers to the probability that level-relevant advertising effects will be accessed at the time of brand choice. In other words, it is not enough to provide level-relevant information: consumers must also have access to that information at the brand purchase occasion. For example, although level-relevant advertising effects may be available in memory, it may happen that it requires a greater amount of effort to retrieve the information in the presence of other sources of information such as past experiences, familiarity or package information at the point of purchase. The ease with which level-relevant information can be retrieved at the point of purchase, relative to other accessible levels of relevant information, will determine the relative accessibility of level-relevant information. The relative accessibility of advertising information **becomes increasingly important** as brand response involvement **decreases**.

Relative relevance. If it is accepted that an advertising effect in a consumer's memory is level-relevant, relative relevance refers to the advertising information's perceived ability to discriminate brand alternatives better and more reliably than other level-relevant information such as package information, salesperson advice, experience and displays. The RAM proposes that, within each of the three levels of information, consumers encode, access, and use information that they perceive to be most reliable. Consumers will also avoid and discount implications of less important information. The relative relevance of advertising information **becomes less important** as brand response involvement **decreases**.

These four prerequisites are added to complete the model (see Figure 4.24).

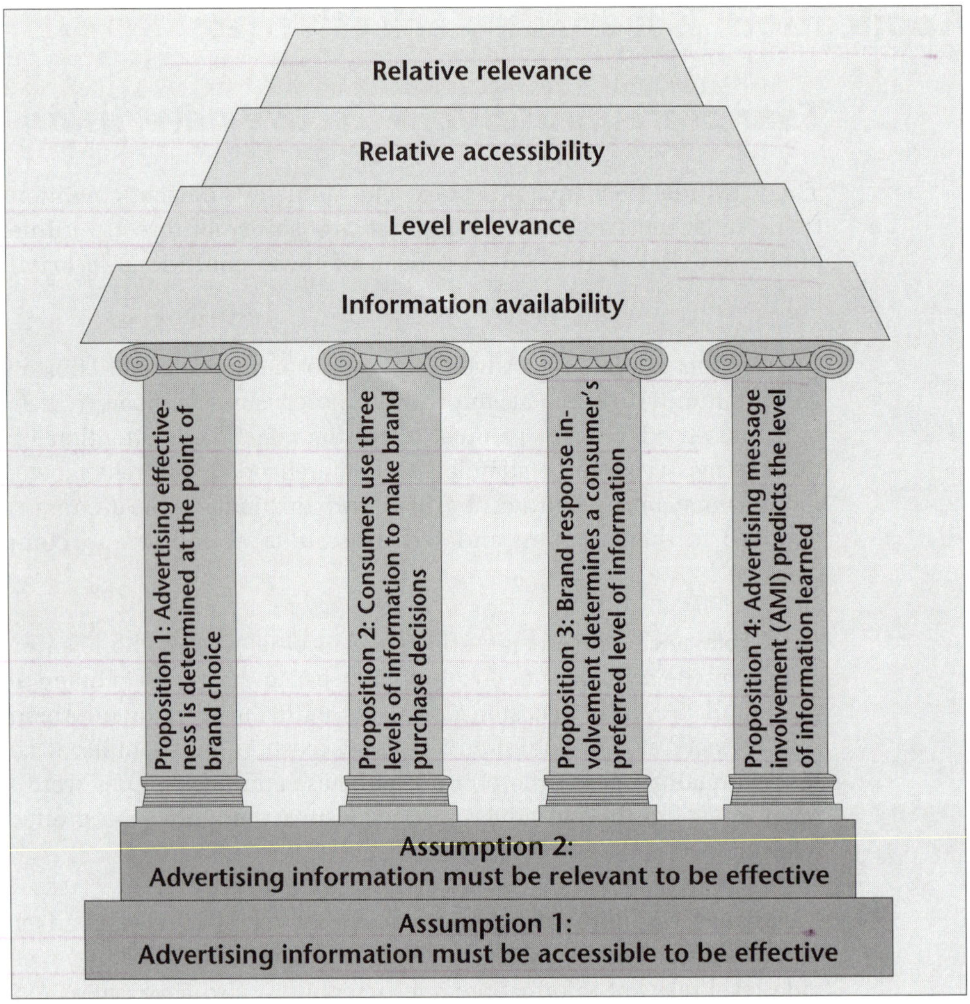

Relative relevance
Relative accessibility
Level relevance
Information availability
Proposition 1: Advertising effectiveness is determined at the point of brand choice
Proposition 2: Consumers use three levels of information to make brand purchase decisions
Proposition 3: Brand response involvement determines a consumer's preferred level of information
Proposition 4: Advertising message involvement (AMI) predicts the level of information learned
Assumption 2:
Advertising information must be relevant to be effective
Assumption 1:
Advertising information must be accessible to be effective

Figure 4.24 **The complete model**

Maximising advertising effectiveness

Baker (1993:78–79) proposes four steps that can be taken to meet the conditions discussed above. A brief summary of the steps is as follows:

Step 1: It is necessary for advertisers to predict correctly the **brand response involvement** of the targeted consumers. The correctly predicted brand response involvement will make it possible to know which level of information to emphasise in advertising. It is possible to predict consumers' brand response involvement by studying the perceived product risk and product differentiation (cf. Proposition 3).

Step 2: It is important that advertising messages communicate **level-relevant** information (cf. Proposition 2)

Step 3: A further condition is to ensure that advertising messages communicate **relatively relevant** information. The expected level of information that the target market will use to make a brand choice will determine which information is relatively relevant. Only research can identify the best quality cue, the most important performance benefit, and/or the best way to associate affect with the brand (depending on the expected level of information). For example, if the brand response involvement for a product (such as an expensive music sound system) is expected to be high, then only research can reveal which **relative brand performance information** is the most important for consumers in order to emphasise that information in an advertisement.

Step 4:   For an advertisement to be effective, the advertising message must be designed in such a way that it will maximise its **relative accessibility** to the consumer target market. Relative accessibility of the advertising message can be improved by, among others:

▶ repeating the message throughout the advertisement with all the elements contributing to and reinforcing the message;

▶ communicating the message in an attractive and arousing way;

▶ communicating the message by involving various sensual modes (e.g. words, sounds, pictures – modern technology even makes it possible to make use of smell in print advertising);

▶ focusing consumer attention on the message (the skilful and beautiful creative elements of the advertisement must not distract the attention of the consumers);

▶ repeating the advertisement (heavy repetition schedules).

4.6   ADVERTISING CAMPAIGNS

Implementing advertising as a campaign

Advertising is best created and implemented within the broader marketing plan in co-ordination with the other promotional elements. The best way of ensuring that the advertising remains integrated with the broader marketing structure and achieves its specific and broader objectives is to manage it within the framework of an *advertising campaign*. See the discussion of public relations campaigns in Unit 2 for an additional discussion of the concept **campaign**.

An advertising campaign comprises one or more advertisements that are related by a central theme, may be presented in different media, and are intended to attain specific communication objectives within a specific time (cf. Wells, Burnett & Moriarty 1995:647). The term **campaign** is derived from the military context and shares with it the concept of a co-ordinated set of activities that have been strategically organised to achieve a particular goal, solve some problem or reap the benefits of some opportunity. Like the military example, an advertising campaign is circumscribed by time and objective parameters. A campaign would be planned for up to a year and would be used to achieve specific marketing goals. An advertising campaign may make use of one advertisement in one medium for one audience, but could also comprise a number of different (but related) advertisements that are placed in different media for different audiences.

Advertising campaigns can be applied to the promotion of products, services or ideas, but to remain as clear as possible we refer only to **products** in this discussion. We also refer only to **companies**, but bear in mind that, as we discussed earlier, any organisation can make use of an advertising campaign.

A number of advertising campaign frameworks exist, but most commonly they would comprise four phases, namely the *situation analysis*; *strategy*; *implementation*; and *evaluation*.

Situation analysis

The first phase of most advertising campaigns is a comprehensive evaluation of the situation of the product, the competition, the target market and the environment. The results of this analysis will largely affect the advertising strategy that is developed in the second phase of the campaign process. The situation analysis comprises the creative interpretation of information that already exists, and it often includes formal research.

Identification of the marketing problem or opportunity

At the outset of the situation analysis the specific marketing problem or opportunity for the advertising is identified by noting what is to be achieved by the advertising campaign and the reasons for its implementation.

The target market

An advertising campaign is aimed at a particular group that may or may not coincide with the target market. The **target market** is the group of people that the company identifies as the focus of its marketing effort. The target of an advertising campaign is termed the **target audience**. This group comprises those people whom the advertiser wants to reach directly through the advertising. The target audience may be the same as the target market, but it could include a different group, such as purchase decision makers or a limited portion of the target market. The needs, problems, characteristics, predispositions and preferences of the target audience are core factors in the creation of the advertising that is to be targeted at them; a clear and accurate picture of this group must therefore be established.

The process of defining the target audience for the specific campaign will include a detailed definition of the audience, and an attempt to create a *profile* of the typical member of the audience. Wells et al. (1995:252) state:

> The attempt here is to identify a real person and make that person come to life for the creative people, who then try to write believable messages that will appeal to this person ... Writers then associate that general profile with someone they know.

The detailed definition of the target audience must be as complete as possible. In our discussion of public relations, we examine some elements of audience definition. The subject is considered here particularly as it refers to advertising. The target audience should undergo cross-sectional analysis (evaluation in the present, at one point in time), and longitudinal analysis (through time, indicating past trends and future expectations). Audiences are described in numerous ways, but the most common are **demographic**, **psychographic**, **geographic**, **behavioural** or **needs** definitions. Refer to Unit 1 for a description of these categories of audience definition.

Target audience definitions may be used alone or in combination with others. The target audience could, for example, be defined in terms of its demographic and sociographic characteristics. It may be defined as predominantly female, 16 to 24 years of age, resident in the Eastern Cape (demographic factors), with membership in professional and amateur theatre and dance groups (sociographic factors).

The product analysis

The product that is to be advertised must be fully described. Attention must be given to its role in the lives of the target market and the methods and reasons for its use. The product's parts, make-up and variations, its constituent and total costs, strengths and weaknesses must be identified. Attention must also be given to the product's distribution channels and availability, the target market's perceptions of the product and the values attached to it. An attempt should be made to determine these values not only in terms of the product's physical properties, such as size, composition or volume, but also in terms of its intangible qualities (including **affect**), such as emotional appeal or expectation of reliability.

Environmental analysis

Information on the social, political and economic environment of the product will benefit the campaign planners. This information would include an evaluation of the competition and aspects such as the conditions of distribution, environmental trends towards the product, and society's view of the advertiser and brand.

The position of the competition within the market is one of the most important factors in the campaign, because the market evaluates the product in relation to similar products. The product tends to be acquired where it offers the best value to the market, with that market determining its own criteria regarding value. Value includes aspects such as the product's physical attributes, but also includes other factors such as availability, after-sales service, cost, image and reputation. The competition should be defined in as much detail as possible. An attempt should be made to gain information that is as detailed as that of the product itself, so that direct comparisons between the different products and brands can be made.

Critical information

The situation analysis concludes with a description of critical information such as the campaign's time schedules (date of commencement, duration, et cetera), the budget, constraints or obligations that may apply to any aspect of the campaign, as well as creative and media parameters. For example, a campaign may be specified for the summer months of December to February; have an overall budget of R1,6 million for production and media; be committed to television advertising worth a minimum of R400 000 because of a prior contract for the purchase of television time, and exclude all animals from the creative execution because of the advertised product's harmful effect on dogs, cats and mice.

ACTIVITY

Imagine that you have just opened a food store in your neighbourhood. You are planning a local advertising campaign. Complete a situation analysis in terms of the criteria that are noted above.

Strategy

4

This is the phase in which a strategy is developed for the advertising. *Strategy* is the range of actions that will be taken to achieve the stated objectives. The foundation of the strategy is the information that has been gained during the situation analysis.

The advertising campaign is implemented to achieve a particular objective (or objectives). Once the objective has been clearly specified, the advertising strategy is devised. Advertising strategy comprises two predominant components, creative strategy and media strategy, but also includes other aspects such as budget allocation, task allocation, and the creation of review mechanisms.

Set the advertising objective

The advertising objective is the set of circumstances that the advertising must achieve. At the outset of the analysis a specific marketing problem or opportunity is identified. The advertising is used to address the problem or opportunity. Despite having identified the problem or opportunity, it may not have been set out as specific objectives for the advertising. The situation analysis may have illuminated some aspects of the problem or objective that were previously unknown or not considered important, and these aspects could affect the advertising objective. The objective may therefore be formulated differently at this point in view of the findings of the analysis. The objective must, however, coincide with longer-term advertising objectives and the broader marketing goals of which it is part, and the objective must be co-ordinated with the objectives of the other marketing components. The product, consumers and market environment evolve in time, making a reassessment of the objective necessary for each campaign.

The advertising objective can be specified after the strengths and weaknesses of the product, its competitive position, and the nature and needs of the market have been considered. The objective must be written. The advertising campaign points out the direction that the advertising will take, makes it possible for everyone who is involved to understand the purpose of the campaign, and acts as a measure of success at the conclusion of the campaign.

The advertising objective should identify the perception that is to be embraced by the target market at the conclusion of the campaign. The objective generally deals with persuasion, awareness, information dissemination or change in the predisposition to behave. It is important to avoid objectives that advertising cannot attain. Such objectives would include marketing goals that are not attainable by communication alone, and behavioural changes that cannot result from communication. If the objectives are to be accurately measured and directly related to the operations and actions of the advertiser and audience, it is preferable to set goals that affect **predisposition to behave** rather than behaviour itself.

Although the ultimate objective of most advertising is to increase sales, the relationship between advertising and sales is generally indirect. The best that advertising can do is to supply the communication that supports and reinforces purchasing behaviour. Advertising can assist in all of the behavioural steps that lead to the purchase by creating awareness, ensuring recall, identifying benefits, publicising availability and cost, reinforcing brand perceptions, et cetera.

The advertising objective must be realistic, acceptable to those who are to achieve it, and include everything that is to be achieved. It should specify the target audience to be reached by the campaign, the perception that is to be created amongst that audience, the time by which the campaign is to attain its objective, and the result that the campaign is to achieve. Specification is more precise if quantified values are given to the objective.

In a campaign to establish the difference between a product and the rest of the products in the product category, an objective could be:

> to create a 70 per cent perception amongst 12 – 24-year-olds by the end of the campaign that the taste of Spring Gum lasts longer than any other chewing gum.

When the advertising objective has been set, the advertising strategy is created.

Advertising strategy

Advertising strategy is the planned means of attaining the advertising objective. The overall advertising strategy is stated in order to place the remainder of the strategic decisions within the overall advertising framework. The advertising strategy statement may specify some or all of the following (cf. Runyon 1984):

▶ budget allocation to the different tasks or audiences;

▶ distribution of the advertising effort in time and place;

▶ the relationship between advertising and the other marketing activities;

▶ specification of what is to be advertised (e.g. specific products in a product line);

▶ the dominance of media or creative considerations in the campaign.

Creative strategy

▶ **The copy platform:** The creation of the copy platform occurs at the outset. The copy platform guides the creative team by specifying the elements that should be included in the advertising and by establishing the focus. It specifies the basic elements of the creative strategy. The copy platform is a written statement that could identify the following (cf. Arens & Bovée 1994; Engel, Warshaw & Kinnear 1994):

Who	–	the most likely prospects for the product
Why	–	the reasons for the advertising (the objective)
		and
		the reasons for the consumer's interest in the product – the needs that the product satisfies (rational or emotional)
What	–	the factors that appeal to the audience (positioning, image, strengths and weaknesses, features)
Where	–	the location and medium for the communication
When	–	the time of the communication
How	–	the style, approach or tone of the advertising.

Very often the copy platform will not contain all the information mentioned above. Much of the detail that could be included in the copy platform may need to be developed in the remainder of the creative process. The market needs that the advertising will address, as well as the appeals, approach, and even the timing and media could be selected at a later stage.

The copy platform is an important starting point in the creative process, but to become advertising it must be translated into an advertising message. The message is created by first establishing the creative concept and the major selling idea (i.e. **what** the advertisement will communicate); and secondly, by establishing the creative execution (**how** the advertisement will communicate).

▶ **The creative concept**: The first step in the creation of the communication message is the establishment of the *creative concept* (in other words, **what** the message will communicate). The creative concept (i.e. the **big idea** or the **major selling idea**) is the one idea that will establish the intended perception of the product in the minds of the target audience. The creative concept should join the benefit of the product to the needs of the consumer in a unique way.

The major selling idea must be the strongest single thing that can be said about the product. The major selling idea must be singular, using only **one** concept. The reason is that in an environment of competitive advertising clutter, a single position must be created in the mind of the consumer. More than one concept will dilute and confuse the message.

The major selling idea can be developed in a number of ways. It can be derived by *positioning*, which Arens and Bovée (1994:G-15) define as "the way in which a product is ranked in the consumer's mind by the benefits it offers, by the way it is classified or differentiated from the competition, or by its relationship to certain target markets". Product positioning may be achieved by (cf. Engel et al. 1994:166):

– association with a specific *attribute* such as strength, health, power or reliability;

– *price* and *quality* – although these are attributes, they are considered separately because they are particularly important;

– use or *application* in specific situations and occasions;

– association with a *product user* or class of users;

– association with a *product class;*

– association with *competitors.*

The major selling idea can also be obtained by *identifying the benefit* that only that product offers. It can be obtained by identifying the *inherent drama* that is unique to the product. The major idea can also be obtained by creating a *brand image* that is particularly useful in product categories where unique product attributes or benefits are not evident. A strong brand image can differentiate the product in the minds of the target audience. The USP, or *unique selling proposition*, is a concept that assists in the creation of the major selling idea. It is the offer of a specific benefit to the consumer that is unique to the product and strong enough to attract the market to it. (Cf. Belch & Belch 1995; Engel et al. 1994; Wells et al. 1995.)

In our example of Spring Gum, the major selling idea could be "the taste that lasts longest". This incorporates a **position**, the USP, and an identification with the product benefit.

▶ **Creative execution**: After the communication planner has decided *what* the message will communicate, it is necessary to determine *how* the message will communicate. This is done by devising the *appeal* and the *execution* of the advertising.

  – *The advertising appeal*: The advertiser selects the *advertising appeal* that will attract the attention of the audience most effectively. Advertising appeal is "something that moves people, speaks to their wants or needs, and excites their interest" (Moriarty 1991:76). It is "the specific approach advertisers use to communicate how their products will satisfy customer needs. The two broad types of appeals advertisers use are rational and emotional appeals" (Arens & Bovée 1994:G-2). The advertiser makes a decision on the use of an emotional or a rational appeal, or a combination of the two.

  If the audience's needs are functional or practical, if information or help are required, a rational appeal will generally be more effective. The need will be logically addressed, often with the use of facts. Examples of rational appeals are economy, health, safety, performance, earnings and savings potential. If the audience's needs are social or psychological, an emotional appeal and the inducement of feelings such as satisfaction, pleasure, excitement, arousal, curiosity, comfort, romance, pride, sympathy, esteem or recognition may be more effective.

  Message approaches are not all emotional or rational. They could, for example, act as reminders or use a combination of rational and emotional appeals.

  – *The execution*: The execution is the actual presentation of the appeal to the audience. It is the vehicle that communicates the message to the audience. The execution must be appropriate to the audience and the media that will be used. The campaign's message can obviously be executed in any number of ways. It may be an announcement, humorous, factual, a demonstration, a dramatisation, based upon the product image or brand, a testimonial, a fantasy, musical, based upon personality or authority, a personal recommendation, presented as technical or scientific evidence, an offer, animation, a lifestyle demonstration, or a "slice of life" (a drama that demonstrates the solution to a problem).

Media strategy

The media strategy is, together with the creative strategy, a core consideration of the overall advertising campaign plan. Media are the communication channels through which the campaign message is transmitted.

The most expensive part of an advertising campaign is normally the purchase of media space and time. All media must be selected with the target audience and communication objective in mind. The primary criteria in media selection include cost, access to the target audience, and ability to convey the campaign message. The media that offer the greatest reach, frequency, and impact on the target audience at the best cost and at the right time will gain preference during media selection.

Reach refers to the total, unduplicated number of people who are exposed to the advertisement, and may refer specifically to the target audience. *Frequency* refers to the number of times that one person (or the average member of the target audience) is exposed to the advertisement.

Impact refers to the strength or power of a medium to convey a message. The greater the medium's impact, the greater the effect of the message upon the audience. Impact is a property of media, but also a property of the message itself. A good message has a far greater impact on one medium than a poor message would have on the same medium.

As media selection criteria, reach, frequency, and impact can be illustrated by the media triangle. The size of the area within the triangle denotes the amount spent. Careful planning and selection can, however, extend the reach, frequency and impact which may be obtained for a specified budget. Media planning is an attempt to obtain the greatest reach, frequency and impact for a given amount of money.

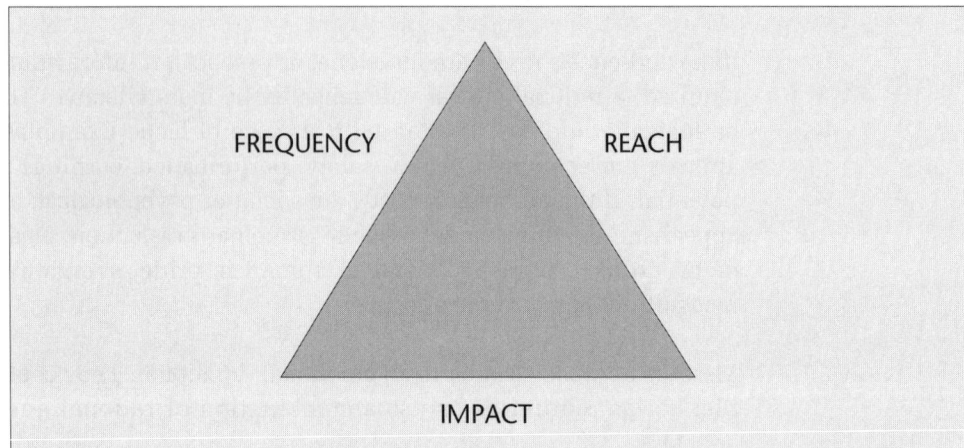

Figure 4.25 **A media triangle that demonstrates an equal expenditure on reach, frequency and impact**

Certain advertising contingencies require greater reach, frequency or impact. The amount spent on one component may therefore be increased or decreased, with a correspondng fluctuation of expenditure on the other components.

Certain media are more effective in delivering each of the components of the media triangle. Personal media have greater impact, but greater expense and lower reach. Mass media, although expensive in terms of total budget, generally cost very little per person reached.

▶ **Print**: Print permits detailed explanation and the opportunity to return to the advertisement as often as the reader pleases. Writing, graphics and pictures are possible, and advertisements are read specifically because of the reader's interest in them. Magazines reach specialised audiences and offer high-quality reproduction, but are relatively expensive, rarely reach the full target audience, and require long lead times before they reach the audience. Newspapers offer the advertiser a wide variety of colour, size and placement opportunities. Advertisements can be placed at short notice. However, newspapers offer lower reproduction quality and relatively high wastage – not all newspaper readers see or pay attention to every advertisement.

▶ **Electronic media**: Electronic media – radio and television – tend to reach mass markets, but in South Africa, as in many other parts of the world, electronic media audiences are becoming fragmented as the variety of media options increases. Electronic media are gaining more of the characteristics of specialised and personal media as narrower audience niches become available to the advertiser. For example, Teletext, faxes and the Internet have made possible the individual interaction between advertiser and prospect.

The sound and visual characteristics of radio and television make it possible to convey emotional messages effectively, but these messages are transient. The electronic media attract large audiences at little cost per person reached, but costs can be very high per commercial.

The opportunities offered by the sight and sound of television permit great creativity, but repetition of commercials is normally required to attain results. The proliferation of television advertising has resulted in clutter that reduces the effectiveness of the individual commercial. The production costs of television advertisements are generally high, as are the placement costs at peak times when mass audiences are viewing.

Radio can be listened to while participating in other activities and travelling. It is a versatile and mobile medium that reaches fairly distinct market segments. It has low impact, however, with the result that radio advertising may not gain the attention of all listeners. Radio advertising is relatively inexpensive to produce and place.

▶ **Cinema**: Cinema has the audio and visual advantages of television. These advantages tend to be increased because the audience is captive, has few distractions, and is faced with the greater visual and sound impact of a large screen and good acoustics. Cinema advertising is expensive to produce, although it may be combined with the production of television material. Cinema does not have access to mass markets, tending towards regional and young adult audiences.

▶ **Outdoor**: Outdoor advertising such as billboards and signs reaches large audiences at low cost. The creative possibilities and the complexity of the message that can be conveyed are, however, limited. Outdoor advertising is therefore effective in building brand awareness and supporting other media messages.

▶ **Direct marketing**: Direct marketing includes a range of media and methods that go a lot further than direct mail, which was one of the original methods for inducing a direct sales response from the market. Direct mail, stickers, posters, telemarketing, press, electronic media and even door-to-door calling can be used for direct marketing. Fill (1995:331) defines direct marketing as "all media activities that generate a series of communications and responses with an existing or potential customer".

Unlike most advertising, direct marketing offers a direct measure of the sales response to each burst of advertising. It offers the audience the result of the full marketing mix. The promotion, sale and distribution of the product all exist within the direct marketing mechanism. An ongoing direct marketing programme does, however, require the development of a particular structure to maintain and manage the direct marketing process. The definition of the target audience becomes very important, with increasing importance being placed upon the creation of effective customer databases.

▶ **Other media**: The media spectrum does not only include mass media such as radio or magazines, but in less formal environments could also include unconventional media such as theatre, folk and traditional media, vehicles, buildings or public spaces.

A campaign's media may be divided into *primary* and *secondary media*. Primary media have the primary task of delivering the advertising message to the target audience, while the secondary media support the delivery of the message.

Resource and task allocation

The people, groups and companies that are involved in the creation and execution of the communication campaign are identified, and the resources for its implementation are allocated to them.

ACTIVITY

Having completed a situation analysis in the last activity, you are now ready to create your food store's advertising campaign. Using the components of the model described above, devise the advertising strategy, focusing especially upon the overall, creative and media strategies.

Implementation

Implementation is the phase in which the advertising is created and delivered to the target audiences at the planned time in the selected media.

The campaign should ideally run exactly to strategy, but the advertiser should be prepared to adapt some elements of the plan if necessary. During implementation the advertiser pays particular attention to production, timing, media and budget control.

Production

The advertising material that is to be used in the media is produced. This is generally done by specialist companies. An important consideration is the budget framework that has been set for production.

Timing

Good planning is fruitless if it is not implemented at the correct time, in the right place and for the necessary period. The media exposure (in the press, on television or outdoor) must be timeously purchased according to the framework given in the media plan; material must be delivered to the media before the material deadlines; and the advertising must be monitored to ensure that it is given exposure at the right time, place, and for the right duration.

The timing of the advertising may need adaptation if the target audience is not being reached. Resources permitting, the advertiser may repeat or extend parts of the campaign.

Budget control

The advertiser must review costs throughout the campaign. Budget control is easier with formal media, because the costs are contractually stipulated. Cost control is more difficult where informal media are used because the pricing of services may be variable, and contingent upon the particular situation.

Evaluation

Evaluation occurs at the end of the campaign. The **specific** and **measurable** criteria that were set for the campaign in the advertising strategy are evaluated. The advertiser determines whether the advertising campaign's objective has been attained, if any corrective action is necessary, and the actions that will follow the campaign's completion.

Objective attainment

The advertiser determines whether the overall campaign objective and its component objectives have been attained. These could include aspects such as target audience reach, average frequency and information transfer. The advertiser must further decide whether the campaign has attained the set budget, media and creative objectives. The research methods that will be used to evaluate the overall effectiveness of the campaign are then selected and implemented.

Corrective action and follow-up

If the advertising campaign has been successful, the next step should be decided upon. The results of the advertising campaign will be incorporated in the situation analysis that lays the groundwork for the next campaign.

If the campaign has failed partially or completely, actions that can rectify the problem must be identified, and corrective action planned.

ACTIVITY

Having completed the situation analysis and strategic plan for your food store's advertising campaign, you are now ready to implement the campaign. Give a brief outline of the steps that you would follow, and the criteria that you would use to implement and evaluate your campaign.

4.7 CRITICAL RESEARCH ISSUES IN ADVERTISING

Key terms to understand and remember

active outward orientation
basic research
S-M-C-R model

applied research
passive inward orientation

The focus of advertising research

Companies advertise to achieve specific marketing goals. As we noted earlier, interest in advertising is therefore focused primarily upon its applications, and advertising research reflects this. Far more attention is given to the acquisition of knowledge that will lead to immediate benefits in a particular advertising project than to the underlying "laws" of the field.

The underlying principles of advertising lie in the sciences that form its foundations such as communication, sociology, psychology and economics. Most of the *basic research* or *theoretical research* in advertising therefore extends from these fields, although the advertising phenomenon does receive some attention from scholars who wish to learn more about the field as a whole. The greatest research attention is not, however, given to basic research. Far more attention is given to specific, *applied research* in areas of advertising such as media selection, audience profiling and copy testing. The bulk of the investigation into advertising can therefore be classified as applied research.

The research issues in advertising can be described in terms of the *S-M-C-R model* of communication. Research tends to focus upon questions related to the *sender* (communicator or advertiser) and the product of that advertiser; the *message* or advertisement; the *channel* or medium through which the advertisement is sent; and the *receiver* or target audience of the advertised message.

The major questions that are addressed in advertising research are discussed here in terms of the S-M-C-R model. Particular attention is paid to research that has a bearing upon *communication*, and less attention is devoted to the marketing, economic or psychological components of advertising.

The advertiser and product

The advertiser can be viewed as the sender in the advertising communication process, and research at this level focuses upon the advertiser and the advertiser's products.

The advertiser

The company that advertises has an important effect upon the target audience's perception of its advertised products. The perception of products is largely affected by a company's **personality**. Research into the company's character, **personality** and culture delivers important information for the advertising plan. The situation analysis that precedes the development of the advertising strategy should include the findings of research into the company. Fill (1995:162–176) identifies five areas that should be addressed in organisational analysis.

Firstly, corporate strategy and its communication should be evaluated. The degree to which corporate strategy is communicated within the company affects the degree to which its members embrace that strategy. A company that incorporates and expresses its corporate strategy within its operations tends to create within its environment a perception that reflects that strategy. The degree to which the company's corporate strategy can be implemented and will be accepted is determined by the company's ability to attain its objectives, its past performance, the effectiveness of its communication; and the credibility of its chief executive officer (cf. Fill 1995:164–165).

Secondly, corporate culture should be evaluated (see the discussion of corporate culture in Unit 2). Angelopulo (1990) proposes that organisational culture is a phenomenon that can be expressed along a continuum of basic assumptions. At the one extreme, companies can be defined as *passively inward oriented*. Their personnel view their roles within the company in isolation from the rest of the staff; largely ignore the potential and importance of the environment in the success of the company; do not disseminate important information and do not actively seek new information; view their company as a whole that is closed from, and unaffected by, the environment; and react to, rather than actively engage the environment. *Actively outward oriented* companies have staff and management who view their roles as interrelated parts of the greater company; attempt to understand their environment fully; seek and distribute important information; realise the reciprocal influences of the environment and their company; and actively engage the environment. Companies that are actively outward oriented tend to grasp the communication requirements for the solution of problems and the maximisation of opportunities that the environment offers.

Thirdly, the company's identity and image should be considered. According to Fill (1995:169), companies "project their personality through their identity. The audience's perception of the identity is the image they have of the … corporate body." The concepts **image** and **identity** must be seen in the light of the discussion of these concepts in Unit 3.

The fourth component is an evaluation of the company's most recent communications with its target audiences. The research can comprise the findings of communication campaign evaluations and independent communication assessments, and these findings can be accumulated over time to determine key communication requirements and the position of the company and its products in relation to the competition. An ongoing assessment makes it possible to establish the effectiveness of past strategies, corporate image and objective attainment amongst important audience segments.

The fifth element is the evaluation of the company's functional capability, which largely determines the extent and content of its advertising. Fill (1995:175–176) identifies three areas that should be assessed: the financial, manufacturing and marketing capabilities of the company.

The product

The importance of understanding the product that is to be advertised, and the target audience's awareness and perception of the product, have been noted in the earlier discussion on the advertising campaign.

Important product information includes the role that it plays in the lives of the target market, the needs that it satisfies, the methods and reasons for its use, its make-up, cost, strengths, weaknesses, distribution, availability, presentation, its tangible and intangible attributes and values. Each of these factors has a bearing upon the target audience's perception of the product, which is one of the central issues in advertising.

"Positioning is often the most critical element in a firm's marketing strategy because it defines the perception the firm intends consumers to have of its product. In addition, positioning directs the entire marketing mix of the firm" (Engel et al. 1994:164). *Positioning* is "the way in which a product is ranked in the consumer's mind by the benefits it offers, by the way it is classified or differentiated from the competition, or by its relationship to certain target markets" (Arens & Bovée

1994:G-15). The existing position of the product, the position that is intended for it, and its position in relation to competitive products, are central considerations in advertising. The success of the product depends upon accurate positioning. Effective advertising requires the foundation of an accurate product position – the remainder of the advertising process deals with the execution that will best establish that position.

Effective positioning is directly linked to effective research. "Positioning is only as good as the research it is based on" (Burnett 1993:59). Research must establish the value that the market places upon the individual and combined attributes of the product and its competition. Research is applicable throughout the development of a product's position, which Engel et al. (1994:167) see as a seven-step process:

▶ identify the competitors;

▶ determine the market's perception of the competitors;

▶ determine the relative positions of the product and its competitors;

▶ identify open positions or positioning gaps relative to consumer needs;

▶ select the desired position for the product;

▶ implement the marketing and promotional strategy to attain the desired position;

▶ monitor the product's position in the market.

Research is particularly valuable in steps 1 – 4 and in step 7. One of the most effective research tools for the positioning process is the perceptual map. Perceptual maps are used to establish the market's needs in the product category and the relative position of the products in the category. Perceptual maps are created by positioning products or attributes on a grid. Each axis of the grid represents a product attribute. For example, a perceptual map could identify the relative position of particular models of cars in consumers' minds, relative to two attributes – quality and performance. Figure 4.26 depicts such a perceptual map.

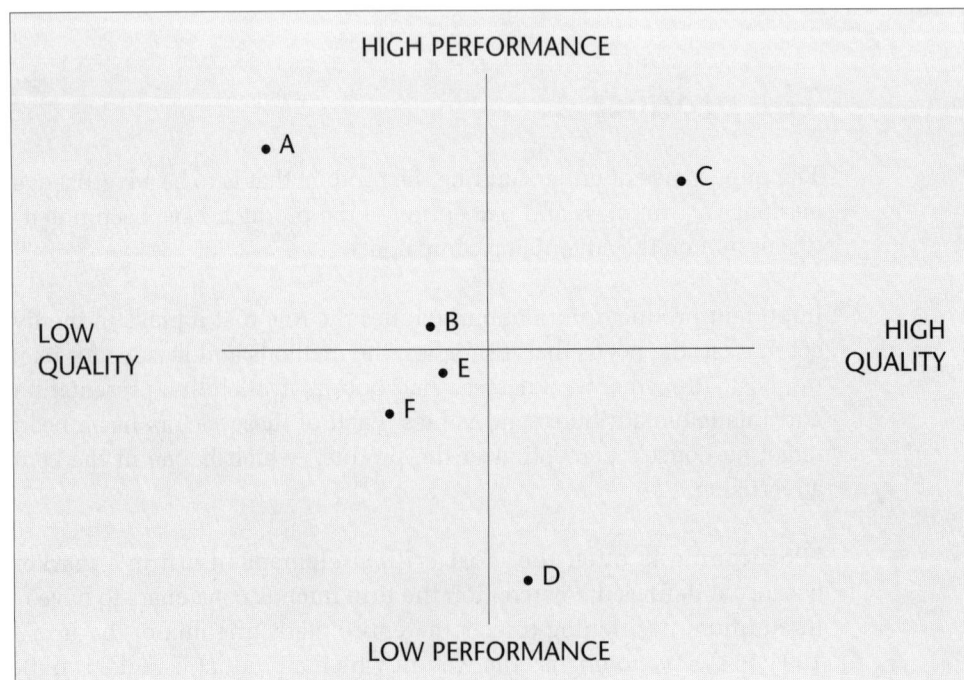

Figure 4.26 **Perceptual map for the car market**

Model A is therefore perceived to have high performance but low quality, model C is perceived to have high performance and high quality. The closer the grouping of products, the greater the competition and the more difficult it is to compete in that particular sector (e.g. models B, F and E); the wider the grouping, the greater the product differentiation and the greater the opportunity for the introduction of a product with a unique position in the market. Positioning strategies are most commonly based upon product features, price/quality, use, product class dissociation (dissociation with an uninteresting or inferior product class), product users, competitors, benefits, and cultural symbols (cf. Fill 1995:245–248).

Positioning can be obtained by a number of methods. Qualitative methods such as focus groups, and quantitative methods such as cluster analysis and multidimensional scaling can be used. Two-dimensional maps such as the one in Figure 4.26 are not the only ones that are used. Perceptual maps may include a number of dimensions.

ACTIVITY

Consider any product that you regularly use. Attempt to analyse this product in terms of the theoretical criteria that have been discussed above, focusing upon the company that manufactures the product and the product itself.

The advertisement as the message

The advertisement is the message in the advertising process. Evaluation of the creative product is contentious because it is extremely difficult to evaluate the effects that the ideas within advertisements generate. Evaluation of the communication component of advertisements can, however, generate usable data (cf. Sinclair & Barenblatt 1993). Research into the advertisement itself can generally be divided into two categories, pre- and post-testing. Pretesting is implemented before the advertisement is exposed in the media, and post-testing is implemented after exposure.

Pretesting is used to evaluate the elements to be included in the advertising and to test the creative product prior to its implementation. Research that precedes the creative process is closely related to, and in some cases incorporates the research that has been discussed above. The needs of the market, evaluation of the product, and the position of the product in relation to the competition are all factors that must be considered before the creative strategy is developed.

During the creative process and prior to its implementation, research can be used to develop and refine the advertisement, and to establish whether it achieves its communication objectives. The trial advertisement can be ranked with others in order of best-liked to least-liked; and it can be paired with individual advertisements to permit direct comparison. Words or images can be left out of the trial advertisement in a *cloze procedure*, where respondents are asked to complete the sentence or image – if this is successfully done, the advertisement is deemed to convey its message well. *Copy tests* and *theatre tests* evaluate the copy and imagery of print and television advertisements for readability, comprehension, degree of liking, and even the degree to which the advertisement may induce a sale (cf. Jugenheimer & White 1991:41–44).

Post-testing is research that attempts to establish the effectiveness of existing advertising and the direction that the advertising should follow in the future. Research typically deals with *recognition* and *recall* of advertisements and their parts; *awareness* of the product that the advertisement advertises; *knowledge* of the product that is advertised; and *association* between the advertisement and the product. Each of these can be tested at one point in time or over time with a *tracking study*, during which changes in the performance of the advertisement can be evaluated (cf. Jugenheimer & White 1991:44–47.)

The media

Advertising media are the channels of advertising. They receive extensive attention in advertising research because of their central position in the delivery of the advertiser's message to the target audience. Media research is used primarily to assist in *media planning*. "The purpose of media planning is to conceive, analyse, and select channels of communication that will direct the advertising message to the right people in the right place at the right time" (Arens & Bovée 1994:366). Also important in media planning is the selection of media at the most economical rate for the benefits derived.

Although media planning is the task of advertising that is most easily quantified and measured, it remains a creative process. Many media placement decisions can be planned and evaluated on the basis of measured standards, but the qualitative dimension of media placement and the selection of media combinations require creativity and experience that cannot be quantified. Nonetheless, the media planner makes extensive use of research in the selection of the media channels to use for each campaign. The research that is most commonly sought by the media planner focuses on sales and market data, competitive advertising, consumer data, media audience, distribution and cost information (cf. Engel et al. 1994:315–333; Jugenheimer & White 1991:232–235).

The critical research issues in media planning are therefore concentrated around the areas that the media planner focuses upon most closely – the placement of advertising in media that will reach the greatest portion of the target audience with the greatest frequency and impact as economically as possible. Research must deliver information on the extent, geographical characteristics and timing patterns of consumption of the advertised product and the product class as a whole. The amounts spent on advertising and the advertising patterns of competitors, and the characteristics of the target market (demographic, sociographic, psychographic and other information such as product and media usage) will affect the media plan. The available media must be evaluated in terms of the audience size and percentage of the total audience that they deliver. The cost of placing advertising in each medium must be evaluated in terms of cost per person reached and the total cost of placement.

ACTIVITY

Analyse the advertising for the product that you considered in the previous Activity. Evaluate its effectiveness (with yourself as the sole respondent) in terms of recall, recognition, and likeability. Without taking the budget into consideration, critically evaluate the media selection of the advertising campaign for the product. If you believe that the schedule could be improved, explain how and why; if not, give your reasons for believing that the existing media schedule is best.

The target audience

The receivers in the advertising process are the members of the target audience. A component of the market orientation that was described earlier is the delivery of products to consumers that they want and need. Central to marketing, and the advertising that is part of it, is therefore the accurate definition of the market and its needs. In the context of advertising, this permits the positioning of products that the market wants in a way that appeals to that market.

Very few products appeal to the mass market as a whole. It is therefore necessary that the advertiser identifies the market to be targeted for a particular product, and then creates advertising that will reach that market effectively. The identification of viable sections of the market and the advertising audiences within it is achieved by *market segmentation*. The total market is broken into segments that comprise people who have similar product needs. Research is required to define the specific segment to which the advertiser will address the advertising message. A full understanding of this market segment is needed for the development of the overall advertising strategy and the media and creative strategies.

The research that is used for audience segmentation uses a number of bases. *Geographic segmentation* is based upon the geographic position of audiences. Criteria for *demographic segmentation* are variables such as age, gender, level of education, income, dwelling and family size. *Psychographic segmentation* uses lifestyle and personality variables, and *sociographic segmentation* uses group, political and social affiliations as the segmentation criteria. *Behaviouristic segmentation* divides audiences on grounds of usage (product type and level of usage), buying patterns and product loyalties; *benefit segmentation* does so using the categories of benefits that audiences search for in products; *audience type segmentation* divides audiences into end-user, decision-maker, business-user and industrial-user groups. These categories are not mutually exclusive, and are used separately or in combinations.

The information that is obtained in the segmentation process is used to build a *profile* of the target audience. A profile is a description of the target audience that is meaningful to the advertiser. The information derived from the segmentation process may comprise statistics and data which have little meaning in themselves. Profiling interprets this information and permits the advertiser to describe a "typical" member of the audience for whom advertising can be written and media purchased. The findings of the research into audiences is used extensively in the positioning, creative and media processes.

ACTIVITY

Using only the elements that have been described above and your own critical ability, attempt to specify the audience profile of the advertising for the product that was described in the last Activity.

Key terms to understand and remember

brand value	business cycle
consumer demand	hierarchy of effects
sales effects	the abundance principle

Advertising in society

So far we have discussed advertising as a value-neutral phenomenon. Advertising is seen as a part of the marketing process, assisting in the supply of need-satisfying products to consumers. From this point of view, advertising has a number of functions, and certain powers are ascribed to it. These are not always seen in a neutral light, however. Largely because of its visibility in the social and economic arenas, the societal influence of advertising has received much attention. The impact of advertising upon society tends to be discussed in terms of psychological, economic and ethical effects. Advertising is specifically evaluated in terms of sales effects, its hierarchical effect upon the behaviour of consumers, the value that it adds to products, profitability, the effect upon pricing, consumer demand, competition, the business cycle and overall economic impact.

Sales effects

One of the primary functions of advertising is to assist in the generation of sales. Although the link between advertising and sales is tentative in most fields outside direct marketing, sales remain one of the main reasons for the use of advertising. Advertising is assumed to affect sales because, as a form of communication that has a psychological impact, it can affect the audience's predisposition towards the purchase of the advertised product (cf. Burnett 1993:286). It is also assumed to lower the cost of the sales process by reaching the potential market with the sales message much more economically than alternative means such as personal selling (cf. Arens & Bovée 1994:23).

Hierarchy of effects

As a psychological phenomenon, advertising is also perceived to generate a hierarchy of effects in audiences. Advertising is seen to draw the audiences into a relationship with the product through a series of effects that may typically begin with the creation of awareness and culminate in the sale. Advertising communicates product information, induces trial of the product, and promotes increased usage (cf. Arens & Bovée 1994:23).

Value

One of the major reasons for advertising is to add value to products and brands (cf. Burnett 1993:291). The intention is to establish brand loyalty, to create an appropriate image, and to add values that would be difficult to achieve without the symbolic ability of advertising. Arens and Bovée (1994:22) describe as the most basic marketing function of advertising "to identify products and differentiate them from others".

Profitability

Although the relationship between advertising and sales is difficult to establish, research has identified a relationship between advertising and profitability. It has been found that businesses that spend more on advertising as a percentage of sales have a higher return on investment, and market share is related to the businesses' relative expenditure on advertising (cf. Burnett 1993:294).

Pricing

Because advertising is expensive, it is often assumed to increase the price of advertised products. The price of advertising is built into the cost of the product, so it is ultimately paid for by the consumer.

The argument on pricing is not, however, simple. It has been pointed out that the amount spent on advertising as a percentage of most products' price is small. Sinclair and Barenblatt (1993:59) point out that a small percentage of consumption spending is allocated to advertising – in 1992 the figure in South Africa was only 1,5 per cent. Because advertising contributes to mass production, it indirectly results in the lowering of the unit price per item, and this results in lower cost to the consumer. Retail advertising tends to lower prices because it promotes price competition, while product advertising promotes features and thereby supports higher prices (cf. Arens & Bovée 1994:31).

Advertising has a particular relationship with the pricing of one product category to which it is closely related – that of media. Because of its economic support of the media in which it is carried, advertising covers a proportion of the media's costs that otherwise would have been paid for by the consumer. Advertising therefore reduces the cost of media to the consumer.

Competition

It has been proposed that advertising promotes monopoly and oligopoly, and restricts competition because new entrants in the market cannot compete against the advertising voice that is projected by the large, existing firms. The establishment of monopolies and oligopolies could result in price inflation; advertisers' retention of the money saved by economies of scale instead of passing the benefits on to the consumer; no product improvement; intercompany collusion; and barriers of entry into the market (cf. Sinclair & Barenblatt 1993:56).

Intense competition does result in the reduction of the number of participants in a market sector, but advertising may play a smaller role than poor service, an inferior product, poor pricing or inadequate distribution in this process. No advertiser, no matter how large, can support advertising media to such an extent that it can dominate a market. Arens and Bovée (1994:31) point out that regional companies and unadvertised house-brands compete successfully against large national advertisers. In markets that are characterised by heavy advertising expenditure, advertising does tend to inhibit new entrants. But this is also the case with heavy expenditure levels in other areas of business such as plant and machinery.

Consumer demand

Advertising and consumer demand have often been associated with each other. Although a relationship does exist between promotional activity and aggregate consumption, there is little consensus on the extent of this relationship. When compared to other social and economic influences such as education, income and lifestyle, advertising has comparatively less effect upon overall consumption. Advertising appears to reinforce greater societal trends rather than guide and determine them. It has not, for example, been able to alter declining fashion trends or the use of products that are no longer sought after; but it has assisted in the acceptance and consumption of new products such as computers. "In growing markets, advertisers generally compete for shares of that growth. In mature, static, or declining markets, they compete for each other's shares" (Arens & Bovée 1994:32).

A second aspect regarding consumer demand is the ability of advertising to promote worthless products and to mislead. The promotion of such products is inevitable in any market, and although controls exist in most markets to prevent identifiably fraudulent business practices, the promotion of faulty products and untruthful advertising, markets themselves tend to prevent widespread and continuous consumption of products that do not meet the needs of consumers. "The ultimate test of the quality of any product takes place in the marketplace ... Advertising ... cannot hypnotise ... [the market] into continuing to buy a product that does not satisfy" (Kaufman 1987:508).

Business cycle

Advertising has an effect upon business trends, but the extent of this effect is disputed. At best, advertising can be seen to ameliorate or reinforce the overall business cycle, but it has never proved to be a major determinant in the cycle. Sustained advertising cannot avert an overall business downturn, and it cannot reverse overall business trends. Advertising has, however, benefited companies that maintain their advertising during recessionary times during the economic upturn that follows.

The abundance principle

The overall economic impact of advertising in societies that produce more than they can consume is described as the *abundance principle*. This states that advertising promotes competition among companies and keeps advertisers informed of product choices in these societies. Advertising cannot, however, maintain products that consumers do not want, or products that are priced at levels that consumers are not prepared to pay.

ACTIVITY

Briefly consider the relative position of Coca Cola and Pepsi Cola in your market. Evaluate the advertising of each brand in terms of the criteria that have been noted above, and describe in your own words the impact of the brands' advertising upon their relative market position, the cola and soft drink market, and their economic sector.

Summary

In this unit we considered advertising from a number of perspectives. We began by looking at the historical development of advertising from its earliest origins up to the present. We also considered the position of advertising as it has evolved in South Africa.

Because advertising is so closely affiliated to marketing, we considered marketing and the marketing approach, paying particular attention to the wide and narrow definitions of marketing. The position and role of advertising within the marketing process was considered.

The classification of advertising was considered by discussing various categories of advertising. The theoretical foundations of advertising were considered, and Baker's model of advertising effectiveness discussed in detail.

Most advertising is intended to achieve certain goals within a certain period. Such advertising is best approached within the framework of the advertising campaign. The concept of an advertising campaign was discussed, and a detailed model for the planning, implementation and assessment of an advertising campaign described.

The primary areas of research in advertising were considered in the light of the fact that most research is applied, with comparatively little that could be considered basic or theoretical. Advertising research was discussed in terms of the areas in which it is most focused, those of communicator, message, channel, and receiver. Advertising is widely seen to possess certain economic and social "powers", and for this reason it receives much attention. In this unit we critically considered the primary psychological, economic and ethical effects that are ascribed to advertising.

SUGGESTED READING

Affinity Advertising and Publishing. 1993. *Brands and branding in South Africa: key success stories*. Johannesburg: Affinity.

Arens, W.F. & Bovée, C.L. 1994. *Advertising*. 5th edition. Burr Ridge: Irwin.

Barenblatt, M. & Sinclair, R. 1989. *Make the other half work too*. Halfway House: Southern.

Burnett, J.J. 1993. *Promotion management*. Boston: Houghton Mifflin.

Fill, C. 1995. *Marketing communications*. London: Prentice-Hall.

Percy, L. & Woodside, A.G. 1983. *Advertising and consumer psychology*. Lexington, Mass: Lexington.

Presbrey, F. 1968. *The history and development of advertising*. New York: Greenwood.

Sinclair, R. & Barenblatt, M. 1993. *The South African advertising book*. 3rd edition. Halfway House: Southern.

Skinner, S.J. 1994. *Marketing*. 2nd edition. Boston: Houghton Mifflin.

Sutherland, M. 1993. *Advertising and the mind of the consumer*. St Leonards, Aust: Allen & Unwin.

Wells, W., Burnett, J. & Moriarty, S. 1995. *Advertising*. 3rd edition. Englewood Cliffs, NJ: Prentice-Hall.

Sources

UNIT 1

Arens, W.F. & Bovée, C.L. 1994. *Advertising*. 5th edition. Burr Ridge: Irwin.

Ayres, J. & Miller, J. 1994. *Effective public speaking*. 4th edition. Dubuque, Ia: Brown & Benchmark.

Berlo, D.K. 1960. *The process of communication. An introduction to theory and practice.* New York: Holt, Rinehart & Winston.

Biagi, S. 1992. *Interviews that work: a practical guide for journalists*. Belmont, Calif: Wadsworth.

Boyd, A. 1994. *Broadcast journalism. Techniques of radio and TV news*. 3rd edition. Oxford: Focal.

Bredenkamp, C. 1996. An introduction to persuasive communication, in *Introduction to communication: course book 4 – communication planning and management*, edited by R.S. Rensburg, Cape Town: Juta.

Brown, M. & Brandreth, G. 1986. *Suksesvolle onderhoude*. Cape Town: Tafelberg.

Burke, K. 1969. *A rhetoric of motives*. Berkeley, Calif: University of California Press.

Cathcart, R.S. 1988. *Post communication. Rhetorical analysis and evaluation*. 2nd edition. New York: Macmillan.

Clevenger, T. 1966. *Audience analysis*. Indianapolis: Bobbs-Merrill.

Corbett, E.P.J. (ed.) 1984. *The rhetoric and poetics of Aristotle*. New York: Random House.

Damer, T.E. 1987. *Attacking faulty reasoning*. 2nd edition. Belmont, Calif: Wadsworth.

Davis, W.A. 1986. *An introduction to logic.* Englewood Cliffs, NJ: Prentice-Hall.

DeVito, J.A. 1990. *The elements of public speaking*. New York: HarperCollins.

De Wet, J.C. 1991. *The art of persuasive communication*. 2nd edition. Cape Town: Juta.

De Wet, J.C. & Rensburg, R.S. 1989. *Evaluation of public speaking*. Cape Town: Juta.

Du Plooy, G.M. 1991. *500 communication concepts. English/Afrikaans*. Cape Town: Juta.

Ehninger, D. 1965. Historical development of speech, in *Introduction to the field of speech,* edited by R.F. Reid, Oakland, NJ: Scott, Foresman.

Freeley, A.J. 1993. *Argumentation and debate. Critical thinking for reasoned decision making.* 8th edition. Belmont, Calif: Wadsworth.

Gronbeck, B.E., German, K., Ehninger, D. & Monroe, A.H. 1992. *Principles of speech communication.* 11th edition. New York: HarperCollins.

Hurst, B. 1992. *The handbook of communication skills.* London: Kogan Page.

Hyde, S.W. 1995. *Television and radio announcing.* 7th edition. Boston: Houghton Mifflin.

Koehler, J.W. & Sisco, J.I. 1981. *Public communication in business and professions.* St. Paul, Minnesota: West.

Lee, R.E. & Lee K.K. 1989. *Arguing persuasively.* New York: Longman.

Littlejohn, S.W. 1992. *Theories of human communication.* 4th edition. Belmont, Calif: Wadsworth.

Mandela, N.R. 1994. Inauguration speech as president of South Africa. 10 May, Pretoria.

Mandela, N.R. 1995. Speech at a pitso. 13 May, Maseru.

Mandela, N.R. 1996. Speech at the football banquet. 1 March, Pretoria.

Maslow, A.H. 1954. *Motivation and personality.* New York: Harper & Row.

McCroskey, J.C. 1978. *An introduction to rhetorical communication.* 3rd edition. Englewood Cliffs, NJ: Prentice-Hall.

Miller, G.R. 1972. *An introduction to speech communication.* 2nd edition. Indianapolis: Bobbs-Merrill.

Naidoo, J. 1996. Speech at Dr Knak Primary School. 22 March, Alexandra.

O'Donnell, L.B., Hausman, C. & Benoit, P. 1987. *Announcing. Broadcast communication today.* Belmont, Calif: Wadsworth.

Osborn, M. & Osborn, S. 1988. *Public speaking.* Boston: Houghton Mifflin.

Packard, V. 1960. *The hidden persuaders.* Harmondsworth: Penguin.

Rafe, S.C. 1991. *Mastering the news media interview: how to succeed at television, radio and print interviews.* New York: HarperBusiness.

Rensburg, R.S. (ed.) 1996. *Introduction to communication: course book 4 – communication planning and management.* Cape Town: Juta.

Schutte, P.J. 1990. *Debattering en redevoering.* Pretoria: Academica.

Schwartz, S.P. 1994. *Fundamentals of reasoning.* New York: Macmillan.

Sinclair, R. & Barenblatt, M. 1993. *The South African advertising book. Make the other half work too.* 3rd edition. Halfway House: Southern.

Skinner, C. & Von Essen, L. 1991. *The handbook of public relations.* 3rd edition. Halfway House: Southern.

Steinberg, S. 1994. *Introduction to communication: course book 1 – the basics.* Cape Town: Juta.

Terrell, D.B. 1967. *Logic: a modern introduction to deductive reasoning.* New York: Holt, Rinehart & Winston.

Toulmin, S.E. 1958. *The uses of argument.* Cambridge: Cambridge University Press.

Toulmin, S., Rieke, R. & Janik, A. 1979. *An introduction to reasoning.* New York: Macmillan.

Tulloch, S. (ed.) 1993. *The Reader's Digest Oxford complete wordfinder.* London: Reader's Digest.

UNIT 2

Bahl, S. 1995. Whither Asian public relations? *Media Asia. An Asian Mass Communication Quarterly* 22(3):136–143.

Baskin, O. & Aronoff, C.E. 1992. *Public relations. The profession and the practice.* 3rd edition. Dubuque, Ia: Wm. C. Brown.

Bell, Q. 1991. *The PR business. An insider's guide to real-life public relations.* London: Kogan Page.

Bell, S.H. & Bell, E.C. 1976. Public relations: functional or functionary. *Public Relations Review* 2(2):47–57.

Bernays, E.L. 1923. *Crystallizing public opinion.* New York: Boni & Liveright.

Bernays, E.L. 1952. *Public relations.* Norman: University of Oklahoma.

Bernays, E.L. 1955. *The engineering of consent.* Norman: University of Oklahoma.

Black, S. 1995. A tribute to Edward Bernays – father of public relations. *International Public Relations Review* 18(2):28–32.

Botan, C. 1993. Introduction to the paradigm struggle in public relations. *Public Relations Review* 19(2):107–110.

Botan, C.H. 1989. Theory development in public relations, in *Public relations theory,* edited by C.H. Botan & V. Hazelton, Jr., Hillsdale, NJ: Lawrence Erlbaum.

Botan, C.H. & Hazelton, V. Jr. (eds) 1989. *Public relations theory.* Hillsdale, NJ: Lawrence Erlbaum.

Center, A.H. & Jackson, P. 1990. *Public relations practices. Managerial case studies and problems.* 4th edition. Englewood Cliffs, NJ: Prentice-Hall.

Cohen, P.M. 1987. *A public relations primer. Thinking and writing in context.* Englewood Cliffs, NJ: Prentice-Hall.

Cutlip, S.M. 1994. *The unseen power: public relations. A history.* Hillsdale, NJ: Lawrence Erlbaum.

Cutlip, S.M., Center, A.H. & Broom, G.M. 1985. *Effective public relations.* 6th edition. Englewood Cliffs, NJ: Prentice-Hall.

Endres, F.F. 1976. Public relations in the White House. *Public Relations Review* 2(3):5–12.

Goldman, E.F. 1948. *Two-way street.* Boston: Bellman.

Grunig, J.E. 1989. Symmetrical presuppositions as a framework for public relations theory, in *Public relations theory,* edited by C.H. Botan & V. Hazelton, Jr, Hillsdale, NJ: Lawrence Erlbaum.

Grunig, J.E. (ed.) 1992. *Excellence in public relations and communication management.* Hillsdale, NJ: Lawrence Erlbaum.

Grunig, J.E. & Grunig, L.A. (eds) 1989. *Public relations research annual. Volume 1.* Hillsdale, NJ: Lawrence Erlbaum.

Grunig, J.E. & Hunt, T. 1984. *Managing public relations.* New York: Holt, Rinehart & Winston.

Hallahan, K. 1993. The paradigm struggle and public relations practice. *Public Relations Review* 19(2):197–205.

Harlow, R.F. 1975. Management, public relations, and the social sciences. *Public Relations Review* 11(1):5–13.

Harlow, R.F. 1988. Building a public relations definition, in *Precision public relations,* edited by R.E. Hiebert, New York: Longman.

Heath, R.L. 1992. The wrangle in the marketplace: a rhetorical perspective of public relations, in *Rhetorical and critical approaches to public relations,* edited by E.L. Toth & R.L. Heath, Hillsdale, NJ: Lawrence Erlbaum.

Hiebert, R.E. (ed.) 1988. *Precision public relations.* New York: Longman.

Hunt, T. & Grunig, J.E. 1994. *Public relations techniques.* Fort Worth: Harcourt Brace College.

Kendall, R. 1992. *Public relations campaign strategies. Planning for implementation.* New York: HarperCollins.

Lesly, P. 1987. Report of the special committee on terminology. *International Public Relations Review* 27(2):5–9.

Long, L.W. & Hazelton, V. Jr. 1987. Public relations: a theoretical and practical response. *Public Relations Review* 13(2):3–13.

Lucas-Bachert, U. 1992. Public relations in Europe. *International Public Relations Review* 15(3):11–15.

Marston, J.E. 1963. *The nature of public relations.* New York: McGraw-Hill.

Miller, G.R. 1989. Persuasion and public relations: two "ps" in a pod, in *Public relations theory,* edited by C.H. Botan & V. Hazelton, Jr, Hillsdale, NJ: Lawrence Erlbaum.

Moscardi, M. & Honiball, A-M. 1993. Public relations in southern Africa. *International Public Relations Review* 16(1):2–6.

Murphy, P. 1991. Limits of symmetry: a game theory approach to symmetric and assymetric public relations, in *Public relations research annual, Volume 3*, edited by L.A. Grunig & J.E. Grunig, Hillsdale, NJ: Lawrence Erlbaum.

Nager, N.R. & Allen, T.H. 1984. *Public relations management by objectives.* New York: Longman.

Newman, W. 1993. New words for what we do? *IPR Journal* 16(2):12–15.

Newsom, D., Scott, A. & VanSlyke Turk, J. 1989. *This is PR. The realities of public relations.* 4th edition. Belmont, Calif: Wadsworth.

Olasky, M.N. 1987. *Corporate public relations. A new historical perspective.* Hillsdale, NJ: Lawrence Erlbaum.

Opukah, S. 1993a. Development and challenges in public relations in Africa – a call for professionalism. *International Public Relations Review* 16(4):12–16.

Opukah, S. 1993b. FAPRA addresses public relations development on the African continent. *IPR Journal* 16(2):15–17.

Rensburg, R.S. (ed.) 1996. *Introduction to communication: course book 4 – communication planning and management.* Cape Town: Juta.

Rensburg, R.S. & Angelopulo, G.C. 1996. *Effective communication campaigns.* Halfway House: International Thomson.

Rensburg, R.S., Mersham, G.M. & Skinner, J.C. 1995. *Public relations, development and social investment. A southern African perspective.* Pretoria: J.L. van Schaik.

Seitel, F.P. 1995. *The practice of public relations.* 6th edition. Englewood Cliffs, NJ: Prentice-Hall.

Skinner, C. & Von Essen, L. 1995. *The handbook of public relations.* 4th edition. Halfway House: Southern.

Van der Meiden, A. 1993. Public relations and 'other' modalities of professional communication: asymmetric presuppositions for a new theoretical discussion. *International Public Relations Review* 16(3):8–11.

Van Ommen, H., Sterk, R. & Van Kuppenveld, E. 1990. *De PR-methode.* Groningen: Wolter-Noordhoff.

Wolter, L.J. & Miles, S.B. 1983. Toward public relations theory. *Public Relations Journal* 39(9):12–16.

UNIT 3

Baskin, O. & Aronoff, C.E. 1992. *Public relations. The profession and the practice.* 3rd edition. Dubuque, Ia: Wm. C. Brown.

Bell, S.H. & Bell, E.C. 1976. Public relations: functional or functionary? *Public Relations Review* 2(2):47–57.

Bivins, T.H. 1992. A system model for ethical decision making in public relations. *Public Relations Review* 18(4):365–383.

Botan, C. 1993. Introduction to the paradigm struggle in public relations. *Public Relations Review* 19(2):107–110.

Broom, G.M., Lauzen, M.M. & Tucker, K. 1991. Public relations and marketing: dividing the conceptual domain and operational turf. *Public Relations Review* 17(3):219–225.

Budd, J. 1995. Communications doesn't define PR, it diminishes it. *Public Relations Review* 21(3):177–179.

Cutlip, S.M., Center, A.H. & Broom, G.M. 1994. *Effective public relations.* 7th edition. Englewood Cliffs, NJ: Prentice-Hall.

Grunig, J.E. (ed.) 1992. *Excellence in public relations and communication management.* Hillsdale, NJ: Lawrence Erlbaum.

Hallahan, K. 1993. The paradigm struggle and public relations practice. *Public Relations Review* 19(2):197–205.

Kaye, M. 1994. *Communication management.* Englewood Cliffs, NJ: Prentice-Hall.

Littlejohn, S.W. 1996. *Theories of human communication.* 5th edition. Belmont, Calif: Wadsworth.

Lubbe, B.A. & Puth, G. (eds) 1994. *Public relations in South Africa. A management reader.* Durban: Butterworths.

Moffit, M.A. 1994. Collapsing and integrating concepts of 'public' and 'image' into a new theory. *Public Relations Review* 20(2):159–170.

Moore, H.F. & Kalupa, F.B. 1985. *Public relations. Principles, cases, and problems.* Homewood, Ill: Irwin.

Newsom, D., Scott, A. & VanSlyke Turk, J. 1989. *This is PR. The realities of public relations.* 4th edition. Belmont, Calif: Wadsworth.

Overton-De Klerk, N. 1994. Corporate social responsibility, in *Public relations in South Africa. A management reader,* edited by B.A. Lubbe & G. Puth, Durban: Butterworths.

Parsons, P.H. 1993. Framework for analysis of conflicting loyalties. *Public Relations Review* 19(1):49–57.

Pearson, R. 1989. Albert J. Sullivan's theory of public relations ethics. *Public Relations Review* 15(2):52–62.

Pratt, C.B. 1991. PRSA members' perceptions of public relations ethics. *Public Relations Review* 17(2):145–159.

Rensburg, R.S. (ed.) 1996. *Introduction to communication: course book 4 – communication planning and management.* Cape Town: Juta.

Seitel, F.P. 1995. *The practice of public relations.* 6th edition. Englewood Cliffs, NJ: Prentice-Hall.

Steinberg. S. 1994. *Introduction to communication: course book 1 – the basics.* Cape Town: Juta.

Sullivan, A.J. 1965. Toward a philosophy of public relations: images, in *Information, influence and communication. A reader in public relations,* edited by O. Lerbinger & A. Sullivan. New York: Basic.

Van Deventer, A. 1995. Public relations within a policing context in South Africa. *Southern African PR Journal* 1(9):16–18.

Van Riel, C.B.M. 1995. *Principles of corporate communication.* Englewood Cliffs, NJ: Prentice-Hall.

Verwey, S. 1994. Communication theory, in *Public relations in South Africa. A management reader,* edited by B.A. Lubbe & G. Puth, Durban: Butterworths.

UNIT 4

Affinity Advertising and Publishing. 1993. *Brands and branding in South Africa: key success stories.* Johannesburg: Affinity.

Angelopulo, G.C. 1990. The active outward orientation of the organisation. *Communicare* 9(1):5–10.

Arens, W.F. & Bovée, C.L. 1994. *Advertising.* 5th edition. Burr Ridge: Irwin.

Baker, W. 1993. The relevance accessibility model of advertising effectiveness, in *Advertising exposure, memory, and choice,* edited by A.A. Mitchell, Hillside, NJ: Erlbaum.

Barenblatt, M. & Sinclair, R. 1989. *Make the other half work too.* Halfway House: Southern.

Belch, G.E. & Belch, M.A. 1990. *Introduction to advertising and promotion management.* Boston, Mass: Irwin.

Belch, G.E. & Belch, M.A. 1995. *Introduction to advertising and promotion.* 3rd edition. Chicago: Irwin.

Bredenkamp, C., De Wet, J., Du Plessis, D. & Rensburg, R. 1991. *Communication: intercultural, political and organisational communication, public relations and advertising.* Pretoria: University of South Africa. (Only study guide for CMN208–5)

Burnett, J.J. 1993. *Promotion management.* Boston: Houghton Mifflin.

Coulson-Thomas, C.J. 1987. *Marketing communications.* London: Heinemann.

Davis, H.L. & Silk, A.J. 1978. *Behavioral and management science in marketing.* New York: John Wiley.

Du Plooy, G.M. 1991. *500 Communication concepts. English/Afrikaans.* Cape Town: Juta.

Engel, J.F., Warshaw, M.R. & Kinnear, T.C. 1994. *Promotional strategy*. Burr Ridge: Irwin.

Fill, C. 1995. *Marketing communications*. London: Prentice-Hall.

Goodrum, C. & Dalrymple, H. 1990. *Advertising in America: the first 200 years*. New York: Harry N. Abrams.

Gorton, M. 1996. Hoe verandering in die media almal gaan raak. *Beeld* 22 February: S16.

Jefkins, F. 1992. *Advertising*. 5th edition. Oxford: Butterworth-Heinemann.

Jugenheimer, D.W. & White, G.E. 1991. *Basic advertising*. Cincinnati: South-Western.

Kaufman, L.C. 1987. *Essentials of advertising*. San Diego: Harcourt Brace Jovanovich.

Koekemoer, L. 1991. *Marketing communications management*. Durban: Butterworths.

Kotler, P. 1981. A generic concept of marketing, in *Marketing classics*, edited by B.M. Ennis & K.K. Cox, Boston: Allyn & Bacon.

Lears, J. 1994. *Fables of abundance: a cultural history of advertising in America*. New York: Basic.

Mitchell, A.A. (ed.) 1993. *Advertising exposure, memory, and choice*. Hillside, NJ: Erlbaum.

Moriarty S.E. 1991. *Creative advertising: theory and practice*. 2nd edition. Englewood Cliffs, NJ: Prentice-Hall.

Nelson, D. 1990. *A pictorial history of advertising in South Africa*. Cape Town: Don Nelson.

Nolte, L.W. 1979. *Fundamentals of public relations*. New York: Pergamon.

Overton-De Klerk, N. 1996. Vergelykende reklame verg deeglike besinning. *Beeld* 22 February: S16.

Percy, L. 1980. *Advertising strategy: a communication theory approach*. New York: Praeger.

Percy, L. & Woodside, A.G. 1983. *Advertising and consumer psychology*. Lexington, Mass: Lexington.

Presbrey, F. 1968. *The history and development of advertising*. New York: Greenwood.

Rensburg, R.S. (ed.) 1996. *Introduction to communication: course book 4 – communication planning and management*. Cape Town: Juta.

Runyon, K.E. 1984. *Advertising*. 2nd edition. Columbus: Charles E. Merrill.

Russel, J.T. & Lane, R. 1990. *Kleppner's advertising procedure.* 11th edition. Englewood Cliffs, NJ: Prentice-Hall.

Sandage, C.H., Fryburger, V. & Rotzoll, K. 1983. *Advertising theory and practice.* Homewood, Ill: Richard D. Irwin.

Schein, E.H. 1987. Defining organizational culture, in *Classics of organizational theory,* edited by J.M. Shafritz & J.S. Ott, Chicago: Dorsey.

Shimp, T.A. 1993. *Promotion management & marketing communications.* 3rd edition. Orlando: Dryden.

Sinclair, R. & Barenblatt, M. 1993. *The South African advertising book. Make the other half work too.* 3rd edition. Halfway House: Southern.

Skinner, S.J. 1994. *Marketing.* 2nd edition. Boston: Houghton Mifflin.

Sutherland, M. 1993. *Advertising and the mind of the consumer.* St Leonards, Aust: Allen & Unwin.

Wells, W., Burnett, J. & Moriarty, S. 1995. *Advertising.* 3rd edition. Englewood Cliffs, NJ: Prentice-Hall.

Wigston, D. 1994. The new South African broadcasting environment. *Dialogus: newsletter of the Department of Communication, Unisa* 1(2):5–6.